Islamic Theology and the Problem of Evil

Islamic Theology and the Problem of Evil

Safaruk Chowdhury

The American University in Cairo Press
Cairo New York

First published in 2021 by
The American University in Cairo Press
113 Sharia Kasr el Aini, Cairo, Egypt
One Rockefeller Plaza, 10th Floor, New York, NY 10020
www.aucpress.com

ISBN 978 1 617 97993 4

Library of Congress Cataloging-in-Publication Data

Names: Chowdhury, Safaruk
Title: Islamic theology and the problem of evil
Identifiers: LCCN 2020037109 (print) | LCCN 2020037110 (ebook) |
    ISBN 9781617979934 (hardcover) | ISBN 9781649030559 (epub) |
    ISBN 9781649030566 (pdf)
Subjects: LCSH: Good and evil—Religious aspects—Islam. | Islamic ethics. |
    Theodicy. | Suffering—Religious aspects—Islam.
Classification: LCC BP188 .C48 2021 (print) | LCC BP188 (ebook) |
    DDC 297.2/118—dc23

1 2 3 4 5   25 24 23 22 21

Designed by Newgen India

Contents

Acknowledgments

There are a few acknowledgments that must be made. First, I thank Tarek Ghanem, formerly at AUC Press, for initially taking interest in this work and seeing it take off and second, Nadia Naqib and the team thereafter steadily and with incredible patience ensuring it made a sound landing. I really appreciate the warm encouragement given by Kevin Timpe when I contacted him and Ramon Harvey as well as Arnold Y. Mol for reading draft chapters of the book and providing me with very helpful comments. I especially appreciate the meticulous feedback of an anonymous reviewer that has greatly improved the structure, accuracy, contents, and style of the book. I have endeavored to incorporate as much of the reviewer's suggestions as I was able to.

Introduction

On June 14, 2017, in the month of Ramadan, around 1:00 a.m. London local time, when many residents were asleep in their homes, but a number of Muslims were either waking up for the predawn meal before the commencement of the next day's fast or finishing their late-night prayers, the emergency services received a distress call that a fire had broken out on a twenty-four-story tower block in West London called Grenfell Tower. This fire tore through the exterior cladding of the building in a matter of minutes, and within an hour, despite the heroic efforts of the fire service personnel, the fire had become an uncontrollable blaze claiming the lives of thirty people trapped in the top floors. By early morning, a couple of hours later, the victim tally had doubled and the injury count quadrupled, and the fire in the Tower was now raging fiercely. The night unfolded with destruction and devastation as everything succumbed to the fire's blazing reach. It took over a full day to put out the fire and begin the preliminary investigative procedures. Embattled, weary, and traumatized, both the emergency services and Grenfell Tower survivors could not comprehend how and why such a tragedy occurred. This was the deadliest structural fire in the United Kingdom since the 1988 Piper Alpha disaster and the worst recorded residential fire accident since the Second World War. All that remains, other than ethereal memories and traumatized survivors, is a hollow and charred corpse of a building in full view of the regular commuters on the Hammersmith and City line. Even while writing this introduction, two consecutive terrorist attacks took place at mosques in the city of Christchurch, New Zealand, during the Friday prayer on March 15, 2019, killing fifty people and seriously injuring fifty more. The terrorist was a white supremacist ideologue from Australia motivated specifically by a worrying global ascendancy of anti-Muslim

1

hatred. He streamed his actual shooting on Facebook live, relaying the horror and carnage in real time. It marked the deadliest mass shooting in modern New Zealand history and the most merciless mass killing by a single perpetrator against Muslims in recent times. In many respects, Grenfell and Christchurch and innumerable tragic cases like it provoke many generic questions like: why do people suffer in horrendous ways? What purpose is served by instances of pain, suffering, and agony? Why do innocents like babies and children suffer? Why are acts that harm others allowed to occur? Why is there so much tragedy, sorrow, destruction, and distress in the world? In light particularly of the last question, one would be forgiven for concluding that the world is grim, brutal, hopeless, and full of *evil*.[1]

Yet, Muslims (as well as their faith neighbors Jews and Christians) believe with conviction that the world was created by a transcendent and personal Creator—God—who is absolutely powerful, has knowledge of all things, is fully Merciful, and is perfectly Just and Wise. Muslims also believe that the world and everything in it has been offered as an entrusted gift to us and that it is providentially guided by God for the specific ends and purposes He has determined. Muslims further believe that the evils of pain and suffering can be explicable, and intelligible to our minds and experience, and therefore not a reason to either doubt the existence of God or lack conviction in His specific attributes just mentioned. Are Muslims correct to believe that the world as it is and God so described are compatible? This question gets us to what has been called the 'problem of evil.' This book is an attempt to argue that the existence of evil is at least logically compatible with God as revealed in the Muslim sacred scripture of the Qur'an. The attempt is carried out bearing in mind that according to some observations, the project of theodicy may not have been a priority within Islamic theological discourse.[2]

In this book, I take theodicy as a worthy project of elaborate consideration. This means first and foremost I consider the problem of evil as a serious *theoretical* (intellectual) problem, acknowledging as well that there is an *experiential* (existential) component that has layers of complexity different in its severity and implications as well as a *practical* (functional) component that involves ways to eliminate what is identified as evil or bring about some desirable goal. Both these components are entirely different (and no less important) than a discursive engagement with theological and philosophical concepts that involve solving a logical problem. The experiential and practical dimensions of the problem of evil require a distinct and separate approach—one that I have not made the aim or focus of this book—and so for present purposes, I will not explore them (though I have something to say about this in the conclusion). I have restricted my examination of the problem of evil to four major versions. They are: (1) the problem of why innocents suffer, particularly persons with disabilities, (2) the problem of animal pain and suffering, (3) the evolutionary problem of evil, and (4) the problem of hell. The approach I take in this book is to offer different ways Muslims might respond to these four formulations of the problem of evil using the resources of their own intellectual tradition in order to demonstrate the logical compatibility between the existence of evil and the core attributes of God. The methodology I employ is that of analytic theology where the tools of conceptual precision, argumentative rigor, logical coherence, and systematic reasoning borrowed from the storehouse of analytic philosophy define the style and communication of the content. This method is appropriate for a work that seeks to analyze concepts, claims, and arguments on a range of Islamic theological doctrines. Moreover, as a method, analytic theology has marked similarities with the medieval Muslim scholastic or rational theology called *kalam*, where definitions, fine distinctions, syllogisms, and dialectics defined the manner in which the discipline was presented and practiced. Before outlining the structure of the present book, let me first situate its significance and relevance within the field of Islamic theodicy.

Key Works on Theodicy

Watt, in an article nearly forty years ago, noted how, compared to Judaism and Christianity, early Sunni Muslims "paid little attention to the problem of theodicy," it being a project undertaken exclusively "among heretical Muslims" by which he was referring primarily to the Mu'tazilites.[3] It is inescapably obvious that in comparison to contemporary Christian and Jewish theological and philosophical works at least, the Islamic theodicy literature produced among academic writing in English is considerably less. In what follows, I briefly survey some of the key works on Islamic theodicy and then situate this book within the academic territory. I restrict my scope to only book-length treatments written in English that take evil and theodicy as an exclusive subject of enquiry. I am aware that there are other English works with sections or chapters that usefully analyze evil and theodicies. In addition, titles in Arabic, Farsi, and Turkish that address the topic have also been omitted from the review. My reason for doing this is that, first, space permits me only to be brief. Hence, I had to make a decision on selection and scope. Second, each book I survey here has contributed a substantively novel thesis or increased information on the overall understanding of the topic from the Islamic sources, and third, this current book builds on the merits of these earlier works and explores avenues not directly addressed by them.

One of the first works to thoroughly examine theodicy is Ormsby's *Theodicy in Islamic Thought* where he undertakes a rigorous analysis of Arabic theological sources related to the controversy surrounding al-Ghazali's statement that the actual world is the best possible one. Ormsby unpacks the central claims underpinning its controversy and the constellation of secondary problems arising from it, setting out the core scholastic arguments and counterarguments. Particularly helpful is the analysis and presentation of the significance of God's omnipotence, divine wisdom and benevolence, and the metaphysical notions of possibility and necessity, and how ideas about them impacted and shaped the theological debate over a number of centuries subsequent to al-Ghazali. The book is filled with rich analysis and translations, making it indispensable as a reference for understanding the various reactions and embedded discussions and how Muslim scholars grappled with the perennial issues confronting any articulation of theodicies or indeed a doctrine of optimism from the dictum of one man. Ormsby's approach, although not analytic theology, is no doubt one of the earliest to give a systematic and methodical exposition of a theme very much different from the then prevailing method of historical analysis within Islamic Studies.

A decade and a half after Ormsby's publication, two important works were published related to evil: Heemskerk's *Suffering in Mu'tazilite Theology* and Inati's *The Problem of Evil*. To mention Heemskerk first, her monograph analyses the way the Basran Mu'tazilite theologian al-Qadi 'Abd al-Jabbar systematically gave an exposition of the etiology, function, and purpose of creaturely pain and suffering and how that fits into an overall divine eschatological compensatory scheme. Building her study on the extant editions of 'Abd al-Jabbar's *al-Mughni* as well as the works of his disciples Mankdim (d. 425/1034) and Ibn Mattawayh (d. 469/1076), Heemskerk meticulously examines the familiar ambit of related metaphysical issues over divine motivations, power, justice, goodness, and human freedom that had crystallized by the fourth H/tenth CE century from extended theological polemics. She then explores how 'Abd al-Jabbar attempts to reconcile these attributes with the existence of human and indeed animal pain and suffering within his account of divine imposition of creaturely responsibility (*taklif*). Although there is little by way of comparison with other theological schools, thinkers, and religious traditions or any novel venturing in interpretation, Heemskerk nevertheless offers a detailed exposition of 'Abd al-Jabbar's welfare-oriented account of divine agency where a greater good (afterlife compensation) ultimately guides God's reason for permitting pain and suffering.

Inati's book presents a detailed analysis of the nature of evil, its types, etiology, and justification from specifically Ibn Sina's philosophical perspective. Inati constructs and then assesses the arguments and metaphysical commitments behind seven theses Ibn Sina proposes for the justification of evil in the world and how there is no incompatibility between God's goodness and power with such evils. Inati shows how instrumental Ibn Sina's thoughts on this topic are on later developments in both Muslim and Christian theological and philosophical thinking just like his own thinking was influenced by his Neoplatonic predecessors. The various 'Avicennan theodicies' and their effectiveness are thoroughly explained by Inati but argued by her to ultimately fail. Nevertheless, the presentation of Ibn Sina's material with close-text analysis is extremely useful, and the theodicy proposals offered by him constitute the core ones subsequently amplified by Islamic theologians and philosophers.

A decade later, Sherman Jackson published a seminal study called *Islam and the Problem of Black Suffering* that sought to situate black American existential concerns into dialogue with the intellectual resources of primarily premodern Sunni theology in order to explore whether these resources are robust enough to meaningfully offer solutions to the black experience—especially the reality around historical collective black pain and suffering raised by the controversial work of William R. Jones *Is God a White Racist?* written in the post–civil rights 1970s. Jackson offers a broad typology of major Muslim theological denominations and surveys the core postulates of each regarding divine omnipotence and benevolence followed by examining whether investing their intellectual capital into the problem of black suffering yields any fruitful deliberative gains. Although the overall answer is in the affirmative, it is nevertheless complicated and merely a human effort where theological arguments may not be enough. Jackson's scope and depth of analysis as well as the unique step in bringing a dialogical format to the field of study allows insights to be teased out from theologically opposing views. Jackson's lucid and in-depth presentation of the doctrines underpinning classical Muslim denominational theodicies for the black predicament is a helpful template for applications to other contexts and communities.

One final book to mention is Ozkan's *A Muslim Response to Evil*. Ozkan's book is in two parts: part one outlines the meaning of evil from the Qur'an, early mainstream Muslim theological accounts of it—especially key thinkers like Ibn Sina, Ibn Rushd, and al-Ghazali—summarizing analyses from earlier books in the theodicy literature. Part two is a deeper dive into the thought of Said Nursi (d. 1960) related to the metaphysical nature of evil as well as its teleology. Ozkan presents a detailed overview of the intricate and often novel ideas developed by Nursi that demonstrates the eclectic and comprehensive approach he took in order to address the problem of evil beyond merely an abstract and theoretical reflection to one grounded in practical and moral engagement with it. Ozkan's treatment is wide in scope and allows for accessing a broad range of perspectives from within the Muslim theistic outlook and this makes it a helpful and convenient repository. However, this breadth also prevents any possibility for systematically assessing specific theodicies in order to bring out wider implications or make detailed comparisons with Nursi and other thinkers.

Cumulatively, all the above works offer valuable information and analysis on how the concept of evil was conceptualized by Muslim theologians and philosophers and how pain and suffering as phenomena were to be explained. They form a strong set of works, with divergent approaches, and constitute a core body of references in English on the topic. Each work has deepened the appreciation of specifically Islamic perspectives on evil, which is still very much absent from the general philosophy of religion literature. However, some areas were neither examined in detail nor addressed at all and it is these areas I particularly focus on in the current book. One area is that of a disability theodicy where I attempt to survey different ways disabilities have been explained from Muslim sources and offer a novel framework to instances of horrendous-difference disabilities and thereby allow a hitherto absent disability perspective into the conversation. Another area is that of animal pain and suffering. Although explored in a section by Heemskerk and briefly discussed by Ozkan, there is no detailed theological treatment that appropriates current philosophical and animal psychology literature that both surveys possible Islamic arguments and proposes independent tentative explorations. In addition, the strong trend toward a convergence of science and religion with particular interest in Darwinian evolution has meant God's agency and the theological issues like the problem of evil being reassessed and reexamined in light of categories defined by the biological sciences. What possible account of evil can be made on an evolutionary model of creation with specifically Islamic insights is a neglected area of exploration and so preliminary foray into such an account is attempted in this book. Finally, none of the reviewed works address one of the most difficult questions and that is the theodicy of hell.[4] This book will examine such a problem from an integrated account drawing on Islamic theological heritage and the recent works in analytic theology. Thus, the current book is in a sense an extension of the body of existing Islamic theodicy works that hopes to bring new arguments, angles, explorations, and a missing approach to the mix—analytic theology.

Chapter Summaries

The structure of the book is as follows: in Chapter 1, I first outline the idea of evil generally and then specifically from the Qur'an. I then present a broad account of evil within the thought of Ibn Sina followed by a survey of four prominent conceptions of God within the formative period of Islamic theology and the understanding of good and evil that arises out of those respective conceptions. These will constitute the broad theological frameworks within which my own thinking, proposals, and analysis will operate. I thereafter sketch core aspects of what are called 'theodicies' and give a candidate list of the major ones articulated by medieval Islamic thinkers. I also briefly discuss the 'anti-theodicy position'—those who reject religious theodicies and the traditional formulations of the problem of evil.

In Chapter 2, I examine the first of the four versions of the problem of evil, which is the problem of why innocents suffer, taking my specific subgroup of innocents—those persons with disability. I focus on the problem of horrendous-difference disability. I attempt here to outline the etiology of disability according to Islamic primary sources of the Qur'an and Hadith and then propose a few theodicy models culminating in one specific model for those given life-debilitating impairments to defeat this challenge based on incorporating the Islamic concept of hospitality (*diyafa*) into the person with disability's cognitive outlook and subjective meaning-making process.

Chapters 3 and 4 are separate but also related chapters. Muslim scholars had discussed at length the nature, status, and destiny of nonhuman animals. This also meant they did not exclude discussions on the reasons why animals suffer and whether such suffering had an overall purpose. Chapter 3 thus examines the second of the four versions of the problem of evil, which is the problem of animal pain and suffering. I analyze possible animal theodicies and offer some novel speculative explanations of my own based on the theological ideas and precepts of some Muslim theologians. Chapter 4 introduces the third of the four versions of the problem of evil and that is the evolutionary problem of evil sometimes dubbed the 'Darwinian' problem. Hitherto unexplored within Islamic theology, I propose an Islamic evolutionary theodicy drawing on the works of some major contemporary theologians and philosophers as well as precepts and precedence within the Qur'an and Muslim theology in order to construct possible reasons why God may allow such things as death, predation, and extinction in nature based on the evolutionary paradigm involving selection, adaptions, and accidents.

Chapter 5 assesses the fourth version of the problem of evil and that is the problem of hell. Here, a methodical and detailed analysis of the morally sufficient reasons why God would create hell and the overall validity of the retributive nature of its punishment will be tackled. Various positions in the Islamic theological literature will be examined that attempt to reconcile how what can be called the 'Mainstream View' of hell that upholds unending conscious torment of hell's inhabitants is compatible with the core attributes of God. The chapter will conclude with a short section on the soteriological problem of evil, namely, why God would allow some persons to suffer eternal punishment in hell for either never having heard the message of Islam or willfully rejecting it.

The concluding chapter discusses the findings and outlines of the book with suggestions for exploring a different avenue related to the topic of theodicy and evil that is either not addressed in this work or departs from its framework and methodology.

The different theodicies and defenses mentioned and discussed in this book are offered as responses to the various iterations of the problem of evil. They are meant to cumulatively offer theoretical explanations for why there might be pain, suffering, and other adverse states of affairs detrimental to the proper ways God Himself desires human and nonhuman living and flourishing to be but nevertheless is logically compatible with His core attributes. This, all the while acknowledging that "the Muslim theodicist has his task cut out for him"[5] because not only is there few rigorous contemporary Islamic philosophical and theological works (from which to draw intellectual stimulation and ideas) contributing to the plethora of religious voices on the issue but often the enterprise of theodicy itself is under attack for doing nothing to ameliorate evil and suffering.

There are some justifications I need to make regarding the style and form of this book. First, I have broadly attempted to adhere to gender-inclusive language but have clearly avoided it in the case of God, which I type with a capitalized 'G' and treat as a proper noun reflecting the original Arabic masculine. I have also avoided it for hadith where in most cases examples appear grammatically masculine in the Arabic but assume the feminine as well. This meant that I have not modified the English translation of the original Arabic with gender-neutral pronouns or terms. Second, I have omitted translating Arabic formulaic eulogies often found after the name 'Allah,' the name of the Prophet Muhammad, his family members, companions, or any scholarly figure. This decision is more to allow for a steady and unbroken rhythm of reading than any disagreement with eulogies as a practice. Third, in some chapters, the material is undertaken with formal analysis that is then presented in logical form. This is to allow the reader to see an argument of a particular author or my own arguments in a series of steps. Because of the technical nature of the subject and the methodology adopted for the book, these logical forms are inevitable and arguably an important feature of grasping the specific claims within the arguments. Ordering claims into premises that constitute an overall argument is an effective way to visually trace the movement and pattern of the core reasoning. However, I have attempted to keep the logical machinery to a minimum so that there is no impression of unnecessary obfuscation often leveled at works of analytic theology. Fourth, a point on references. The problem of evil is a topic with a vast written literature produced within Anglo-American philosophy of religion and this 'plagues' the author (in a manner of speaking) with choice. What I have endeavored to do is reference those works that are collative or summative in nature, meaning they contain other studies that the reader can consult, saving me the need to make extensive citation of references. Where I do make extensive citations, it is mainly due to my reliance on such works for an argument, a particular angle on some issue, or it being important I feel for the reader to understand and explore.

All translations in this book are mine unless otherwise stated and acknowledged.

1

The Problem of Evil: Outlines

In this chapter, I outline a number of issues related to the study of theodicy. First, I summarize the current state of the problem of evil within the analytic philosophy of religion. This is followed by examination of the concept of evil in the Qur'an, the thought of Ibn Sina, and major theological denominations in the formative development of Islam. I then conclude with a survey of key areas that link to the topic of theodicy such as its definition, core questions, criteria, types, and detractors.

The Current Situation

The problem of evil *broadly* conceived is the challenge of attempting to reconcile the existence of evil and imperfection in the world with commitment to the positive existence of justice, goodness, and harmony. In its *narrow* (theistic) conception, it is more specifically the problem of reconciling the existence of an absolutely perfect being with the evil of sin and suffering.[1] The brief outline I give here in this section is that of the contemporary treatment within the tradition of analytic (Anglo-American) philosophy of religion because it has defined much of the scope and parameters of how this problem is understood and addressed by current theologians and philosophers across the three theistic traditions of Judaism, Christianity, and Islam. The standard approach of the analytic tradition is as follows:[2] God is conceived in a particular way, namely that He is one and exists uniquely. This God is a personal being and must be characterized as the proper object of religious worship. The grounding for this proper religious worship is God's perfection, where perfection is conceptualized as maximal greatness: a being than which there is no possible greater one. This bare or minimal conception of divinity constitutes a common departure point for all the Abrahamic theistic traditions and is often referred to as "perfect being theology."[3] From the idea of God's maximal greatness, a set of necessary core or essential attributes are deduced that are constitutive of God's nature because such attributes are great-making properties and, combined, would entail there is no other type of being greater. These great-making properties or essential attributes of God (which He would have to a maximal degree) include:

1. Omnipotence: the power to bring about any state of affairs that is logically possible.
2. Omniscience: knowing everything that is logically possible to know.
3. Perfect goodness: the supreme source of morality and what is good.
4. Aseity: ontologically independent, self-subsistent, and sovereign over everything.
5. Incorporeality: possesses no body or finite dimensions.
6. Eternity: is either timeless or everlasting.
7. Omnipresence: wholly present in all space–time.
8. Perfect freedom: nothing external to God determines His actions.

This conceptualization of God (call it 'standard theism,' or *ST* for short) is then challenged by bringing it into conflict with certain formulations of or ideas about evil. This is done in order to cast doubt over God as a perfect being. However, as we will see in the subsequent chapters, it is primarily 1 and 3 from the attribute list above that were the sites of contention most heavily played out within Islamic theology.

A distinction is commonly made between, on the one hand, evil in relation to God as an *experiential* problem and, on the other, its relation to God as a *theoretical* problem. The former problem generally concerns itself with how individuals face personal and practical difficulties in knowing and experiencing suffering or are victims of events and acts of evil. It may also involve the practical modalities of combating and eliminating injustice and evil from society. On a specific level, the experiential problem may relate to personal crises of faith in religious adherents in how evil becomes a factor that undermines love, confidence, and trust in God because of one's inability to process and compute the complexity and disturbing effects it generates. This category of the problem is often excluded by philosophers who see it more as the domain of work reserved for religious leaders, social workers, and health professionals.

The latter problem by contrast is a purely discursive and intellectual engagement that examines the impact the existence of evil may have on the truth-value or epistemic validity of God on *ST*. This theoretical problem of evil is generally subdivided into two types: (1) the logical problem, also labeled as the *deductive* problem, and (2) the evidential problem, also labeled as the *inductive* problem. Trakakis explains the difference:

> The logical problem consists in removing an alleged logical inconsistency between certain claims made by *ST* and certain claims made about evil (e.g., that the existence of the God of *ST* is logically incompatible with the existence of certain kinds of evil). The evidential problem, on the other hand, takes it as given that the question of logical consistency has been or can be settled, and focuses instead on relations of evidential support, probability, and plausibility: the question here is whether the existence of evil, although logically consistent with the existence of God, counts against the truth of *ST* insofar as evil lowers the probability that *ST* is true.[4]

Philosophers like J. L. Mackie[5] and H. J. McCloskey[6] set out formal arguments attempting to demonstrate the logical incompatibility between God and evil, meaning neither can coexist, but it is generally held by contemporary philosophers that this attempt was unsuccessful and that there is a plausible internal consistency between *ST* and formulations of evil. A pivotal point that marked the transition from the logical to the evidential problem was the seminal paper written by atheist philosopher William Rowe published in 1979[7] that advanced an "intuitively appealing argument" that was "crucially predicated on the inductive step that, given the countless instances of apparently pointless suffering found in the world, it is highly likely that at least some of these are in fact instances of pointless suffering."[8] Theistic responses to this evidential problem consisted of two maneuvers. The first maneuver was to construct theodicies and the second was to retreat into a view known as *skeptical theism*.[9] Theodicies involve vindicating God's justice and goodness by offering plausible reasons or justifications of why God allows evil in the world. Skeptical theism is the view that "the limitations of the human mind are such that we are in no position to be able to discern God's reasons for permitting evil—and hence, the fact that we cannot identify such reasons should not surprise us and should not count against the truth of *ST*."[10] Both maneuvers characterize the current state of play within the philosophical literature on the problem of evil, and the disagreement among philosophers of religion has assumed a hardened and entrenched form with little possibility of moving beyond mere adaptations, nuanced reformulations, and reiterations of already existing arguments, although recently there has been a move toward a more imaginative and innovative redirection of the problem with a whole new set of parameters and presuppositions guiding the discussions.[11] I have tried to appropriate to some degree these imaginative insights in this book that also build on from earlier works in theodicy within Islamic studies.

Evil in Islamic Theology and Philosophy

This section will situate the term 'evil' and its related topics specifically within the Islamic context. First, the concept will be presented generally, then as it occurs in the Qur'an before sketching Ibn Sina's view because it encapsulates much of the direction and thinking of theologians who came after him. Thereafter, a summary of the main theological contours of God and evil as expounded in the major Muslim theological schools will be given.

There is clearly a reality to evil. Despite knowing, experiencing, and recognizing its reality, the word is notoriously difficult to define with any precision. There is no single statement or meaning that captures the entire range of uses and cases and no description that reflects all its complexities. Muslim theologians did not offer technical definitions for evil but gave extended lists of examples that included broad notions like maleficent acts, pain, and suffering. Evil used in this sense will be generally intended throughout the book.[12] In addition, the standard classification of evil into *moral* and *natural* will be assumed as they are reflected in the Islamic theological and philosophical literature. The former type of evil is that which results from the actions of a person held to be morally accountable or blameworthy that harm others and oneself such as acts of terror and torture or defects in one's character like dishonesty and vanity, whereas the latter type does not relate to moral agents but naturally occurring events or disasters like floods, hurricanes, illnesses, diseases, and disabilities that are not due to the choices and actions of a moral agent. What both types have in common is that their token instances bring about suffering, harm, or adverse states of affairs in creatures.[13]

Turning to the Qur'an, the key Qur'anic passages that give us an idea of the core notion of evil within Islamic belief include: (1) al-Baqara, verses 30–34: creation of Adam and Iblis's refusal to obey God's command to prostrate; (2) al-Hijr, verses 32–42: Iblis's recalcitrance manifested in his arrogant disobedience of God's command to prostrate before Adam. He is then pronounced accursed but is granted powers by God to misguide humanity; (3) al-Baqara verse 36: Adam and Hawwa disobey God's command not to approach the tree. The Qur'an thus offers a prehumanity historical account that indicates a few things for us about the nature and etiology of evil including:

1. Evil is not a directly created entity by God but a secondary outcome from the free agency of Iblis and subsequently post-Adam—humanity in general.
2. Evil is not destroyed by God (as Iblis is allowed to persist) but is integrated into His total providential plan and governance of the world.
3. Evil is caused by a metaphysical agent like Iblis.
4. Evil is caused by the exercise of free will or choice.
5. Evil's purpose is to test humanity—whether they will obey God and be faithful to His commandments and covenant (*mithaq*) or follow Iblis and his cohorts.
6. Evil is suggested to be whatever is contrary to the Divine will and command.[14]

Ozkan has extensively surveyed the semantic field of the Qur'anic term "sharr" from the root *sh / r / r /*—often translated into English as 'evil'—and has shown the diverse contextual range of meanings. Her list includes the following:[15]

1. Parsimony (*bukhl*): withholding in miserly fashion from God's bounty and gifts as an evil.
2. Going astray (*dalal*): to veer away from God's path.
3. Rejection of God (*kufr*): disbelief in God and His revelation.
4. Idolatry (*shirk*): associating deities and partners with God in His divinity.
5. Violation of a covenant or treaty where a promise is made but then betrayed.
6. Turning away from God (*i'rad*): having an aversion to what God institutes and commands.
7. Slander (*ifk*): spreading malicious rumours.
8. Transgression (*tughyan*): exceeding all bounds and limits in iniquity, wickedness, arrogance and aggression.
9. Trials and tests with evil.
10. The situation in hell.
11. Satan/evil inclinations.

Ozkan concludes that there is no singular portrayal of evil in the Qur'an because it occurs in a plurality of contexts. Also, there is no ontologically precise category for evil in the Qur'an and so she argues that it seems more abstract like a *relation* as in a relation of loss, for example, especially in human actions and situations rather than an actual and separate existence of some entity.[16] This account of evil in the Qur'an is somewhat different from that generally articulated by Muslim philosophers who no doubt inspired by the Qur'anic insights adopted a stronger metaphysical framework to explain the etiology and ontology of evil. One of the most influential philosophers of the medieval period to do this was Abu 'Ali b. al-Husayn Ibn Sina (d. 428/1027).[17] He discussed at length the notion of evil under the doctrine of divine providence (*'inaya*; *tadbir*).[18] He believed evil was willed by God insofar as it is a corollary of what He creates. If God knows and wills everything that He creates, and if evil is something encountered in the created order, then it must follow that evil is known, willed, and created by God. But Ibn Sina, in agreement with his Neoplatonist predecessors, states that the existence of evil is not a positive existence but a negative one—a privation (*'adam*)—meaning it is an absence of or lack of some perfection in something that occasionally arises rather than a recurrent and fixed substantive reality. In other words, evil is accidental, which would mean God's creation of evil is accidental. This is not to say as McGinnis explains that not just any privation or absence is an evil, but only a privation of some perfection required by the nature of the thing, where the perfections in question are grounded in the very species and nature of the thing. Thus, there is nothing evil about the fact that a rock cannot see. Only in something of which sight is one of the perfections and goods of that kind of thing is the absence of sight and blindness an evil.[19]

For Ibn Sina, evil occurs as a reality ultimately because of matter. The physical world is one that is characterized by change (generation and corruption) and that entails it is susceptible of privation. When matter is not compliant with how it is to be shaped or pressed into receiving form, this shortcoming is what gives rise to evil. Matter is unavoidably evil because it is by its nature always characterized by potentiality.[20] To give an analogy as mentioned by Seeskin, if God is like a surgeon, then the "essence of what the surgeon does is to heal," but in order for the surgeon to "accomplish this end, the surgeon must cut into the body and produce pain." It is arguable that the surgeon is responsible for the pain but it is "accidental to her mission or what we might call her primary intention." Similarly, God is responsible for privation but "only as a concomitant factor of creation."[21]

Regarding naturally occurring evils (nonmoral or 'surd' evils), Ibn Sina, being a Neoplatonist, argues that God creates good for its own sake because He is the Ultimate Good. Because He is pure good and pure perfection, all things desire God and are themselves perfected insofar as they seek their fulfilment in Him. Through an emanative process, God creates good from His own essence. Evil, however, is an accidental creation as mentioned but has a sort of existence in relative terms. What this means is that when things occur in nature, they create certain effects. A person S judges these effects relative to how S perceives them to be, which is either harmful, adverse, or negative (–), or beneficial, favorable, or positive (+). But when some naturally occurring object or event x is "considered merely in itself or essentially as the kind of thing that it is, then its performing the functions characteristic of its kind is a good or perfection of x." If, for example, fire burns or when rain falls and puts a fire out, they are being a good instance of their kind, and "that things should be good instances of their kinds in fact contributes to the order of the good. Therefore, natural things considered in themselves or essentially are not evil but good." However, if x is judged by S to prevent some other object y from obtaining some good or x appears to remove some good from y, then x is considered an evil relative to or accidentally to y. Thus,

> when someone is burned by a fire, the fire is perceived as a cause of evil relative to the one burned, for certainly if that same person were freezing the fire would be perceived as a good. Conversely, if rain were to prevent a freezing person from starting a fire, the impediment to and absence of the fire would be perceived as an evil.[22]

In other words, "inasmuch as x is considered relative to y, and relations are accidental, x's being a cause of some evil for y is accidental." What Ibn Sina wants to argue is that the natural order and its constituents are not essentially a cause of evil or an evil cause. "Considered in themselves and essentially, they are all good" because natural evil resulting from external causes "is an accidental consequence of natural things performing their necessary and proper activities."[23] Therefore, evil cannot per se be attributed to God's creative activity but only as a necessary consequence of creating good.

On moral evil, Ibn Sina states very little. He does uphold that acts done by individuals that bring about harm or bad are based on choices. These choices are brought about by the individual thinking that the act possesses a good that is expected to result from it. These faulty judgments—in reality *ignorance*—about what are expected goods in actions arise when the soul is unable to resist matter, giving in to its inclinations and desires. Thus, it is only when the soul is separated from the trappings of matter that it can free itself from ignorance and thus become moral.[24]

Given the above account, Ibn Sina addresses the problem of why there is evil in the world in several ways as Inati has discussed and they are:

1. evil does not have positive existence,
2. evil is part of the providential ordering of creation,
3. good outweighs evil,
4. evil is inevitable and unavoidable as it is a consequence of there being good,
5. evil is a necessary means for realising good,
6. evil is a necessary part of creation, and
7. evil is caused by free will.[25]

These various solutions also capture the broad range of approaches taken by Muslim theologians before and after Ibn Sina although he systematically presented it within a specific metaphysical framework. Thus, his theodicies deliver a broad and effective package of understanding and explaining evil and suffering that can be employed and elaborated for further theodicies or defenses.

Mainstream Theological Perspectives

In this remaining part of the section, I will merely outline the core doctrines underpinning the ideas about evil and God's essential attributes as conceptualized and articulated within the major theological schools that emerged within the formative period of Islam restricting the scope to the Mu'tazilites, Ash'arites, Maturidites, and Traditionalists. I avoid here a historical analysis of the development of these schools, which have been extensively done by others,[26] and so the account is minimalistic, not going beyond the relevant points related to the issue.[27]

The Mu'tazilites:[28] Generally, primacy was given by this group to God's justice ('adl) and benevolence, which is the principal attribute by which all other aspects of God had to be reconciled—especially His motives and actions. God's justice and benevolence meant human beings possessed libertarian free will in order to undertake genuine moral choices and thus be causal agents of evil because if God is the direct cause of actions, He would also be the cause of evil actions and that would compromise His goodness and transcendence. It would also mean He would hold humans accountable for acts that He has effectively determined—something they believed was palpably unjust and obviated human responsibility. God in this way was exonerated from either causing or cooperating with evil. God's justice and benevolence also entailed that God's actions are welfare oriented, meaning God was obligated to maintain whatever is optimal (aslah) for all creatures. This further entailed that God cannot act arbitrarily but is morally bound to guide His actions so that it averts harm or secures tangible goods for creatures. These moral goods that guide divine actions are independent of Him and hence amenable to human reason and were the means by which humans could come to recognize God as just. God and humans both, therefore, are governed by the same moral paradigms. In addition, this notion of the optimal would further entail God was obligated to create the best possible world because anything less would be to act contrary to what is optimal. All this, therefore, allowed the enterprise of theodicy as viable because God's actions were now scrutable and so various explanations could be sought justifying them. The problem of evil and suffering on the Mu'tazilite account would primarily be explained due to human free actions, and God's permission of it would mean He would be duty-bound to recompense that with something equal or greater in goodness and pleasure—especially in the Hereafter.

The Ash'arites:[29] Broadly, on this theological orientation, divine will and power were attributes prominently situated into the center of what essentially defined and characterized God's activity. There are no values, principles, or norms that are independent of His self-determined dictates. Any move to constrain God's activity with His benevolence, Ash'arites argued, is entirely misplaced. God is under no obligation to direct any act or create anything based on promoting human welfare; *that* He does is purely from a contingent act of benevolence. God's power and prerogatives are unbounded and so everything is subordinated to them. Ultimately, God's will, sovereignty, and autonomy determine everything in creation—including human actions and history. Humans have a slender margin of involvement in performing their actions. Only the will directed at performing some action is properly attributable to humans and the remaining requirements to execute the act like capacity, connectivity between will and act, and any other necessary circumstance are all enacted by God and acquired by (*kasb*) humans. This high providence and strong determinism also meant evil was created by God. However, because evil on this view has no objective existence but is relative to the subjective experience and judgments of individuals, it meant that God could not be attributed with evil acts or wrongful acts per se because there is no ontologically independent reality that is evil. Moreover, God is not obligated to recompense or balance any affliction of harm, injustice, or adverse states of affairs that He causes with some equal or greater reward because there is no moral index that checks God's motives or actions. Thus, any temporal or human categories of judgments are not applicable to God. Put another way, God has no duties to anything in a kingdom He is sovereign over. In fact, God is the very source of moral duties in that they are grounded in His issued commandments recorded in scripture. It would further follow on this view that instances of suffering in the world are not really amenable to explication simply because divine motives and actions are not grounded in any overarching goals or purposes. Searching for explanations then is ultimately futile, which would make the project of theodicy pointless. Their stance is an anti-theodicy one. However, for Ash'arites, the existence of or the fact of evil does not translate as God's approval of evil: only that its existence cannot be beyond His will and control.

The Maturidites:[30] There is considerable overlap in this theological school with the account of Ash'arism just given, although there are some significant and nuanced differences. One difference, for example, is that although Maturidites would sympathetically share the commitments, motives, and reasoning that underpin the Ash'arite arguments for divine power, sovereignty, and human finitude, they would situate at the forefront of their theology God's absolute wisdom (*hikma*). This attribute can constrain God's omnipotence although how exactly the relation between both attributes plays out is not always clear. One thing that is clear is that God's actions are guided by wisdom and so there are no pointless or aimless divine acts. Wisdom is generally defined as acts that are either commensurate with their rightful purpose or that which promote beneficial and praiseworthy results. This consequentialist consideration, however, is also—paradoxically—inscrutable because although God must act based on wisdom, the precise substance of this wisdom is nevertheless unknowable. Another difference with Ash'arism (and indeed Mu'tazilism) is that God, on Maturidism, can commit evil. God can bring about, cause, sponsor, and cooperate in evil. Thus, causing suffering, harm, or adverse states of affairs in the world does not compromise His goodness and justice. However, God does not do these actions arbitrarily because that would not appear to serve any wise purposes and it is impossible for God to act gratuitously (*'abath*). This suggests that if evil or suffering did serve wise purposes, then God could permit them. Here, the general Maturidite account of evil clarifies this doctrine, namely, that evil is always proximate and never ultimate. In other words, God's actions in the end cannot be evil even though immediate human experience may judge something adversely. Evil then is teleological. On the Maturidite view, evil, bad states of affairs, suffering, and hardship have instrumental value in that they serve a number of ends like enabling spiritual growth or exemplifying God's great attributes. The ends serving evils are directed by God's wise purposes and, although may not necessarily materialize in the fullness of a patient's life, nevertheless will reveal itself within a greater teleological scheme.

The Traditionalists:[31] Although often positioned antithetically to the more overt rationalist orientation of Muslim theological groups like the three just surveyed, Traditionalist theology in some respects has considerable overlaps with them. God, for example, is held to have complete sovereignty over human agency, nature, and history but not everything that is constituted by God's ontological decree or will is reduced to God's deontological decree or will: God decreeing x does not mean God approves of x. The complete extension of God's power over human acts nevertheless does not negate meaningful moral agency because of the psychological event of choice (*ikhtiyar*). This means that the etiology of moral evil is ultimately traced to the human self (*nafs*) and Satan, and not God. In this way, divine cooperation in evil is avoided while preserving omnipotence. The way omnibenevolence is upheld is that God by definition cannot enact pure evil (*sharr mahd*) because it has no ontology. Only relative or proximate (*idafi*) evil exists and that too because human subjective evaluations judge something as such based on contextual factors like time, place, and circumstances. The proximate evils that God permits are guided by His infinite wisdom, mercy, and goodness: an axiological matrix that governs divine choices and decisions in order to realize some greater good. This welfare-oriented motive guiding divine actions is a defining feature of God's relation with His creation. A qualification, however, is that God not only acts with consideration of creaturely welfare but acts based on self-vindication and self-consideration because wisdom entails that an actor acts in her own interests as well. God acting based on self-consideration amounts to ensuring He is adequately and properly worshipped as that generates His approval and pleasure. Evil on this view is also teleological and not gratuitous. The existence of suffering serves a wise purpose, which is educative such as awakening humans from ignorant slumber and heedlessness of God to a reorientation toward Him.

From the above theological schools and their core postulates, several points about evil can be inferred, which include:

1. Evil is part of God's creation.
2. Evil is neither desired nor approved by God.
3. Evil is a privation.
4. Evil has a reality.
5. There is no absolute evil only relative evil.
6. A minor evil can avert a greater evil.

Given Ibn Sina's account of evil as well as that of the mainstream theological groups, we can set out a preliminary list of identifiable theodicies found in the works of both. These will recur in the subsequent chapters in various forms, details, and iterations. Some of these theodicies no doubt overlap, whereas others do not and, in fact, may not even be fully consistent when in conjunction with each other. The theodicy list then includes:

1. There would be no (appreciation of) good without evil.[32]
2. Evil is caused by human free choices.[33]
3. The actual world is the best possible world.[34]
4. Evil is necessary.[35]
5. Evil is a privation and hence has no actual being/existence.
6. Ultimately, there is no evil because what is thought to be evil is in the end disguised goods.[36]
7. Reward in the afterlife outweighs earthly pain and suffering.[37]
8. Evil is a means to a greater good.

It remains to look at what exactly the concept of a theodicy is. To this I now turn to the final section of this chapter.

Examining Theodicy

Theodicy, in general terms, refers to the attempt to explain evil in the world.[38] These explanations may vary in sophistication and detail but they all have the same basic objective, which is to reconcile justice and goodness with the ubiquitous reality of evil, injustice, pain, and suffering. The term 'theodicy' itself is a neologism, being a combination of two Greek nouns θεός (God) and δίκη (justice). G. W. Leibniz in the eighteenth century transliterated them into the French word *théodicée* in his book on the subject *Essais de Théodicée sur la bonté de Dieu, la liberté de l'homme et l'origine du mal*. This definition has retained its original sense of the vindication of divine justice, as illustrated by Immanuel Kant's explanation where he writes, "by 'theodicy' we understand the defence of the highest wisdom of the creator against the charge which reason brings against it for whatever is counterpurposive (*das Zweckwidrige*) in the world."[39] Theodicy, in the narrow, technical, and theistic sense, "explores logical strategies to vindicate God from moral culpability for evil." In short, "theodicy seeks to 'justify the ways of God to men.' It does not simply refute the accusation of injustice; it demonstrates God's justice."[40] Metaphysician Peter van Inwagen summarizes the point as follows: "a theodicy is not simply an attempt to meet the charge that God's ways are unjust: it is an attempt to exhibit the justice of his ways."[41]

Some philosophers differentiate theodicy from what is called a 'defense.' One way of demarcating this difference is to say that in a theodicy, the theodicist makes the strong claim of knowing God's actual reasons for allowing evil, whereas the proponent of a defense argues with a weaker and more cautious claim that for all we know, a particular explanation *could be* (might possibly be) the reason why God permits evil and that possibility is sufficient for establishing the compatibility between divine goodness and justice with varieties of evil. Another way of demarcating the theodicy–defense difference is by highlighting the aims of each. On a theodicy, the theodicist seeks to argue how theism makes plausible sense of evil and suffering by demonstrating how God's actions based on His power, knowledge, wisdom, mercy, and love to permit evil are fully justified, whereas a defense seeks to show how evidentialist arguments against God on the basis of evil are unsuccessful in undermining belief in theism. Meister and Taliaferro explain the difference like this:

> A *defence* can be used in two different ways: first, when deployed as a response to the logical problem of evil, in which it is argued that there is a logical inconsistency between certain claims about God and evil, it attempts to establish that it is rational to believe that God exists; and second, when it is deployed as a response to the probabilistic or evidential problem of evil, in which it is argued that it is implausible to believe certain claims about God and evil, it attempts to establish that the existence of evil does not make it improbable that God exists. With a *theodicy*, the objective is to demonstrate that it is reasonable to believe that God exists and, while not typically attempting to account for every evil, to offer an overarching structure in which to make sense of evil in the world as an aspect of an overall good.[42]

Theodicy as an overarching approach relates religious/theological and philosophical questions about evil in order to present a framework or applicable model to explain how evil is compatible with God. These core questions of theodicy are as follows:

1. Origin of evil: How does evil originate? Who is responsible?
2. Nature of evil: What is the ontology of evil? How does it exist?
3. Problem of evil: How does evil pose a problem for theology?
4. Reason for evil: Why does God permit evil? What is the morally sufficient reason?
5. End of evil: How will God end evil and/or ultimately bring good out of evil?[43]

A theodicy does not have to address each question in a sequential or methodical way (religious texts like the Qur'an, for example, do not do so but nevertheless suggest answers to these questions) nor even in a definitive way, but a robust theodicy would nevertheless effectively address these core questions.

A further issue of theodicy is determining what exact or clear criterion establishes a valid and robust model that accounts for the compatibility of evil with God and the vindication of His goodness and justice. Here, I adapt the five-point criteria offered by Scott for a criterion for Islamic theodicies:[44]

1. Fidelity: is the theodicy grounded in the appropriate sources of theology, like the Qur'an, Hadith, and early authoritative theological tradition?
2. Coherence: is the theodicy logical and internally consistent with other core and definitive and fundamental Islamic doctrines?
3. Relevance: does the theodicy meaningfully address, connect, and relate to contemporary experiences of evil?
4. Creativity: Does the theodicy imaginatively and innovatively engage the problem of evil?
5. Humility: Does the theodicy recognize its inherent limits and scope?

Any theodicy constructed from the Islamic tradition must first and foremost be congruent with its own sources and consistent with it and its set of foundational doctrines and claims. Establishing this, a theodicy ought then to be assessed for its degree of usefulness in addressing the issue at hand followed by how interpretively imaginative and innovative it is (although constrained somewhat by what the theological sources may possibly allow). Finally, the theodicy must be modest about the extent to which it can address or apply to its case(s).

A relatively new contender in Anglo-American discussions on the problem of evil is a position called 'anti-theodicy.' Although anti-theodical views are not merely a product of recent decades, there are novel aspects that have defined it to be a specific posturing regarding the entire theodicy endeavor and enterprise. As Trakakis notes, anti-theodicy is not a uniform doctrine nor is it driven by an identical set of attitudes. Nonetheless, there are identifiable themes that consist of a spectrum of engagements from critical disdain to constructive skepticism.[45] The core overlapping objections constituting the anti-theodicy position are:

1. Moral insensitivity: theodicies do not take suffering seriously because they make an equivalence between all types of evils. Horrendous evils on a mass scale (like genocide) and a personal tribulation (like an

accident), for example, are explained in exactly the same way by appeal to some greater good, which abandons any distinction in degree, quantity, and severity of an evil like suffering.

2. Moral blindness: theodicies often are formulated in such a way as to occlude the radically cruel and merciless nature of evil—even unconscionable evil.

3. Licenses evil: theodicies license evil because by explaining them away, justifying them, or ameliorating them removes any or at least weakens moral responsiveness. The status quo therefore remains unchanged and so evil is allowed to persist in existence and process.

4. Impersonal: theodicies involve a detached logical approach when making moral assessments and calculations. The analysis of evil within theodicies is expressed in a formal manner, removed from a subjective appreciation or engagement of its severity and impact.

5. Dysfunctionality: theodicies do not understand how morality works because the logic governing the explanatory basis for evil reduces to excessive utilitarian considerations like outweighing factors rather than the victims.

6. Instrumentalization: theodicies make people means to an end rather than significant ends in themselves because evil is explained in teleological terms. Theodicies seem only to work effectively if humans are utilized as a tool for a calculated end.[46]

Anti-theodicy in the Islamic theological context refers to the rejection of offering theodicies because God is entirely different from creaturely predilection and fathomability. In fact, on this view—espoused mainly by the Ash'arites and Zahirites[47]—it would be religiously inappropriate—indeed improper—to seek ultimate explanations and reasons because this would be delving into divine motives, which is inscrutable to human understanding, and involves questioning those motives, which humans have no right to do. A few philosophical arguments were given by Muslim anti-theodicists to reject seeking explanations and justifiable reasons why God might permit evil:

1. A cause cannot ground divine actions because causes are temporal and originated events. Temporal and originated events have prior causes, whereby each cause has a prior cause ad infinitum. Thus, "if God acted on account of a cause or wise purpose, this would entail an endless chain or infinite regress (*tasalsul*) of causes, which the Ash'arites deem impossible."[48]

2. Positing a cause that guides or grounds God's actions implies a lack of

need. If God is sovereign, unbounded in His prerogative, unrestrained in the exercise of His will, and is absolutely powerful, He cannot require causes because acting due to a specific cause will mean He be perfected by it, "because if the occurrence of the cause were not better than its nonexistence, it would not be a cause. One who is perfected by another is imperfect in himself. This is impossible for God."[49]

3. God's commandments ground morality. They are not grounded in any standard external to Himself. If this is the case, then it implies that morality that is constructed by human beings based on subjective formulations is inapplicable to God because He is above any such standards—He *is* the standard.[50]

4. There are no divine obligations so nothing can impose itself on God such that failing to do it, He would be responsible for a fault, wrong, or blame. Such categories cannot apply to God as He owes nothing to anything in what is His creation and kingdom.

5. Explanations for why evils occur only arise if one believes God is motivated to act for what brings about the optimal benefit or good for creatures in any given instance or scenario. Hence, only if one assumes that God is akin to an act-utilitarian being is a theodicy necessary but not if God is a voluntary agent.[51]

The attitude and reasoning of the Muslim anti-theodicist view are starkly captured by the medieval Andalusian exegete and jurist Abu Bakr Ibn al-'Arabi (d. 543/1148):

If it is asked how God can punish creatures without any of them committing any sin or chastise them based on what He had intended for them or had written and determined for them, we will reply by saying what is to prevent Him from doing that—whether rationally or according to the law? If they reply to that by stating the most merciful and wise would not act in such a way, we will reply to that as follows: above is one who commands him and prohibits him. Our Lord may not be questioned about what He does; rather it is *they* who are questioned. It is not permitted to analogise the creation with the Creator nor is it allowed to judge the Creator's actions according to the actions of His creatures. In reality, all actions belong to God and His creation belong to Him; thus, He can do with them as He pleases; judge between them how He sees fit (author's emphasis).[52]

Conclusion

Muslim thinkers engaged deeply with the question of how to meaningfully situate the existence of evil in a world they believed was created for the benefit of human beings. The additional problem they grappled with was how the various token instances of evil like pain, suffering, and horrendous states of affairs are consistent with God's attributes of mercy, compassion, wisdom, and justice. Although many theologians were skeptical of the whole enterprise of theodicy, others did offer explanations—often elaborate and detailed. The remaining chapters will explore some of these elaborate and detailed theodicies.

2

Disability, Suffering, and Four
Theodicies

In this chapter, I will examine four theodicies traceable within the
Islamic primary sources of the Qur'an and Hadith that offer possible explanations why it is that God permits persons to suffer disabilities of various types. This will be followed by a general critique of
their effectiveness from other critical and disability perspectives, with
less emphasis on the formal theological and philosophical underpinnings
that in large part drive the discussion. In this way, the analysis is guided
more by the contents of the Islamic source texts and not analytic theological speculation. This means that the various theological frameworks
that preoccupied the discussions in Chapter 1 are not specifically applied here for addressing the present issue. Although it is arguable that
the Qur'an and Hadith may contain other possible explanatory models
for why some people suffer disabilities (like a free will theodicy or a
communion theodicy), I have restricted myself to only four that I feel
are prominent but often overlooked. The four theodicies I will briefly
examine include:

1. Retribution theodicy
2. Therapeutic theodicy
3. Greater-Good theodicy
4. Educative theodicy

I will then elaborate on the fourth theodicy, offering a version that attempts to afford a way to defeat ostensibly destructive forms of disability
drawing on the Islamic virtue of hospitality or *diyafa*.

Preliminaries

I feel a preliminary observation is necessary before I proceed, which relates to the state of study regarding disability and Islamic (philosophical) theology, law, and spirituality. Much like the attitude toward persons with disability, the Islamic academic cosmos has situated disability studies on the peripheral orbit.[1] This is a mistaken positioning. The current engagement of Euro-American Islamic studies with the field of disability studies is tentative and marginal. At present, other than a few academic monograph-length treatments and a finite set of book chapters or journal articles (some of which are cited in this chapter) little substantial development seems forthcoming.[2] If this is the forecast trend, then it is a costly oversight for a number of reasons. I will briefly mention only three. First, many Muslims have disabilities and many Muslim academics and religious scholars are persons with disabilities and so there is a fact of disabled experience that needs room to work out thinking on Islam from a disability perspective, which will inevitably involve new and divergent methodological and hermeneutical considerations from the inherited premodern interpretive traditions and their corpus. Second, the rich and diverse Islamic scriptural and intellectual resources (historical and current) can bring into conversation precepts, ideas, and arguments that can be utilized in interrogating and contesting the philosophical and anthropological assumptions grounding the field of current Western disability studies concepts and activist practice and propose instead alternative perspectives for consideration. This will not only erect a dialogue between contrasting assessments of what disability is and its related areas of inquiry but also offer an Islamic critical lens that will no doubt enrich disability scholarship. Last, and perhaps more fundamentally, the Qur'an itself thrusts disability into the center frame of the Islamic message—most explicitly in the account of the blind man (*a'ma*) whom the Prophet Muhammad "frowned" and "turned away" from due to annoyance on being interrupted in conversation. The entire 80th chapter of the Qur'an was pointedly named after that incident as "'Abasa" ("He Frowned"). The unnamed blind person in the Qur'anic chapter is identified as 'Abd Allah ibn Umm Maktum who sincerely and eagerly approached the Prophet seeking religious instruction and learning but was ignored as the Prophet was preoccupied with addressing Islam to a hardened and powerful elite group of Meccans. As a result, a "deft and pithy set of verses" were revealed to the Prophet for failing to give proper attention to 'Abd Allah ibn Umm Maktum—something the Prophet subsequently regretted his entire life.[3] Whenever he would see 'Abd Allah ibn Umm Maktum, he would remark, "welcome o dear one about whom my Lord reproached me (*'atabani rabbi*)" and in honoring him would extend his robe for him to wear.[4] Sa'diyya Shaikh has highlighted some of the important lessons to be learned from the incident,[5] but it is the reordering of priorities with disability in focus that is particularly pertinent. On this, Shaikh comments:

> As such, this narrative does not simply help us to illuminate the margins but also functions discursively to pivot the disabled person into the heart of the ethical discourse about moral subjectivity. The narrative renders Abdullah's impairment (blindness) or "difference" from the able-bodied persons fully visible while simultaneously asserting his complete moral agency and total equality within the community of believers.[6]

What this account of 'Abd Allah ibn Umm Maktum results in is that the Qur'an "invites him and by extension all forms of disability and 'otherness' that might be placed at the social margins into an egalitarian centre of shared human value," one that allows a blind man—a person with disability—to occupy "the focal point of the divine gaze, a gaze that sees fully and clearly and renounces alterity and calls for life-giving and nurturing forms of sociality."[7] Given this centrality, the alliance between Islamic studies and disability studies needs further strengthening so that Muslim persons with disability can claim their scripture and appropriate their disability discourse in a meaningful and critically constructive way. The present chapter is a small attempt at forging this alliance between both disciplines for a productive engagement but all too aware that, in so doing, it was done with enormous shortcomings.

Disability

Many verses of the Qur'an and numerous reports from the Prophet that form the Hadith do not address a special category of "disability" as the modern English term is understood, defined, and used by the World Health Organization (WHO) or related institutions.[8] In fact, it is arguable the concept of disability in the conventional sense may not be found in the Qur'an in that there is not a single term that encompasses the impairments typically associated with disability in the modern English context. Rather, two senses seem to be used in the Islamic source texts: the first sense is something approximating a person (or category) who is in a socially disadvantaged state or condition where the requisite values and qualities necessary for living and interacting as a member of society are absent or minimally present.[9] Generalized adjectives referring to persons with such states and conditions include orphans (*yatim*), the weak, (*da'if*), the oppressed (*mustad'af*), the destitute (*miskin*), the sick (*marid*), the poor (*faqir*), and the traveler (*musafir*). The second sense is instances of specific impairments, whether (1) sensory impairments like muteness (*kharas*), blindness (*'ama*), and deafness (*samam*); (2) physical impairments like being immobile (*a'raj*); or (3) mental impairment like loss of sanity (*majnun*) or cognitive functioning,[10] although leprosy does receive a comparatively extensive treatment in the literature than others.[11] The benefits of this kind of terminology have been noted:

> First, the lack of a term comparable to disability in the classical Islamic sources affirms the moral neutrality and normalcy of disability as a fact of life. There is no stigma or evil associated with any term to describe individuals with disabilities. Indeed, the words used are entirely descriptive. Moreover, whereas the English term *disability* contains an explicit denotation of "lacking ability" and is laced with a negative connotation, the classical Arabic words do not contain an indication of "absence," thereby avoiding the creation of an implicit norm that excludes disability. Second, the classical sources recognise disability in the context of both individual condition and social disadvantage, using the relevant terms in discussion of individual rights as well as obligations of societal responsibility and service.[12]

Owing to this lack of singular all-encompassing term, it could be considered that disability and any spectrum of genetic, congenital, and acquired disabilities be taken as subtypes subsumed under the general adverse states of afflictions and misfortunes (*musiba*) mentioned in the Qur'an or, alternatively, as a fact of diversity in creation (the "normalcy of difference")[13] as mentioned in al-Rum, verse 22 and other chapters that invite the readers to reflect on that diversity. Disability on the theodicy models to be examined in this chapter is broadly conceived as something that is a cause of not only pain and suffering but also dysfunction and loss, meaning that disability causes psychosomatic distress and agony, hinders functionality, and curtails opportunities and possibilities to flourish as a social agent in a lived context.[14] These outcomes are involuntary and externally imposed whether by God determining that as part of His decree (*qada'*), through the agency of another by infliction of harm, or through the socially constructed apparatus that creates and imposes states of exclusion. Despite these tangible adverse realities, disability will be argued to have multiple instrumental value beyond the parameters of the person with disability. Thus, an assumption here is that the task of theodicy discussed in the previous chapter is a feasible enterprise, meaning that if

God's acts and motives are guided by His wisdom, mercy, and justice, and these are amenable to a certain degree to human reason, some possible explanations can be given that may justify God's permission of disability. The chapter will for the most part refer to persons with disability who are not constituted by impediments to their functioning and positioning as legally and morally obligated persons before the law (*mukallafin*).[15] Thus, disability here primarily focuses on those without severe sensory, cognitive, and intellectual disabilities that considerably diminish meaningful human functioning or modalities of disability that fail to reach some defined minimum threshold of such functioning. However, mention will be made of those who do suffer from such challenging states and conditions where it becomes especially pertinent for the discussion or where the theodicy directly relates to it.

In Islamic theology, the discussion regarding why specifically persons with disability are made to endure pain and suffering falls under the general topic of why the righteous or innocent suffer. Those considered righteous include divinely inspired Prophets and Messengers who are impeccable (in that they do not commit sins) as well as saints (*awliya'*) and general pious believers. Those categorized as innocent include children, the severely disabled, and animals—those lacking the requisite capacity for legal and moral obligation before the law (*ghayr mukallafin*). The deep theological problem of disability raised questions in the minds of early Muslims. The arch heretic within Muslim heresiographical literature al-Jahm b. al-Safwan (d. 128/746), for example, believed God acted solely based on His power and not out of His mercy or wisdom and so we ought not to be surprised if we see distressing phenomena. Ibn Taymiya relates an incident about Jahm gathering his students around lepers and in mocking fashion points at the lepers, remarking that they are a result of the work of an absolutely merciful God:

> It was related regarding him that he [Jahm] would go out among the lepers exclaiming "look at what the Most Merciful does to such people!" denying [God] the attribute of mercy and alleging that He acts solely on His will unguided by any specific wise purposes.[16]

The general problem of unmerited suffering for persons today makes them "doubt God's goodness" and "does little to placate a righteous person's fear of earthly misery and suffering." Indeed, the idea of a person's "predetermined suffering implicates God in the authorship of an act that seems to cause both physical and moral evil."[17]

This chapter therefore will primarily focus on the interrelated connections between sin, punishments, and the grueling circuit of existential trials and tribulations as they relate to innocents like persons with disability and how that can be explained within an Islamic scriptural and value-framework.

Retribution Theodicy

Some verses of the Qur'an suggest that physical disabilities arise out of some prior committal of sin that forms the reason for God punishing communities or individuals in various ways. Disability on this reading—although not a demonological symbol—is nevertheless a signifier of God's wrath and discipline. This indeed is how some of the companions of the Prophet Muhammad interpreted their personal experiences with afflictions believing that God individualized His punishment by specifically meting it out on them. Advocating this kind of theodicy rests on a retributive idea of God's justice, which is a supernaturally originated but temporally enacted chastisement that is not primarily for corrective purposes but a direct recompense for wrongdoing. Michael Murray explains the multiple functions of this divine punishment: "Defenders of the punishment theodicy have argued that pain can be good for one (or more) of four things: *rehabilitation, deterrence, societal protection*, and *retribution*."[18] Abdulziz Sachedina explains this retributive view as "a divinely sanctioned evil inflicted to teach humanity in general—as opposed to a particular person—a lesson in humility."[19] Sachedina also notes the human irresponsibility that brings about just deserts where "the guilt and suffering that attend the evil perpetrated by a human free agent are often viewed as the just deserts of the wrongdoer" and therefore a nature "correlation is drawn between the freely committed evil and the personal suffering endured by the human author of evil."[20]

In contrast, Rispler-Chaim in *Disability in Islamic Law* optimistically claims that "it is never proclaimed that the disease is predestined by Allah so that the ill Muslim has an opportunity to repent or that disease is a way of punishment for certain sins." In fact, she insists, nowhere does it mention "in the Qur'an, Sunna or fiqh" any "clear causality established between Allah and on the onset of a disease and/or disability in a believer."[21] Sara Scalenghe also shares this optimistic view. She writes that "the central tenets and overarching moral framework of the Qur'an display many similarities to those of the Bible, but the notion of impairment as a product of divine retribution does not feature prominently in Islamic theology" and hence the overall "link between impairment and sin was decidedly de-emphasized," explaining the main reason being due to the "function of the absence in Islamic theology of the doctrine of original sin, of human as inherently sinful beings, which is central to Christianity."[22]

This kind of view that imputes the cause of disability to endowed human agency and not God, of course, assumes that the Qur'an endorses an anthropology of *autonomy* and not an *anthropology* of determinism. Yet, Qur'anic verses do seem to establish a causal link between various types of affliction (personal or communal) and sin. This would be how many premodern Qur'an commentators have read the verses. If disability falls under afflictions and misfortunes and if they are caused because of sin, then disability would be caused because of sin. In al-Nisa', verse 79, for example, it reads that *what comes to you of good is from God, but what comes to you of bad, is from yourself.* The term "good" (*hasana*) is often interpreted to broadly equate with divine favors like prosperity, health, and well-being, and the word "bad" (*sayyi'a*) is taken as a counterpart to good and is broadly equated with "misfortunes" (*musiba*) like calamities and infertility.[23] It is God who is ultimately responsible for inflicting suffering, not human beings, and the suffering can be the conferral of disability. Sachedina notes some of the theological problems this view or language about God's permission of afflictions and suffering creates such as imputing evil to God, "in other words," on this kind of view, "both the Qur'an and Muslim traditions treat suffering as both an inevitable aspect of human experience, and as a problem of faith or theodicy, as it is ultimately the Almighty Creator who causes evil or suffering."[24]

On the causative aspect of the verse, one reading of "*from yourself*" is "on account of your sins" and in a second reading it is more generally, "on account of your actions."[25] Another verse purported to establish a link between afflictions and sin is in al-Rum, verse 41: *corruption has appeared throughout the land and sea by [reason of] what the hands of people have earned so He may let them taste part of [the consequence of] what they have done that perhaps they will return [to righteousness].* Ibn al-Jawzi (d. 597/1200) interprets *what the hands of people have earned* as "due to the acts of sin such people committed."[26] Moreover, in al-Shura, verse 30 states that *And whatever strikes you of affliction—it is for what your hands have earned; but He pardons much.* Al-Razi equates afflictions in this verse with illnesses among other things. He comments, "what is meant here by 'afflictions' (*musiba*) are disliked states and conditions like pain, long-term illnesses, being drowned or struck by lightning and similar disasters."[27] Al-Baydawi (d. 685/1286) interprets *what your hands have earned* as "due to your sins and acts of disobedience (*ma'asikum*)."[28] Ibn Kathir (d. 774/1373) in his commentary of this verse alludes to the gravity of sin and its cause for divine retribution through affliction:

[The verse means] whatever misfortune befalls you, O people, is because of evil deeds that you have already done, and "*He pardons much*" refers to evil deeds—He does not punish you for them but He pardons them. "*And if God were to punish men for that which they earned, he would not leave a moving creature on the surface of the earth.*"[29]

This scriptural connection between possible blighted bodies, physical affliction, and sin was also a personalized connection made by early Muslims. The companion of the Prophet 'Imran b. al-Husayn (d. 52/672) is an example as related by the Egyptian polymath Jalal al-Din al-Suyuti (d. 911/1505) who directly attributes his physical disease to his religious failings:

> Some of the companions [of 'Imran] went to see him. He had been afflicted with a disease on his body. They remarked when they saw him: "we feel really sorry for you because of what we see on you." ['Imran] replied: "don't feel aggrieved because this is due to a sin but God pardons more" and then he recited the verse "*and whatever strikes you of affliction—it is for what your hands have earned.*"[30]

The Qur'an commentator of Andalusia Ibn 'Atiya (d. 541/1146) relates a few incidents involving early Muslim pietistic figures and how they explained the cause of their various afflictions being sin:

> Al-Hamdani said: I saw once on the palm of Shurayh's hand a small ulcer. I asked him: O Abu Umayya, what is this? He replied [reciting the verse]: "*it is for what your hands have earned; but He pardons much.*" Ibn 'Awn said: when Muhammad b. Sirin was saddled with debt, he became distressed because of it. He said [in his condition]: I know why I am in this distress; it is due to a sin I committed forty years ago. Ahmad b. Abi al-Hawari said: Abu Sulayman al-Darani was asked: what is with the virtuous (*fudala'*) in removing any blame from the bad that befalls them? He replied: they know very well that God Most High is testing them due to their sins and then he recited the verse, "*it is for what your hands have earned; but He pardons much.*"[31]

There are also many cases reported in various hadiths of specific afflictions of disability or diseases explained due to improper actions, misdemeanors, or wrong actions. One explicit example is that of Prophet Sulayman who on account of failing to utter "God willing" (*insha' Allah*) for his ambition to produce offspring with his numerous wives that will become warriors in God's path was granted "half a human baby" (*shiqq al-ghulam*) from one wife as a chastisement,[32] which may be understood as a baby with dysmorphic features. Another example includes the case of Jamra bint al-Harith (or Harath) b. 'Awf al-Muzani whose father tried to excuse her from being proposed to by the Prophet by claiming that she had leprosy (*baras*). The Prophet on realizing this stated that she will be afflicted with leprosy due to this blatant false explanation and it occurred. Al-Ghazali reports this under the closing section on the Prophet's miracles and signs from *The Book on the Etiquette of Living* in *Ihya' 'ulum al-din*:

> The Prophet proposed to a woman but her father said that she had leprosy in order to prevent the proposal from taking place when she in fact did not. The Prophet on account of this said, "she will have that." She as a result became a leper known as the mother of Shabib b. al-Barsa' the poet and there are many other examples of his miracles and signs.[33]

In a narration reported in Abu Dawud's compilation, Yazid b. Bahram recounts how he became crippled (and was called the "seated one" [*al-muq'ad*]) for cursing the Prophet: "I saw a crippled man at Tabuk. He (the man) said: 'I passed riding a donkey in front of the Prophet who was praying.' He said (cursing him): 'O God, cut off his walking!' Thereafter, I could not walk."[34] The esteemed Hadith critic Ibn Abi Hatim al-Razi (d. 327/938) relates that Abu al-Bilad recited to al-'Ala' b. Badr verse 30 from al-Shura: "I recited the verse *and whatever strikes you of affliction, it is for what your hands have earned* and he asked: 'why did I lose my eyesight while a young boy?' He replied: because of the sins of your parents."[35] This is one explicit report of an early pious figure interpreting the sins of one's parents as the direct cause of their child's impairment. These examples and others illustrate how a form of retribution theodicy is a way to explain suffering. Disability thereby is explained through merited suffering for the iniquitous. A focal point of the theodicy seems to be that God afflicting individuals or communities with calamities or specific illnesses, diseases, and/or impairments (and thereby causing their disability) does not bring into question His fairness or justice but brings to light the failure of human beings to live by revelatory commandments. The rule of human worldly success is: living by God's stipulations brings about prosperity and success and the contrary brings about misery and affliction. The examples cited from individuals within the early Muslim communities indicate this shift of focus away from God's retribution to the causal agency or culpability of the sufferer. This provides a useful hermeneutical window into the way affliction was understood, framed, and internalized by such a community.

The retributive theodicy generates some serious objections. First, it is extremely restrictive as an explanatory model because by no means is all disability a result of wrongdoing. Hence, merely equating disability with sin in this reductive way is truncated in its explanatory scope. Second, it seems to suggest that persons with disability are entirely or partially at fault for the disabilities they have acquired. This further suggests that there are no other welcome, positive, and beneficial resources within the Qur'an and Hadith to ameliorate the pain, distress, and anxieties caused by disability except divine judgment. Hope and comfort do not seem like possibilities on this model. Third, seeing disabilities as punishment for sins or moral transgressions whether in a prior state of an able-bodied perpetrator or by one's parents and ancestors would be to characterize it as a pollution, an evil, and hence by implication define the very default existence of a disabled person as evil. This would be laying the basis for a kind of regressive theology regarding persons with disability when the Prophet came with a new and transformative engagement with disability to a society that valorized physical prowess, strength, and horsemanship and assumed a physicalist aesthetics. Such a denigrating perspective on disability would also appear to contradict firm Qur'anic principles such as (1) there is no transferal of sin; (2) there is no sin without accountability, (3) no one can bear the burden of another, (4) no one is punished for the crimes of another,[36] and (5) none shall be burdened with more than they can bear.[37] A possible response to this, however, is that the association or causal link between disability (mainly impairments) and moral infraction in the Qur'an and hadiths is profoundly ambivalent. Indeed, there does not seem to be a conscious causal association in these Islamic primary sources between sin and disability. Ghaly points out that verses of the Qur'an and interpretations of the hadiths of the Prophet "indicate that disabilities *may be* but need not *necessarily be* the result of committing sins" and gives examples:

> For instance, when Mu'awiya b. Abi Sufyan was afflicted with facial paralysis, he mentioned three possible reasons, i.e., gaining reward, receiving punishment and finally receiving a disciplinary reproach. According to this view, in the normal course of events disobedient people receive more than one warning before being punished. Disabilities or misfortunes, as punishments, befall those who insist on paying no attention to such

warnings and make no efforts to return to the straight path, declare no repentance to God and continue their disobedience.[38]

This association between disability and sin is perhaps more to do with how specific companions of the Prophet interpreted their own realities of disease, disfigurement, and impairments through the prism of sin rather than it being a scripturally espoused normative conceptual framework for understanding the etiology of disability in general.

Therapeutic Theodicy

This way of explaining the existence of disability is to characterize it as curative, meaning it serves to contribute to the overall afterlife well-being of the sufferer. The disability would be a temporal means to securing pardon of sins or afterlife reward. Rispler-Chaim notes:

> Disease is not perceived by Muslims as an expression of Allah's wrath or as punishment from heaven either, but as a test which can atone for one's sins. Health and sickness become part of the continuum of being, and prayer remains the salvation in both health and sickness. A Prophetic tradition asserts "Whoever dies in any illness is a martyr." This attests that an illness may have some redeeming powers, such as atoning for sins and the like.[39]

Ghaly describes this as a "cathartic function," a process whereby God provides positive spiritual relief for any persons with disability from his/her strong experiences of suffering "by purging the sinner from his sins and bringing him relief from greater torment in the Hereafter."[40] The Prophet is reported to have mentioned many times the therapeutic nature of hardship, suffering, pain, and affliction. In one version of the narration, the Prophet states as reported by Muhammad b. Khalid al-Sulami: "From his father and his grandfather who was a companion of the Messenger of God who said: I heard the Messenger of God say: 'When God has previously decreed for a servant a rank which he has not attained by his action, He afflicts him in his body (*ibtala Allah fi jasadihi*), or his property or his children.'"[41] The representation of bodily affliction to encompass physical disability in this context actually becomes a token of God's benevolence and mercy toward a person with disability. This is underpinned by God's desire for their afterlife elevation in religious rank. In another narration, reported by the companions Abu Sa'id al-Khudri (d. 74/693) and Abu Hurayra (d. 58/678), the Prophet assures that "no fatigue, nor disease, nor sorrow, nor sadness, nor hurt, nor distress befalls a Muslim, even if it were the prick he receives from a thorn, but that God expiates his sins for that."[42] The Hadith equates an acquired disability with atonement of sins. Although God on the majority theological understanding is the cause of all types of afflictions and misfortunes, the causes are for the benefit of the recipient because it constitutes an automatic atonement for any sins. Even more explicit regarding the therapeutic nature of disability is the following narration attributed to the companion 'Abd Allah ibn Mas'ud (d. 83/702): "loss of eyesight is a means for forgiveness; loss of hearing is a means for forgiveness, and any bodily impairment will receive a similar recompense."[43] Ibn al-Qayyim elaborates on the wisdom behind this kind of therapeutic theodicy:

> Were it not that The Most Glorified treats (yudawi) His servants with the remedy of trials and calamities, they would transgress and overstep the mark. When God wills good for His servant, He gives him the medicine of calamities and trials according to his situation and circumstances, so as to cure him from all fatal illnesses and diseases, until He purifies and cleanses him, and then makes him qualified for the most honourable position in this world, which is that of being a true servant of God and for the greatest reward in the Hereafter, which is that of seeing Him and being close to Him.[44]

Here as well, there is overlap, with disabilities being explained through a communion theodicy,[45] where in this case God determines or creates a person with specific disabilities as a means to allow them to draw nearer to Him. The temporal struggle through life for any person with a severe disability and indeed for their committed carer is compensated with God's pleasure and proximity. Thus, in the midst of suffering, the afflicted may draw closer to God in the end.

I mentioned above how the retributive theodicy model explains disability as a possible chastisement for temporal commission of sin; there are, however, alternative suggestions whereby the disability is actually a beneficent means of reward from God (and not a chastisement) as affirmed by the Prophet in several narrations. This would mean that any disability in reality is a sign of God's mercy and not His wrath. In a hadith, the Prophet comments:

> Whatever befalls you of illness, punishment or misfortune in the worldly life is because of what your hands have wrought, but God is more tolerant than doubling the punishment [by inflicting it again] in the Hereafter. As

for what God has pardoned in [the worldly] life, [one should know that] God is more bountiful than reverting [to punishing] after His pardon.[46]

This narration also suggests that God does not punish after pardoning; that is, God may reward in multiples but never punishes in multiples. This beneficence is further brought out in how those with disability lose no opportunities to gain divine favor or reward due to their disability. A principle of continuity in rewards is employed by God regarding a person's predisabled state with their postdisabled state. Ghaly explains:

Another sign of God's mercy mentioned in the tradition in this regard concerns the rewards of good deeds that the afflicted person did before the affliction hindered him/her from continuing to do them. In Hadith collections, one finds separate chapters on the reward of the sick (*ajr al-marid*). These chapters comprise a number of prophetic traditions suggesting that the rewards of such deeds continue to be recorded as if they were still being done.[47]

One such narration Ghaly is referring to is:

No Muslim would be visited with an affliction in his body save God would order the Guardians [Angels] who guard him by saying, "Write down for My servant every day and night the equal [reward] of the good [*khayr*] he was doing as long as he is confined in My fetter [i.e., sickness]."[48]

Here, any good action by which a person accrues reward as an able-bodied person will continue to accrue the same or more reward as long as they remain in their acquired state of disability. It would be as though they were directly committing the action as an able-bodied person. Ghaly writes:

By extension to disability, we may conclude that a person who used to listen to a specific portion of the Qur'an every day and later on was hindered from doing so by deafness is a further example. The divine rewards accorded for this pious act would go on being counted as if he were still in the habit of listening to the Qur'an every day.[49]

Hence, although physical disabilities can affect the overall modality of engaging with stipulated and mandatory religious injunctions pertaining to ritual and behavior, insofar as the spiritual quality and afterlife compensation are concerned, nothing whatsoever diminishes. This theodicy shifts perspective away from God's agency as it relates to the cause and affliction of disability and appears to locate significance more in scripturally grounded imaginings of how God relates to His creatures through His exemplification of various names and qualities (*al-asma' wa-l-sifat*) such as love, benevolence, mercy, and compassion. These grounded imaginings convey how persons of disability are meant to understand the way the afterlife reward scheme operates for any pain and suffering incurred in this life and how that ultimately embodies gain and not loss.

Critical remarks from a disability perspective on this theodicy include how, for example, it rests at core on a principle of delayed reward. God propositions a person with disability with a deferred reward of a purgative state for enduring the agony of suffering in the world. Yet all the while, the time delay between a person's temporal suffering, its purportedly curative work, and the final reward it brings about suggests God recedes into the background of the suffering, becoming a hidden observer to the person of disability instead of their healer—approximating more a *deus absconditus* instead of the *deus revelatus*. Moreover, the theodicy creates dissonance in persons with disability rather than strong optimism. It fails to facilitate any requisite congruence between one's *concepts* of God and one's *images* of God.[50] The former constitutes the cognitive beliefs about God that a person with disability acquires through discursive learning and being taught about the divine from various social and institutional sources—in short, the theology they adopt. The latter forms the emotional and relational experience of God that develops as a latent construct primarily through the way God relates to the lives of persons with disability. The pain and suffering arising from disability generates a discrepancy between the concept of God and the image of God that seems not to be filled by descriptive notifications of the therapeutic function of disability. God would want to minimize the dissonance a person has between these concepts about Him and the images of Him as this would alleviate the cognitive suffering.

Greater-good Theodicy

This model attempts to explain the pain and suffering caused by disability based on a higher value obtained in the afterlife. God will compensate the bad arising from temporal hardship of a person with disability with an outweighing good in the eschaton. In other words, God will allow some evil E such as suffering due to disabilities if and only if it can be used to bring about a greater good G. The permission or allowance of disability is necessary for the realization of a greater good. The theodicy rests on a correspondence between persons and their receiving a greater good.

The net bad judged by human beings to have registered in the history or life-course of a person with disability would, in the greater scheme of existence, be balanced or more than exceed the balance. This kind of greater-good (G-G) theodicy can be extracted from numerous narrations attributed to the Prophet that accord divine reward and tributes to those who suffered impairments or loss of human bodily and cognitive assets. The sixteenth-century hadith commentator and theologian Mulla ʿAli al-Qari (d. 1606) composed a small text called *Tasliyat al-aʿma ʿala baliyat al-ʿama* ("Consoling the Blind for the Affliction of Blindness") in which he "gathered forty narrations (*arbaʿun hadithan*)[51] on patience in the face of trials, gratitude for divine blessings, and contentment with the divine decree in times of happiness and hardship"[52] as a way of consoling those afflicted with visual impairments whether congenital or acquired. The greater good rewards and tributes discussed specifically regarding visual and hearing impairments by Muslim theologians are generically applicable to all types of disability as they are subsumed under afflictions. The set of greater goods for persons with disabilities includes:

1. Elevation in the person's rank before God due to the disability.[53]
2. Assurance of Paradise for the person suffering through the disability.[54]
3. Brightening face on Judgement Day on account of patience through adversity.[55]
4. Atonement of sins.[56]
5. Becoming beloved to God.[57]
6. God's tribute for the person before the angelic host.[58]

One could argue perhaps that this model is not theoretically a theodicy as much as it is an eschatology. The suffering and pain arising from disability in this world will find its defeat in the hereafter through a myriad manifestation of God's mercy and beneficence. In this way, the perspective that disability symbolizes some representation of evil is transformed into radiant symbols of dignity, elevation, and laudation in the eschaton. However, this theodicy raises difficult theological issues.[59] One issue is that it may seem like false assurances, a way of deferring the problem into the realm of a later existence which would do nothing to assuage or comfort the person with disability right here and now. In the short-term perspective, it would not seem therapeutic at all. Moreover, on the G-G theodicy model, disability would either have to be *incidental* to or *necessary* for securing the set of afterlife goods mentioned in the hadiths. By "incidental" is meant that the particular set of goods does not need that specific disability. In other words, could God have realized the set of goods for a person in this world without granting that particular disability on them. This would further mean that the disability is purely gratuitous on God's part—the set of goods did not need that bad. If, on the other hand, the disability is necessary for securing the set of goods mentioned, then it would have to be demonstrated how the set of goods mentioned can only be secured through the specific disability of that person. If God is unable to secure those goods without that disability, it would seem to suggest there is something that He cannot bring about, namely a set of goods without a specific disability. This has implications on divine omnipotence. If the set of goods is part of God's eschatological compensation or reward plan, and it cannot be achieved or completed without the disability to secure those set of goods, then God must make disability unavoidably part of His plan. This would mean as well that God wills the disability on people. He would not be able to do otherwise and he would be the cause of evil. Furthermore, it seems that if suffering through disability secures a greater set of goods, then the more a person with disability suffers, the better it would be. It would be better to leave the person with disability to endure the adverse condition by placating them with news of a greater reward in store. Finally (and related to this previous point) on a practical level, if God brings about disability because it will secure a greater set of goods for an individual or group, then there may be a diminished motive for addressing illnesses and diseases through medical intervention. There may be no desire to eliminate or reduce the suffering caused by various disabilities because it is in fact a necessary adverse state for securing a greater set of goods. The result will be an inculcation of passivity in the face of affliction. Sachedina makes this very point, noting how "the Qur'an admonishes human beings to endure adversity patiently" and although enduring such adversity may instill "further confidence in the wisdom of God, who allows affliction as a necessary part of a greater plan" it nevertheless "seems to reinforce Muslim passivity in the face of afflictions."[60] The attitude of passivity becomes an indicator of pietistic resignation to God's overarching program. It would not be right on this logic, therefore, to intervene with medical measures for the care of persons with disability. In the context of medical intervention and application, Sachedina worries that such scriptural references to resignation before God's plans become a "major source of a quietism, and resignation" that will dangerously "impede the seeking of medical treatment in some quarters of Muslim society" because it is God who is regarded as "the only healer, who, if he willed, could cure the illness and eliminate suffering" and a "true believer" would put his/her "trust in God and depend on him and none other for deliverance from pain and suffering."[61] A clear example of this kind attitude is in the incident of Sa'ida al-Asadiya who came to the Prophet and asked him to pray for her well-being as she was prone to seizures because of her epilepsy. 'Ata' ibn Abi Rabah relates the narration in full:

Ibn 'Abbas said to me ['Ata' ibn Abi Rabah]: "Shall I show you a woman of the people of Paradise?" I replied: "of course." He said: "This black lady came to the Prophet and said: 'I get attacks of epilepsy and my body becomes uncovered; please pray to God for me.' The Prophet said [to her]: 'If you wish, be patient and Paradise is yours; or if you wish, I will pray to God to cure you.' [The lady] said: 'I will remain patient,' and added: 'but I become uncovered, so please pray to God for me that I may not become uncovered.' So [the Prophet] prayed to God for her."[62]

One of the most senior hadith commentators of the Mamluk period Ibn Hajar al-'Asqalani (who incidentally had to relinquish his senior administrative post as supervisor due to his recurring ophthalmia)[63] comments on this narration:

This narration contains lessons such as: epilepsy can be something positive. Patience in the face of suffering bequeaths paradise. Adopting the more severe course of action is more meritorious than acting on an exemption for anyone who knows his own ability and strength and will not weaken by adopting that which is more severe. In [the narration] is evidence for the permissibility of refusing medication and that the remedy for any illness is praying to God. Moreover, seeking refuge in God is more beneficial than taking prescribed drugs. Its effects and the body's reaction to it are greater than the physical remedies. However, the beneficial effects only occur if two matters exist: the first is from the aspect of the patient which is true sincerity and intention and the second is from the aspect of the practitioner whose heart must be firm with God-consciousness and reliance. And god knows best.[64]

Here, the lady opted out of choice to endure the difficulty of seizures over the easier option of being healed. She rationalized her preferences based on the two options and judged the alternative to be in her afterlife self-interest. In this way, her relinquishing medical intervention is interpreted as a meritorious and exemplary attitude toward personal disability in the face of hardship. Interestingly, second only to her pain and distress, the lady was extremely mindful of her compromised modesty in public when suffering these seizures and implored the Prophet to supplicate to

God to spare her from that. Her attitude captured the admiration of the Prophet's companions and the subsequent Muslim community in general because she emulated the moral paradigm of the Prophets like Ayyub (Job) who endured undeserved personal suffering with patience without challenging God to explain the reasons behind such afflictions.[65]

Educative Theodicy

The aim under this final theodicy model is to explain disability as possessing a pedagogical purpose. On the one hand, the person's disability becomes an enabling factor for virtue-building as well as cognitive illumination. This means that such persons develop moral properties to become a better servant of God in addition to gaining a better understanding of themselves and their lives, their role as God's temporal representatives (khulafa'), and indeed greater wisdom embedded in God's overarching scheme of creation and purpose through the realization or acquisition of their disability. On the other hand, disability on this model also constitutes a means whereby the Islamic social goods and virtues like hospitality (diyafa) can be structured and developed in order to enable individual and communal flourishing. Disability then despite its connection with vulnerability becomes an instrument of enlightened instruction to develop humility, poverty, and need for others in an interconnected relation of vulnerability and interdependency that collectively seeks to overcome suffering by endowing it with meaning-making significance.

Turning to the first part of the educative theodicy, which is the personal pedagogical context of disability, the explanatory angle here is that through divine trials and tribulations as tests, opportunities arise for augmentation of the self (nafs) in order to nurture it with qualities necessary for becoming a praiseworthy servant and representative of God.[66] Such inner attitudinal qualities, for example, include patience (sabr), gratitude (shukr), reliance on God (tawakkul), and states such as total submission and servitude to God ('ubudiya).[67] Traversing the journey of embracing and coping with disabilities on this account would be an ongoing religious test provided by God to activate that religious growth potential. Rouzati has extensively discussed the cosmological significance of the Qur'anic concept of "bala" (trials and tribulations in prosperity and adversity) as well as its related concept "fitna" (trials, tests, sedition) and has also discussed how both function as a means by which a person intellectually and spiritually augments and develops to overcome hardship and suffering.[68] Specifically on bala' and its cognate ibtila, her hypothesis is that "contrary to popular perception," ibtila is not simply to be understood as "synonymous with suffering"; rather, it is an "all-inclusive connotation" by which "mankind is granted the opportunity to actualize the potential of his inner nature."[69] She continues, explaining the rationale for why God tests human beings through adversity:

> The Qur'an explicitly affirms that man, as part of his human experience, will be put to the "test," *bala*, by various means of "good and bad." Consequently, the test encompasses the "negatives," illness, natural disasters, and loss of livelihood, and the "positives," wealth, and good health. What the Qur'an seems to emphasize, however, is man's behaviour and how he perceives the particular circumstances of his life. Needless to say that, by nature, while man strives for joy and happiness; he resists any undesirable situation which may cause him sadness and sorrow . . . however, from the Qur'anic perspective, adversity, misery, and human suffering, is central to man's spiritual development . . . This notion, which frequently appears in explicit terms in the Qur'an, illustrates that suffering is an instrument in the fulfilment of purposes of God in creation of humankind.[70]

Rumi describes the need for *bala'* in this vivid way:

> When someone beats a rug with a stick, he is not beating the rug—his aim is to get rid of the dust.
> Your inward is full of dust from the veil of I-ness, and that dust will not leave all at once.[71]

Mohammad Mobini gives the metaphor of the world as a "laboratory" for developing the experiential knowledge required for a real harmonious and qualitative relationship with God and creatures making earth "a testing ground for us in which we can test the different manners of existing and see what sort is the best." He notes that "God could have given us all such knowledge without sending us to this testing ground, but this would not have been experiential knowledge." In order to make the "necessary knowledge" God has given human beings about Himself effective, "He has sent them into this laboratory in order that their knowledge be supported and strengthened by experiential knowledge."[72]

Aslan also explains the Qur'anic perspective on the overall pedagogical role of trials and tests as well as the nature of suffering which "has sometimes been treated as a sign of spiritual development by society" and "has functioned as a means of building character and developing spiritually," treating it "as gifts from God," an "indicator which really confirms spiritual perfection."[73] Aslan also comments how the Qur'an accepts that suffering and hardship are "facts of human life, but it itself is there to prepare believers, so that they are spiritually and psychologically ready to overcome such difficulties." The net spiritual profit gives outputs like being able to assess the quality of a believer's faith, testing sincerity of belief, or allowing the believer to evaluate what their true personality is or even what positive qualities they have developed.[74] Thus, on Aslan's view, like Mobini and Rouzati, the summative purpose of suffering is a means of God testing the believer in order that they become spiritually developed.[75]

The disability journey then can be seen as a way of God testing the person with disability in order to gauge whether there is in him/her a clear cognitive (re)orientation to their purpose of life here on earth and whether the adversity forges in him/her the desirable transformative religious qualities or positive internal and attitudinal values such as gratitude, patience, and reliance on God necessary to overcome it and thereby gain God's favor. The Islamic perspective informed by the Qur'an and Hadith is that persons with disability are not less than persons of lower moral standing excluded from the requirement of God's revealed religious agenda. There is no exclusion from a reciprocal relation with God on account of a disability. A person with disability undergoes no less of a religious engagement with God (and no less of a struggle) than a nondisabled person. Both are required to know and come to realize that God's power, will, and wisdom providentially govern the inexplicable working intricacies of the world and that in reality, neither of them have any real autonomy because they are under that sovereign direction of God. Neither have ownership over themselves because they are temporal vassals who have been entrusted with their bodies by God—abled and disabled—to fulfill their proper function: servitude and submission to His commandments. Because the Islamic narrative includes no notion of redemption through a savior, a person's "ultimate responsibility is to live according to the potentials of his inner nature capable of fully manifesting the Divine attributes, and yet, realize that the key element in actualization of these potentials is his 'free volition and choice.'"[76] One's able body therefore does not endow any metaphysical or spiritually significant privileges insofar as it relates to the purpose of existence, interior quality of worship, and the ultimate destination of return for all creatures. In fact, disability may be a stronger way to return back to God and a sharper reminder of the primordial covenant (*mithaq*) between all human beings and God mentioned in the Qur'an.[77] Rumi, following Junayd al-Baghdadi's (d. 297/910) covenantal mysticism, for example, "frequently references the primordial covenant, and points out that man is faced with afflictions and sorrow in order to be reminded of his covenant with God. For him, this is precisely the mission of the prophets."[78] This is why Rumi elsewhere writes:

> In order to pull us up and help us travel, messenger after messenger comes from that Source of existence:
> Every heartache and suffering that enters your body and heart pulls you by the ear to the promised Abode.
> He has afflicted you from every direction in order to pull you back to the Directionless.[79]

In his work *Fihi ma fihi*, Rumi highlights how wealth and health can be two impediments to God and as a result become a severe test. He remarks:

> Between God and His servant are just two veils; and all other veils manifest out of thee: they are health, and wealth. The man who is well in body says, "Where is God? I do not know, and I do not see." As soon as pain afflicts him, he begins to say, "O God! O God!" communing and conversing with God. So you see that health was his veil, and God was hidden under that pain. As much as man has wealth and resources, he procures the means to gratifying his desires, and is preoccupied night and day with that. The moment indigence appears, his ego is weakened and he goes round about God.[80]

Far from disability being an impediment in drawing closer to God, it is able-bodied persons who are veiled from God on account of their functioning abilities because it leads them to haughtiness, which in turn causes them to be ignorant of their true reality and status as created beings. This haughtiness and ignorance also become a reason for their negligence in God's remembrance (*dhikr*). If disability shields a person from that negative consequence, it is actually a blessing. A narration of the Prophet in this regard reads: "The blind are not those who have lost their sight but those who have lost their insight."[81] This statement is supported by the Qur'an in al-Hajj, verse 46: *So, have they not travelled through the earth and do they not have hearts by which they reason and ears by which to hear? For indeed, it is not eyes that are blinded. But blinded are the hearts that are in the breasts.* Qur'anic exegetes interpreted this verse in a figurative sense:

> The heart has been used here [in the verse] as a reference to the intellect by way of synecdoche (*majaz mursal*) because the heart is the organ that

pumps blood—the fundamental object of life—to all the vital organs in the body, most important of which is the brain which is a component of the intellect. That is why in the verse it says *"by which they reason"* because the instrument of reasoning is the brain . . . it is not the eyes that see but the heart, meaning that the eyes and ears are the means by which knowledge is acquired from what is seen and heard. That which fathoms or grasps all that is [sensed] is the brain because if the brain does not contain the intellect, then the seer is like a blind person and the hearer a deaf person. Any problems with these senses are due only to a deficiency in the intellect. The second reference to blindness is metaphorical for loss of grasping what is sensed with the intellect despite the power of sight being sound and functional.[82]

In Islam, there is no default special right granted to able-bodied persons on account of their physicality. The body is not the center and the visible disability is not the peripheral and this is because of the lesser value given to the corporeal within the overall Islamic outlook. This does not mean Islam denies the lived experience of embodiment or even carnality,[83] but that its vision and aim were not a "somatic society"[84] that neither situates the body as *loci* of consumption and contestation nor constitutes it as the physical horizon for proper worship. For God, the only acceptable criterion of worship is the quality of consciousness, fear, and presence of Him within a person and this is an interior matter. In a hadith the Prophet reports that "Verily God does not look to your bodies (*ajsadikum*) nor to your faces but He looks only to your hearts (*qulubikum*)."[85] The commentators highlight how the heart is the emphasis and not the physical limbs. Al-Nawawi, for example, writes:

> This narration means that the outward actions do not of themselves realise God-consciousness (*taqwa*); rather God-consciousness occurs in the heart such as awe of God, fear of Him and vigilance of him. What is meant by "God looking" here is His rewarding and accounting a person, that is on account of what is in their hearts and not how they look on the outside. God's look encompasses everything. The whole point of the narration is that the heart alone is what is considered in all these matters.[86]

As for the second part of the educative theodicy, its core is constructed from an examination of the idea of hospitality within the Islamic tradition[87] drawing on Alasdair MacIntyre's concept of "virtues of acknowledged dependence"[88] in addition to a recent paper by Kevin Timpe and Aaron D. Cobb[89] employing hospitality as a way of God providing means to defeat what Marilyn McCord Adams has called "horrendous evils"[90] and what Scott Williams has called "horrendous-difference disabilities."[91] I will first briefly outline Adams's contention followed by a short account of hospitality within the Islamic tradition and how this may serve as a possible defeater for Adams-style problems of horrendous evils like horrendous-difference disabilities incorporating the insights of MacIntyre, Timpe and Cobb, and Williams.

According to Adams, there is a class of evils that are so pernicious, cruel, appalling, horrific, and abhorrent that they strain any hope of being able to explain God's justification for permitting them; these she calls "horrendous evils" and defines it as "evils the participation in which (that is, the doing or suffering of which) constitutes prima facie reason to doubt whether the participant's life could (given their inclusion in it) be a great good to him/her on the whole."[92] What makes these horrendous evils the very type they are is not only the intense somatic pain they cause but also the destructive force it is to a person's self-worth and dignity. Such evils reach into the layered psyche of a person and break their capacity for meaning-making, that is, they have no way to construct positivity from the suffering that gives them a sense of inherent significance and value. These horrendous evils then make a person feel subhuman. The disturbing examples Adams gives include "the rape of a woman and axing off of her arms" and "psychophysical torture" with the ultimate aim being "the disintegration of personality, betrayal of one's deepest loyalties, child abuse of the sort described by Ivan Karamazov, child pornography, parental incest, slow death by starvation."[93]

When our cognitive faculties are functioning, we are able to construct out of the confusing and disorderly flux of our experiences a coherent and comprehensible narrative. We do this through the matrix of aesthetic valuables such as "unity, integrity, harmony, and relevance."[94] They along with our goals, aspirations, ideals, and relationships help configure our lives into a meaningful whole. When we suffer horrendous evils in our lives, we become destructively disoriented—broken from our wholeness—and are unable to formulate a coherent narrative along those aesthetic lines because such evils "overwhelm meaning-making capacities, prima facie stumping us, furnishing strong reason to believe that lives marred by horrors can never again be unified and integrated into wholes with positive meaning."[95] Adams believes that to overcome horrendous evils, it is necessary to return to divine goodness and how that can be related to the broken and vulnerable human condition. This is why she eschews the popular maneuvering by analytic philosophers involving abstract logical arguments set out in a series of premises and statements seeking to defend any possible global goods that may justify why God permits evil.[96] Utilizing Roderick Chisholm's distinction between "balancing off" and "defeating" evil,[97] Adams argues that God's goodness must ensure that (1) any evils are fully outweighed by or exceeded by the inclusion of a greater quantity of good within the context of an individual's life and more importantly that (2) God *defeats* horrendous evils by endowing the harrowing experiences sufficient positive meaning by integrating the evils within a structure of a greater good subjectively appreciated by the individual.[98] It is worth quoting her view in full:

> My notion is that reason to doubt can be outweighed, if the evil *e* can be defeated. The evil *e* can be defeated if it can be included in some good-enough whole to which it bears a relation of organic (rather than merely additive) unity; *e* is defeated within the context of the individual's life if the individual's life is a good whole to which *e* bears the relevant organic unity. If the evil *e* is defeated within the context of an individual *x*'s life, the judgement 'the life of *x* cannot be worthwhile given that it includes *e*' would be defeated, but the judgement "*e* is horrendous" would stand; this is because *e*'s inclusion in a good enough whole (even where the whole is *x*'s complete life span) to which it is related by organic unity does not prevent it by itself from counting as prima facie reason for doubting the positive value of *x*'s life.[99]

In this way, "God as divine artist must be capable of taking the horror-strewn chunks of our personal narratives and reintegrating them into a context where they can contribute positive value to a beautiful whole."[100] God, therefore, is the only goodness great enough to overcome the evil. Adams writes again that "God is good to a created person if and only if God guarantees to him/her a life that is a great good to him/her on the whole and in the end and defeats any individual horror participation within the frame of that individual's life."[101] It is not enough for her that horrendous evils are outweighed in an arithmetic tallying off (much like the Mu'tazilite idea we will explore in the next chapter); rather, God has to show He is *for* the sufferer and not *against* the sufferer by enabling the horrendous evil to be folded into a story with such indispensable value, significance, and meaning that the sufferer would not want to wish that horror away.[102] It is with this deep and expansive power of meaning-making that horrendous evils are defeated. Those suffering must understand their suffering as encompassed within a narrative that they construe as sufficiently meaningful and good for them. This actual and potential for meaning-making capacities, however, would ultimately render those "severely brain deficient" as unable to fulfill the participation required in order to evaluate the horrendous evil in a way that is meaningfully integrated into a coherent narrative for themselves.[103] Therefore, there would be no way of them overcoming the horrendous evils on their own terms because they are not agents that have any pragmatic or substantive cognitive functioning capacities. Despite this, Adams herself optimistically argues that horrendous evils can be defeated through, for example, the beatific vision—the direct perception of God enjoyed by those in Paradise. God is "a being greater than any other conceivable being, as supreme or infinite goodness" and thus "if Divine Goodness is infinite, if intimate relation to It is thus incommensurately good for created persons, then we have identified a good big enough to defeat horrors in every case."[104] Andrew Chignell helpfully summarizes the structure of Adams's theodicy as follows:

> A theodicy is only successful, says Adams, if for any person p it can offer a logically possible and theologically-sound scenario in which God ensures that p's life is a great good to p on the whole, and any horrendous evils p participates in are made meaningful by being defeated, not merely within the context of the world as a whole, but within the scope of p's individual life. This last move involves a change in perspective. It is not sufficient for theodicy that God deem p's life meaningful. Rather, p must attribute positive value to her life from an "internal point of view," where such an attribution involves p herself recognizing "some patterns organizing some chunks of her experiences around goals, ideals, relationships that she stabilizes in valuing."[105]

Building on this characterization of horrendous evil, Williams suggests a subcategory of disabilities he labels as "horrendous-difference disabilities." Drawing on Richard Cross's modified theory of social disability,[106] Williams locates the particularly difficult "badness" of a disability in its impediment toward a person's functioning based on what they wish and desire. Williams calls this basis of functioning "rational moral wish satisfaction" (RMWS). He comments that "sometimes the human function that we wish for matters a lot to us, so much so that lacking this human function can seem to devastate one" and if this devastation then "seems insurmountable to one, then one would have reason to doubt that one's life can be a great good to one on the whole."[107] Williams then explicates this horrendous subtype of disability generated by an impediment toward one's RMWS as follows:

One has a horrendous-difference disability$_{RMWS}$ if and only if: (i) one has a rational wish for some human function F, (ii) what is wished for is morally permissible, (iii) what is wished for is impeded from occurring because one has an intrinsic impediment to human function F, (iv) there are no extrinsic aids that are practically accessible to the individual that would enable the individual to be or have human function F (or approximately F), and (v) on the basis of (i)–(iv) one has prima facie reason to doubt that one's life can be a great good for one on the whole.[108]

Williams gives an example of a 19-year-old girl called Sally who suffers from a mismanaged bipolar disorder in order to help illustrate and apply his definition. Sally, like any other person, "has a rational, moral, wish for the intimacy of friendship with another person, Madison, with whom she has been friends during adolescence." Although Madison wishes to reciprocate Sally's friendship, "she finds herself unable to cope with the symptoms of Sally's bipolar disorder and breaks off the friendship." These bipolar symptoms include Sally being "excessively needy, angry, irritated, mostly talks about her medical condition, has a non-typical sleeping schedule, and calls Madison at all hours of the night." Based on these issues, "Madison judges that she cannot participate in the intimacy of friendship with Sally anymore because opening herself up that way brings significant and likely harm to herself." Williams then asks the reader to suppose that the symptoms of Sally's bipolar alienates her from her family and others "and that this holds true for the remainder of Sally's life." What has happened, Williams concludes, is that "in effect, bipolar has ruined Sally's life" because Sally has "a rational moral wish for a certain human function F (in this case, being friends with Madison), but her wish is impeded by an intrinsic property (bipolar disorder) and it is impeded by extrinsic circumstances (e.g., no practical access to medicine and ways to manage the bipolar disorder)." In addition to the personal challenges, suppose further that "Sally lives in a society with few social safety nets and so has no extrinsic aids e.g., the relevant medicine, doctors, care-givers, or counsellors—that might be conducive for maintaining friendship with Madison." If this is the overall state of affairs, then Sally would have prima facie reason "to doubt that her life can be a great good for her on the whole." And if Sally's "contingent historical circumstances were different in the relevant ways, then Sally would not have prima facie reason to doubt that her life could be a great good for her on the whole)."[109]

In addition to this subclass of horrendous-difference disability regarding RMWS, Williams adds another related subclass, which is those persons who have severe or what he terms "profound cognitive disabilities" (PCDs) that eliminate any possibility of typical developmental stages during life. This results in an absence within the person of any rational moral wishes for a particular human function F. Further consequences are that owing to a lack of any cognitive capacities for development, such persons have no sense of self-conception, identity, or indexicality. Such complex and compound cognitive deficiencies originate from intrinsic factors (internal makeup) and are not necessarily from externally imposed constraints or impediments (though they too may arise).[110] Such persons, therefore, would not possess the relevant capacities for recognizing their own participation in their suffering necessary to defeat it. This subclass poses a particularly difficult challenge for this aspect of the educative theodicy being proposed. How then can the pain, suffering, and hardship arising out of this horrendous-difference disability—whether involving RMWS or profound cognitive deficiencies—be defeated? One way would be an appeal to Islamic valuables such as hope (*raja'*),[111] love, longing and desire for God (*mahabba, shawq*),[112] trust in God (*tawakkul*),[113] and brotherhood and solidarity (*ukhuwwa*)[114] that may possibly defeat such evils. One particular Islamic valuable that will be explored here is the important notion of 'hospitality' (*diyafa*). The proposal will suggest how it can be a framework by which to understand how the suffering caused by horrendous-difference disabilities may be defeated. In its broad sense, "Islamic hospitality" means "to give voluntarily and without compensation." Hospitality is a form of an "unconditional welcome of the guest" and is made "through acts, words, and objects." Hospitality also indicates "an effort undertaken by an individual, group of people, or organization based on a desire to honour guests as well as to establish or maintain good relationships with people" and further includes "assisting people in times of need."[115] The central motive for hospitality stems from "moral incentives to the self and others."[116] Hospitality is not about "relations between things, but rather about constructing relations between persons as well as with God." Thus, the key idea is that "hospitality strengthens social relationships between people and unites individuals in integrated communities."[117] Mona Siddiqui explains how central hospitality is to Islamic culture:

> Islam holds hospitality as a virtue that lies at the very basis of the Islamic ethical system, a concept rooted in the pre-Islamic Bedouin virtues of welcome and generosity in the harsh desert environment. The concept can be found in the Arabic root *dayafa*. The Prophet is reported to have said, "There is no good in the one who is not hospitable."[118]

However, the horizon of hospitality should not be seen as merely food and drink or offering shelter. The concept is "multilayered," more positively complex, and encompassing. Siddiqui clarifies this complexity and expansive nature. "Hospitality," she remarks, "should not be confused with contemporary understandings of charity or entertainment. This hosting of a person or people as guests is the closest meaning we can give to the Arabic noun *diyafa*."[119] While a *restrictive* understanding of hospitality consists of providing food, shelter, and conversation, an *expansive* or "diverse" concept of hospitality amounts to "something much greater than hosting a guest or welcoming a stranger," it is "a virtue or a combination of virtues which go beyond giving" and involves "a sacred duty to think beyond our immediate selves in a wide variety of contexts and relationships. This includes charity and alms, but is not defined only through the giving of material wealth."[120] Hospitality in Islam then is a *compound* virtue, meaning a number of different virtues converge and intersect through its enactment. It involves transcending a simple social transactional level of exchange between two parties—host and guest—that consists of prolonged indulgence to embracing a higher conceptualization driven by a deep and unshakable human compassion for others. In this way, "'doing hospitality' is not simply about making physical room for others in our homes," but it is essentially an attitude to life, a specific orientation toward how we not only welcome others but also embrace them. This means "we need to make room for others in our hearts and minds, and with our words."[121] This is only possible through genuine openness, love of the other, and compassion. Siddiqui describes this role of compassion in hospitality. Although hospitality "includes notions of forgiveness as well as reaching out to others" its very basis "is compassion, a compassion which shakes our complacency and leads us to think about more generous ways of being with one another." What compassion does is it "creates empathy, solidarity, and has the power to reduce personal and social conflicts."[122] Siddiqui further elaborates on the wider social value embodied by hospitality in ancient and near-Eastern societies and subsequently Muslim societies where hospitality "towards those who were nameless strangers" demanded "a commitment reflected in showing dignity and care to those who are unknown rather than welcoming those whom we wished to know." In this way, hospitality was not only about a minimal transactional giving and receiving "but essentially about the transformation of persons and societies."[123]

Although in the pre-Islamic Arabian context hospitality was inextricably linked to material magnanimity—especially with food and drink—later within Islam, despite a continuity of the pre-Islamic characterization, there was a broader and more underlying significance to hospitality, which was cultivating a set of qualities or characteristics that made a person caring, empathetic, humble, and acutely aware of the need for not only bonding, solidarity, and companionship but a duty to care and to protect those most vulnerable like orphans, the destitute, the weak, and travelers. Hospitality became not only a marker of nobility but also a wider function of interrelated and interdependent social interaction. Siddiqui comments how "much of the Qur'anic emphasis is on giving to those in need, whether through tax, alms or charity, as a way of creating new relationships, a new and more generous social order" but the "themes and persons around which this ethical imperative to give and share is framed are to be found in a pre-Islamic milieu where Bedouin societies already laid an enormous emphasis on hospitality as central to a noble character."[124] The "outlook of the pagan Arabs was Islamicized" such that deeds like "generosity and hospitality became to be seen as distinct virtues, religious duties," but neither the Qur'an nor the Prophet's revelatory example offered "one particular narrative about hospitality" nor "one concept but several concepts involving various kinds of people and various kinds of relationships."[125]

Siddiqui suggests that some of the aims of this newly invigorated concept of hospitality under Islam included:

1. offering food, shelter, and protection to "the vulnerable or uprooted."
2. "creating a relationship with those outside our immediate family and friends."
3. "expanding our social conscience" in a way that engenders an idea of communal obligation of wealth.[126]

In addition to the above, Siddiqui highlights one of the deeper aims of hospitality:

The linking of God and food is to see God as the ultimate provider and our need as mortals to eat. When we eat we should remember that we are dependent on God, and the food in front of us is a result of God's goodness, "Oh you who believe, eat of the good things which we have provided for you and give thanks to God if it is him you worship" (Q2:172). Gratitude (*shukr*) here is not only thanks for the food but essential to the whole belief system of the Muslim. Belief cherishes the conviction that life has a purpose and the goodness of our existence for which we should be continually grateful flows from an infinite goodness which is God. We are reminded to be grateful, but our gratitude to God can never equal his goodness towards us.[127]

The Shafi'ite hadith expert and theologian al-Bayhaqi (d. 458/1066) reports a narration regarding Adam asking God why He created those inflicted with illnesses and impairments from among his progeny and the reply was God wanted to be thanked:

> From al-Hasan [al-Basri] who said: God Mighty and Exalted created Adam when He created him. He brought out [from Adam's loins] the inhabitants of paradise from his right side and brought out the inhabitants of hellfire from his left side and placed them on earth. Of them included those who were blind, [lepers, paralysed],[128] deaf and one suffering various afflictions (al-mubtala). Adam asked: my Lord, why have You created them from my progeny? [God] replied: O Adam, I wanted to be thanked.[129]

The common context in which these narrations are often interpreted is that the manifestation of God's bounty and generosity (ni'am) toward His creatures is to elicit gratitude. This is why in another narration, Adam asks God why He created people with such huge disparities and differences (like rich/poor, weak/strong, healthy/unhealthy) to which the reply came: "I desired that the one who was granted favours should praise Me and thank Me."[130] In other words, some persons will be decreed with disabilities by God in order that those who are able-bodied can offer their gratitude to God for not being made among those ordained with such challenges. Hence, narrations like these are understood and interpreted as a juxtaposition whereby something positive (being able-bodied) is illuminated by its contrary (disability). This gratitude through appreciation of the contrary was as already mentioned in the previous chapter a view proposed by al-Ghazali as one of God's wise planning of and design in creation.[131] However, the above narration may well possibly be interpreted in an additional way. It mentions that God's reason for creating persons with all types of disabilities is to activate gratitude within human beings, but this gratitude does not have to exclusively be defined by a superficial recognition of able-bodied health but could also be on account of the positive value persons with disability have on those who are not. Sincere gratitude is given to God for allowing others the means to realize through the goodness inherent in persons with disability that they are a gift. Persons with disability give and the nondisabled receive because the former are agents of or means for healing, instruction, and deep realization in the latter.

In the midst of the hospitality then, a realization of gratitude, generosity, dependency, and vulnerability emerges. On one level, a person recognizes that they are dependent, needy, and impoverished. All they possess are purely from the bounty and blessings of God and they sleep and rise under the blanket of sustenance that God alone provides. These bounties and blessings of God would cause a host to pour out with compassionate generosity on their guest seeking their comfort and ease as well as alleviating their anxieties, embodying the generosity of God. On another level, one recognizes too the duty of care and compassion toward others who are vulnerable. This duty is most poignantly encapsulated in one of many hadiths of God's presence among dependent, disadvantaged, and vulnerable members of the society. The Prophet Muhammad is reported to have said:

> Verily, God the Exalted, and Glorious will say on the Day of Resurrection: "O son of Adam, I was ill but you did not visit Me." He would say: "O my Lord, how could I visit you and You are the Lord of the worlds?" Thereupon He would say: "Did you not know that such and such a servant of Mine was ill but you did not visit him? Did you not realize that if you had visited him (you would have known that I was aware of your visit to him, for which I would reward you) you would have found Me with him? O son of Adam, I asked food from you but you did not feed Me." He would submit: "My Lord, how could I feed You and You are the Lord of the worlds?" He would say: "Did you not know that such and such a servant of Mine asked you for food but you did not feed him? Did you not realize that if you had fed him, you would certainly have found (its reward) with Me? O son of Adam, I asked water from you but you did not give it to Me." He would say: "My Lord, how could I give You (water) and You are the Lord of the worlds?" Thereupon He would say: "Such and such a servant of Mine asked you for water to drink but you did not give it to him. Did you not realize that if you had given him to drink you would have found (its reward) with Me?"[132]

The hadith mentions how in serving and attending to the ill, weak, poor, hungry, and thirsty—those who are vulnerable and dependent members of the community—one will find God. It also alludes to the moral failure in acknowledging and then addressing their challenges and difficulties. Moreover, the intervention God is demanding from the believing community in this hadith is not to be executed from a position of sterile, disinterested self-reflection and concern, or independence, power, privilege, and security but rather a sense of duty that is of course axiomatically grounded in the desire for God but also from the realization that those commanded to help are vulnerable themselves. God subjects one group to encounter the vulnerabilities of another group in order to bring the former to comprehend their own vulnerability and thereby activate a deep love and empathy toward the latter group. This relationship, bond, or bridging of vulnerabilities is positioned by the hadith at the center of a community's social ethics. For society to function and flourish there must exist this connectivity of care between different community groups; otherwise, the result is neglect and abandonment and a stifling of moral progress. Here, MacIntyre's emphasis on human vulnerability as an essential and intrinsic feature of human existence allows us to frame hospitality as a means to attend to these embedded human vulnerabilities mentioned in the hadith. He writes:

> We human beings are vulnerable to many kinds of affliction and most of us are at some time afflicted by serious ills. How we cope is only in small part up to us. It is most often to others that we owe our survival, let alone our flourishing, as we encounter bodily illness and injury, inadequate nutrition, mental defect and disturbance, and human aggression and neglect. This dependence on particular others for protection and sustenance is most obvious in early childhood and in old age. But between these first and last stages our lives are characteristically marked by longer or short periods of injury, illness or other disablement and some among us are disabled for their entire lives.[133]

MacIntyre describes how in addition to traditional virtues such as courage, justice, and temperance, there are additional virtues he calls "virtues of acknowledged dependence." These are states of character that enable a person to recognize and appreciate the importance of human vulnerability in order to respond with appropriate measures of care and protective provisions. These virtues of acknowledged dependence are situated in MacIntyre's larger account of human teleology characterized in Aristotelian-Thomist terms. For humans to move from dependent creaturely status to become "independent practical reasoners"—meaning becoming individuals who can achieve an independence of mind that enables them to practically reason about what is most suitable to achieve the good—they are dependent on the contributions and help of others toward their well-being.[134] MacIntyre argues that human beings find themselves in social situations based on asymmetrical relations and unequal degrees and levels of contribution. This means they require more from others than what they themselves can contribute. He calls such social relations "networks of giving and receiving."[135] This means that human flourishing to enable practical reasoners requires more than what individuals contribute by themselves; they require others like family, friends, helpers, and teachers. This is where hospitality becomes extremely important. Individuals and societies flourish, as MacIntyre argues, through this network of giving and receiving. The vulnerabilities and dependencies mentioned in the hadith above are opportunities to manifest these virtues of acknowledged dependence. They create forms of possibilities to care for those whose lives among us are lived in frailty and vulnerability. Hospitality framed in this way takes on a transformative power and value. Timpe and Cobb in this regard argue how hospitality especially when "ordered toward individual and communal flourishing" is only possible by people with a "hospitable disposition" as well as a "deepened understanding of themselves in relation to others." Such people "are able to grasp the true locus of value and individual dignity" and are "liberated from the arbitrary boundaries implicit within culturally-grounded views of value." Cognizing about others in this way highlights how hospitality is a "virtue essential to the common good" and "given that we are all fragile and dependent beings, we are all in need of the welcome and provision of others." Hence, any failure on our part to "cultivate and practice hospitality as both individuals and as communities effectively cuts us off from basic goods essential to living well within community" and these goods include "friendship, solidarity, trust, in addition to provision and care for physical, emotional, psychological, and spiritual needs." Most importantly, however, "it severs us from the gifts that the guest offers by her presence within the community."[136] Timpe and Cobb also note how any extension of care and protection to others who are vulnerable or in need is not simply reduced to the host offering "the gift of assistance to the vulnerable guest" in a host-guest dynamic distinction; rather, hospitality more comprehensively "involves dissolving an artificial boundary between the guest and the host" where the host "invites the guest into a shared space and welcomes her as a person deserving of both honour and care." In this sense, then, hospitality involves "erasing divisions" and as an ideal involves "conversion" of the host to a level of illumination whereby "she sees the artificiality of the entrenched social boundaries; she recognizes the value and dignity of the stranger along with responsibilities to tend to her needs; and she comes to appreciate the gift she receives in knowing and serving the other."[137]

This framework of hospitality embedded in acknowledging human vulnerability is especially pertinent to those with disabilities—particularly the horrendous-difference disabilities discussed above. Cobb explains how human frailty can threaten the course of our flourishing as individuals and communities if those most vulnerable and disadvantaged are neglected:

This threat is most pressing for those whose lives are marked by significant disability or impairment. Every human being will, to one degree or another, face these forms of difficulty at some point in his or her life; we are, at best, only temporarily abled. Children who have been diagnosed with significantly life-limiting conditions face these threats from their conception. For most of these children, their conditions will prevent the development of their capacities for reasoning.[138]

Cobb continues:

Flourishing for these individuals does not depend on the actualization of capacities for intelligence or agency; instead, it depends on the extent to which local communities meet their needs. Furthermore, parents who are expecting a child with a significantly life-limiting condition also find themselves vulnerable. And this vulnerability creates responsibilities within their local networks and associations. A virtuous community is one that seeks to discharge these responsibilities by addressing the needs of both the parents and the unborn child.[139]

Timpe and Cobb both explain the core notion of religious or "theological" hospitality toward those who are not familiar—the stranger, the Other—within a context of mutual vulnerability. Being a "stranger" or "outsider" means suffering a double lack: lacking resources to care for one's own needs as well as lacking the "the standing as a member of the community to make claims on the resources of the community to address these needs." This makes them "particularly susceptible to exploitation and abuse; they are, intentionally or unintentionally, subject to discrimination and prejudice from a community who seeks to protect itself from the demands and threats of outsiders." And this mistreatment has been the case historically for persons with disabilities. Thus, "one could argue that many individuals with disabilities are paradigmatic examples of those who ought to receive the care of a hospitable community."[140]

From hospitality, therefore, a number of unique, powerful, and transformative insights arise and they include:

1. It engenders mutual recognition of value and gratitude between host and guest.
2. It creates a genuine presence, relation, and bond between host and guest.
3. It remakes the relationship between host and guest based on vulnerability.

4. It activates God's awareness in the host that drives the duty of care toward the guest.
5. It decenters power by pegging humanizing strength in compassion, empathy, care, and concern.
6. It is a way to reach God and a way God reaches out to us.

In order to see how those suffering horrendous-difference disabilities with capacities for RMWS may be defeated within the account of hospitality given, I will piece together the overall picture of the theodicy.

(a) *Destruction of dignity*: There are persons who suffer horrendous-difference disabilities. These disabilities are so destructive that they threaten to undercut the affected person's ability to see their life as self-validated and valuable. (b) *Value recognition condition*: In order to defeat this horrendous-difference disability, persons with disability must be able to understand and recognize the specific value of their own life constructed from a narrative or account that sufficiently delivers meaning subjectively for them while they are alive. (c) *Hospitality*: a community as carers (the host) that welcomes persons with horrendous-difference disability (the guest) with genuine compassion, love, and concern not as the distinctive and different Other but as one of itself, opening up the opportunity to afford space for the host to realize and understand the guest as a gift bestowed by God. In this way, persons with these disabilities possess real value in how they play a crucial role for the community to manifest the set of virtues to cultivate a disposition of hospitality that imitates divine hospitality in paradise and is necessary for worldly communal flourishing. Their value also resides in how they constitute a means to generate solidarity within the community through its shared understanding of support, aid, care, protection, and duty. Thus, their enriching presence in the life of the community is an overall good. (d) *Meaning-making process*: although the value of a person with disability is an overall good for the communal solidarity and virtue-building of the community, it is necessary that the individual him/herself recognizes that their life is of value to themselves. They have to grasp how their affliction—albeit will remain as an inseparable challenge to their qualitative well-being—nevertheless is central to the overall beauty, goodness, and value to their life. Perhaps it is in God's direct and explicit identification and presence with them that each individual comes to see themselves as an immense source of value, one that is sufficiently great to overcome the suffering arising from their disability. Thus, each person recognizes how they are a value-marker or indicator of God's priorities because God situates them at the center. (e) Those with PCDs or impairments who cannot undergo a meaning-making process may have their suffering defeated in the hereafter.

Those Williams categorized as identified with PCDs do not have any way of integrating their pain and suffering into a positive and meaningful narrative. They are unable to give context to the pain and suffering through their life-course such that they recognize and grasp them as contributing to the goodness for themselves and their lives. Thus, due to the absence of relevant cognitive functioning capacities, persons with PCD have no subjective, first-person perspective on their adverse states. For them, it may perhaps be that the suffering of horrendous-difference disabilities without capacities for RMWS can only be defeated postmortem, that is, in the afterlife transformation that is restorative.

One criticism of this educative theodicy would be that it is tantamount to treating persons with disability as "virtuous sufferers," meaning "those whom God favours with special burdens aimed at enhancing their spiritual capacities."[141] These theodicies no doubt rely on representations of disability as "a vehicle for blessings and a sign of God's grace," presuming that "submission to affliction yields praiseworthy spiritual attributes, such as humility and dependence upon God."[142] Indeed, the implication would be

> an ascetic ethos of self-sacrifice, one that interprets suffering as a redemptive, a testing device that God's children must undergo to mature in faith by relying on God's strength alone, and not their own abilities. The message transmitted through the tradition has often come to mean that human beings must acquiesce to hardship and pain as a divinely designated route to sanctification. In all wisdom, love and power, God allows us to face adversity because God cares for us and wishes for us to enter into a deeper relation of dependence with God that is not possible without experiencing genuine obstacles to our well-being.[143]

This would mean that human beings are created weak, frail, and incomplete within a world that is not welfare-oriented but a Colosseum for spiritual augmentation. Disability is rationalized as part of God's intended plan and purpose. In fact, by characterizing disability as virtuous or redemptive suffering, it is equating it to suffering *simpliciter*. Such a characterization promotes a passivity born out of a form of fatalistic outlook that eschews any need to actively intervene and address the oppression of personal hardship persons of disability undergo as well as the social exclusion and marginalization they experience. Moreover, not only does this kind of theodicy "sanitise impairment by explaining it away in terms of potential goods it produces, it also baptizes the status quo, sanctioning the cult of normalcy."[144] For the practical modality of disabled existence, this "theology of virtuous suffering has encouraged persons with disability to acquiesce to social barriers as a sign of obedience to God and to internalise second-class status."[145] In the end, the trivialization of disability takes place because it imputes the adverse existence of the disability community to God's decree or (pre)ordainment rather than the result of the socially constructed barriers creating a regime of exclusion and oppression.[146]

On specifically the second aspect of the educative theodicy, the view broadly is that able-bodied persons have so much to learn from persons with disabilities. The latter can be highly beneficial pedagogically in that virtues such as love and compassion can be learned through the act of hospitality. The various disabilities then help to make those who care for them better persons. An evident problem with this, it can be argued, is that it "relegates persons with disabilities to a lesser status" because in effect it gives them "a paltry supporting role in the life story of healthy protagonists who come to acquire a richer understanding of the world"[147] thanks to a participation of a person with disability in their lives. In doing this, there is an asymmetry, a failure to see and view persons with disability as moral equals. Their function, it seems, is merely instrumental for the development of able-bodied persons without both disabled and abled perceived as full and equal moral members of the believing community where exclusion of one impairs the moral status of the other.[148] Reynolds echoes this sentiment arguing it trivializes the gravity of disability by romanticizing it in patronizing terms. He comments how persons with disabilities are reduced to objects "upon which non-disabled persons act as benefactors," which essentializes them as a poor and helpless category "in need of grace."[149] The deeper patronizing dimension is that

> non-disabled persons must lower their expectations for disabled persons, who lack the independent resources to participate in the activities of conventional society. Therefore, inclusion in the life of the community involves condescending acts of care and assistance, making special allowances for persons who are otherwise incapable of functioning normally and contributing to the community. Pity becomes the operating mode of attending to persons of disability, a giving of what "we" have in abundance to "them," who are deficient in graces.[150]

Shaikh also notes a similar worry:

> There is a difficult struggle here. On the one hand it is important to have an inclusive theology (and activist practice) which allows for the recognition of frailty and vulnerability. In the other hand, if we use disability as an example of what it means to be frail, may we not be reinforcing the idea that people with disability are particularly frail and vulnerable?[151]

The further difficult question Shaikh asks is:

> How do we recognize the universality of frailty and vulnerability (all people are frail and vulnerable) by using disability as a key example without inadvertently reinforcing a false distinction between the vulnerability of those labelled as having disabilities and those not so labelled?[152]

The answer is not easy but the version of an educative theodicy I offered in this chapter attempted to be palliative in explaining suffering by centering significance for the agent-patient through a kind of cognitive reappraisal framework.

Conclusion

The theodicy models explored in this chapter offer clues into how the Qur'an and Hadith view suffering and pain of persons with disabilities and the possible purposes they serve. An extended analysis of an educative theodicy was also given, incorporating the Islamic notion of hospitality as a framework by which to overcome horrendous-difference disabilities by enabling the person with disability to be part of a welcoming community that reaches out through realization of their own vulnerability as well as duty of care. The embrace of the community indicates not only the love, compassion, care, and concern persons with disability deserve but also the intrinsic value they possess that enriches the lives of the community. This perhaps enables them to see the intrinsically powerful value their disability holds, and if they subjectively realize and endorse this, they would have overcome or defeated their horrendous-difference disability. For those with PCD, the afterlife arrival to God will find Him the most gracious Host offering in His abode "what no eye has seen, what no ear has heard and no heart has conceived."[153]

3

Nonhuman Innocents: Theodicies for the Problem of Animal Pain and Suffering

In this chapter, I will discuss a subset of the problem of evil relatively overlooked as a distinct subject of study by contemporary academics within Islamic studies in comparison to other subjects and that is the problem of animal pain and suffering.[1] I will first survey key theses regarding the status of animals within the Islamic revelatory sources in order to frame the problem itself. This will be followed by accounts attempting to tackle the problem from Mu'tazilite, Asha'rite, and Maturidite perspectives in addition to an account based on the theological ideas of Ibn Qayyim al-Jawziya.

The Nature and Status of Animals in the Islamic Source Texts

The Islamic primary sources, arguably, have a high view of animals.[2] Three core theses relevant for the present chapter are deducible from these primary sources as well as the Islamic theological and philosophical literature. Cumulatively, they establish that animals have an endowed sanctity that ultimately derives its moral force from God who created them in their wondrous diversity and behavior. The three core theses regarding animals are:

1. The welfare thesis
2. The similarity thesis
3. The psychology thesis

The welfare thesis: It may seem that at its core, the Islamic source texts (like that of Judaism and Christianity) are dominated by an ethical anthropocentricism. However, this human-centeredness is modified by ethical principles that guide the life-world of animals as well as their instrumentality within a context of a divinely ordained but reasoned speciesism (read here as favoring humans).[3] In the Islamic sources, human beings are situated at the center of the moral universe with animals put there for their flourishing and edification.[4] However, this does not mean that there is no regulation regarding the treatment and engagement with animals on their own moral terms as independent creatures of God. Animals are morally considered beings who can be wronged. The Hadith literature is thick with references on animal welfare as a priority. Not only does Prophet Muhammad point out the interconnected domains animals and humans share (that brings about a necessary mutual dependence and reliance as well as risks) but there are serious legal and afterlife penalties for mistreating them. Regarding the first point, the Prophet mentions a catalogue of duties as well as a scale of responsibilities for being compassionate toward animals ranging from feeding and sheltering them to ensuring their emotional well-being:[5]

> Animals are to be protected from harm (whether from insect bites to life-threatening danger).
> Animals are not to be distressed (like separated from their families).
> Animals are not to be imprisoned.
> Animals are not to be aesthetically impaired (like cutting the forelock of a horse).
> Animals must not be neglected (like left without due care).
> Animals must not be physically harmed (like over ridden, over-burdened) or abused (like being hit on the face, mutilated or branded anywhere on the body).
> Animals are not to even be treated idly let alone cruelly.
> Animals are not to be made targets.
> Wild animals are to be left totally unmolested (thus, killing animals for sport, commercial interests or gratuitously is expressly forbidden).

Regarding the second point, maltreatment of animals can result in detriment to human salvation in the hereafter. The Prophet recounts for his companions an incident of a woman who was put into hellfire for seriously neglecting a cat (*hirra*) such that it died of starvation.[6] Human beings will be held accountable before God for killing any animal—irrespective of how small it is. The converse is that helping, assisting, supporting, and caring for animals are the means to earn afterlife reward and God's pardon.

Perhaps the most vivid and poignant account of animal protest and complaint in relation to their treatment at the hands of humans occurs in the fictional tale *The Case of the Animals versus Man*[7] by perhaps the most enigmatic medieval eponym Brethren of Purity (Ikhwan al-Safa)[8] where nonhuman animals bring humans to court due to the latter's abuse arising out of their claims to ontological superiority. The text is situated within an evident Neoplatonic metaphysical paradigm and with rich allegory dissects and indeed critiques a myriad of matters related to species hierarchy, anthropocentricism, and animal ethics. The text offers a corrective and innovative way of viewing the animal kingdom and to date is the most unique premodern work that critiques anthropocentricism and anthropogenic evil.

The similarity thesis: Muslim scholars employed a form of argument from analogy in order to establish the similarity between humans and animals. The exegetical discussion revolved around al-An'am, verse 38: *And there is no creature on earth or bird that flies with its wings except that they are communities like you. We have not neglected in the Register a thing. Then unto their Lord they will be gathered.* Here, the direct Qur'anic description of animals being communities or nations like human beings (*umamun amthalukum*) elicited a number of interpretations including:

1. like humans they are grouped and classified with names for identification purposes,
2. like humans in the way they are created beings by God,
3. like humans in how they praise and glorify God,
4. like humans in their biological behaviour and functions,
5. like humans in how they are governed by a divine providential plan,
6. like humans in that they will be resurrected and given their rights and due,
7. like humans in how they are recipients of divine love, mercy and care,
8. like humans in strong physical and behavioural resemblance and
9. like humans in how all their affairs have been recorded.[9]

Muslim scholars were open to extending the similarity between animals and humans to include similarity in minds and even prophetology. Al-Alusi (d. 1854) in his Qur'an commentary *Ruh al-ma'ani* extensively discusses the view that animals are like humans in rationality and prophetology.[10] Some people, he says, especially the Sufis and others among the Muslim philosophers, use al-An'am, verse 38 to prove that animals have a rational soul. He then cites passages from *al-Yawaqit wa-l-jawahir fi bayan 'aqa'id al-akabir* as well as *Durar al-ghawas 'ala fatawa sayyidi 'Ali al-khawwas*, written by the eminent sixteenth-century Sufi master 'Abd al-Wahhab al-Sha'rani (d. 973/1565), who upholds both positions citing a number of evidences. First, on the general rationality of animals al-Sha'rani deduces its reality using a narration that when the Prophet migrated to Medina, his she-camel was wandering around looking for a spot to alight. When it did, he ordered the people to "leave her because she was ordered by God." al-Sha'rani concludes that being ordered (*ma'mura*) by God must mean the she-camel understood the command and to understand commands necessitates having an intellect. If the she-camel has an intellect, then it follows that other animals too have an intellect as there is no difference between one animal and another.[11] Second, a statement is attributed to the Prophet's companion Ibn 'Abbas that the animal communities have an equivalent of every person in the human communities "such that they even have an Ibn 'Abbas like me among them."[12] Third, in another work cited by al-Alusi entitled *al-Ajwiba al-mardiya 'an a'imma al-fuqaha' wa-l-sufiya* ('The Approved Responses from the Scholars and Mystics'), al-Sha'rani relates from his teacher 'Ali al-Khawwas al-Burullusi (d. 939/1532–33) this equivalence between animals and humans includes animals being morally accountable creatures (*mukallafa*). They have been sent with warners (*nadhir*) as well as Prophets (*anbiya'*) to serve as cautionary examples, basing his interpretation on the general import carried in al-Fatir, verse 24 that reads, *And there was no community but that there had passed within it a warner*. Animals being a community (*umma*), therefore, had warners and messengers (*rusul*) dispatched to them as the generality of the import does not exclude them.[13] Finally, the view that animals are like humans in being recipients of Prophets and messengers from among their kind is reported as heretical by al-Alusi (citing Ibn al-Munayyir) and concludes the discussion of the verse with a note of tolerance by stating that although he personally does not incline to such a view he also does not anathematize anyone who does.[14]

This formal discussion by the exegetes is one dimension reflected in the Islamic subject sources. The reality of this Qur'anic description of 'communities like you' is also encapsulated in more observational examples. One notable fourth/tenth-century Iranian mystic of Shiraz Abu al-Hasan 'Ali b. Muhammad al-Daylami[15] marveled at the resemblance between animal behavior and human behavior. Recounting one episode while in Mecca, the author describes the intricate posturing of pigeons courting each other and concludes that all animals (*kull dhi ruh*) display love like human beings. It is worth quoting in full:

> We have seen similar things ourselves. Once, when I was in the sacred
> Mosque in Mecca, I saw a female pigeon walking around a male, flapping

her wings lowering her head for him. But he paid no attention to her. After things had gone on like this between them for a long while, another male pigeon came and made advances to her, strutting around her in a circle trying to seduce her. But she refused him. Indeed, although he continued to circle around her for a long while trying to seduce her, she still refused him. Now, when the first male pigeon perceived her behaviour, he came and offered himself to her. But now that he had come to her, she refused him too. He did his utmost, but she rebuffed him and flew off, and he flew off after her. I do not know what became of them. But I was amazed by the fact that she offered herself to him and no other pigeon, and that she humbled herself before him but disdained the other male. Moreover, I was amazed at the first male. When he saw that another has offered himself to her, while she still inclined to him, he returned to her, seeking to possess her. But when she came back to her, she turned on him and refused him. I have never seen two animals more like human beings.[16]

Although it may be argued that al-Daylami indulged his reminiscing with a dose of embellished "anecdotal anthropomorphism,"[17] clearly the affinity between human beings and animals was something deeply acknowledged among Muslims—an outlook born out of intense wonder and amazement at God's handiwork and manifestation of creative power.

The psychology thesis: The Qur'anic data reveals an enriched animal psychology and life-world where they are ascribed with properties that can only be possible based on possessing advanced mental properties. Tlili has extensively surveyed these mental and related properties under seven broad themes which I group here with only selected examples, deferring the reader to her survey for the details of the exegetical analysis of the Qur'an from various commentators:[18] (1) *Spirituality*: animals are part of the terrestrial creatures mentioned as glorifying and praising God (al-Isra', verse 44; *tasbih*) as well as performing ritual actions of prayer like bowing and prostrating (al-Hajj, verse 18). Birds are given particular mention in al-Isra', verse 79 and al-Nur, verse 41 as speaking and joyously singing God's praises. Fish are also mentioned by the Prophet as seeking pardon (*istighfar*) from the religious scholars (*'alim*) because their knowledge of the legal rulings (*ahkam*) prevents creatures—like them—from being tortured or slaughtered inappropriately by the uninformed and uneducated.[19] Muslim exegetes were on the whole inclined to the possibility of genuine animal language being a meaningful medium for glorifying God—even if the modality of that religious consciousness is not explicable. (2) *Language and intelligence*: animals possessing language is undeniably mentioned in the Qur'an (al-Naml, verse 15). There are a number of references in the hadith too. It is reported, for example, that a cow was being overburdened with a load and turned toward the shepherd objecting in human language, "I have not been created for this but for ploughing."[20] Animal communication through an articulated language (*nutq*) that is species-specific would require the mental preconditions of a language such as intention, concept formation, and intelligence. One of the most exceptional accounts of a conversing nonhuman animal is that of the ant (*namla*) in the story of Prophet Solomon characterized as a believer, intelligent, generous, and poetic (al-Naml, verses 18–19)—all qualities that set it apart as a nonhuman creature.[21] Based on this, majority of the scholars accepted the possibility that animals being language users have species-specific minds of their own. Some scholars even suggested that animals may have concepts like the temporal origination of the world (*huduth al-'alam*) and the unity of God (*tawhid*), but such phenomenal realities are epistemically inaccessible to humans.[22] (3) *Morality* and (4) *Accountability*: the Qur'an does not explicitly mention animals having moral properties because they have not been endowed with moral freedom. Although Muslim theologians like some of the Mu'tazilites acknowledged that animals have choice (*ikhtiyar*), and therefore can choose to harm or benefit (like to attack or not attack their prey), the effects of their actions nevertheless do not carry moral blame.[23] In other words, animals are creatures free from moral accountability (*taklif*) like humans even though the jurists considered that legally their actions may carry a liability. However, as mentioned above, some like al-Sha'rani held animals to have full accountability owing to their possessing a rational soul. (5) *Inspiration*: The Qur'an is unequivocal in mentioning that animals can be inspired directly by God (*awha*).[24] The most explicit example in the Qur'an is that of bees, their hive construction and production of honey (al-Nahl, verses 68–69).[25] Commentators also acknowledge that certain animals are actually inspired by God to know what things benefit them and harm them as well as how to plan and live their lives.[26] (6) *Resurrection*: the Qur'an states in two places that all creatures will be resurrected (al-An'am, verse 38 and al-Takwir, verse 5). Although scholars differed over whether the Arabic word "hashr"[27] in both verses semantically referred to their being caused to die or physical resurrection, there was broad agreement over the view that once they face fair acquittal for their worldly behavior, they would be annihilated to dust (see, for example, al-Naba', verse 40).[28] Not all scholars accepted annihilationism as a doctrine because certain narrations from the Prophet allude to some animals having a postmortem existence in Paradise as a reward and others will exist as God's agents of delivering pain and retribution for the iniquitous in hell.[29] Yet other animals will be inhabitants of paradise that have not survived a temporal existence but created exclusively in order to service the delights of the righteous. Thus, a bull (*thawr*) will be prepared as food for feasts in paradise (in reference to al-Tur, verse 22 and al-Waqi'a, verse 21), sheep (*ghanam*) and bridled she-camels (*makhtuma*) will also inhabit paradise along with white camels (*naja'ib*) and resplendent horses (*faras*).[30] Disagreement among the commentators also lay over the rationale for animal resurrection because lacking moral choices, they would not be culpable for reward or blame. Some held that a lesser form of accountability—a general recompense—will take place postresurrection. Others from the Mu'tazilites like 'Abd al-Jabbar argued that the resurrection is followed by God settling the score for all animals that were wronged in order to administer a compensation (*'iwad*) after which their afterlife existence is closed through annihilation.[31] (7) *Perspectives*: the Qur'an places the voice of animals into words. It clearly positions them as fully articulate subjects to convey contextual information significant for the listener. The hoopoe and ant in the story of Solomon, for example (al-Naml, verses 18 and 22–26, respectively), are depicted as informative and lively. Not only do they speak, but they are represented as insightful with their own opinions and experiences. On the one hand, the ant commanded admiration of the commentators for its forbearance, empathy, and understanding as well as its intellect and wisdom. It overlooked and sought an excuse for Solomon's army when nearly destroying the ant colony while in its charge because a Prophet would never knowingly do such actions.[32] The hoopoe, on the other hand, is genuinely perplexed at the people of Sheba's immersion into misguidance and fails to see why they obstinately reject worshipping God alone. It even offers an argument from divine Omniscience for why God is the being solely deserving of all worship (al-Naml, verse 25).[33]

The outcome from acknowledging human and animal affinity as well as the Qur'anic data in general on animals was that Islamic theology never really succumbed to a form of mechanistic philosophy where animal behavior was explained by mere reflex-driven actions or that they were creatures much akin to automata because they are supposedly devoid of a soul, consciousness, rationality, and thus emotions. Such a conclusion was to define Descartes' characterization of animals in the sixteenth century that essentially eliminated their moral consideration because lacking rationality and a soul meant denying they felt pain or that they truly suffered.[34] al-Juwayni, for example, asserts that orthodox Muslim belief upholds the reality of animal pain and suffering because—as living and sentient creatures—that is what we observe and experience about them:

The Bakriya[35] deny self-evidence (al-darura) and reject intuition (al-badiha). We know self-evidently that beasts and children suffer pains, that they are tormented when they suffer pains, and that they have a strong aversion against what they know will cause them pain. If it were allowed to deny this fact, one could deny also they are alive and proceed to claim that they are inanimate objects (jamadat), unable to feel, or to suffer, or to perceive. But this ought to be enough to refute them.[36]

Al-Razi mentions the Karramiya[37] as also denying the reality of animal pain and suffering in relation to when they are ritually slaughtered. They argued, he says, that God numbs their pain at the moment of their slaughter—a view he rejects as "mere denial of facts."[38] Thus, mainstream Muslim theology on one level affirmed a threshold of psychological complexity in animals based on pretheoretical intuitions about animal mental states through perceiving and inferring from their modes of action. However, it may be argued that the examples mentioned in the Qur'an are exceptional, where a small set of animals are represented within the overall assumed supernatural worldview of Islam (with the existence of an Omnipotent being) and not universalizable claims about all animals. In other words, the truth of these reports is affirmed of a few animals based on trust in the Qur'an as a source and not independently verifiable facts about animals and whether they are minded creatures. This may explain why majority of the Muslim theologians still upheld a marked difference between human and animal minds that ultimately relegated the latter secondary to the former in the hierarchy of the created order.

In the contemporary philosophical and scientific literature, humans, it is argued, uniquely bear two types of mental properties: (1) *reasoning* (like problem-solving) and (2) *phenomenal* consciousness, whereas animals do not; this is what makes one a different kind of being or species than the other.[39] In the case of animal thinking and reasoning, the denial of such mental powers in animals may be stated as follows:

Argument 1:
   (1) Whatever lacks the ability to think and reason, is not a moral agent.
   (2) Animals lack the ability to think and reason.
        a: because they do not have language.
        b: because they do not form beliefs (as they lack perspective on states of affairs).
        c: because they do not form mental concepts.
        d: because they do not communicate their mental contents to others.
        e: because they do not use mental beliefs to define and guide their

behaviour.

f: because they do not exhibit logical reasoning.

g: because they do not show signs of transferring knowledge to novel cases.

h: because they do not have meta-cognitive abilities (thinking about their own thinking).

i: because they do not have intentionality (that is, their thoughts are not *about* a thing).

(3) Therefore, animals are not moral agents.

(4) Therefore, animals do not suffer, from (3).[40]

In the case of phenomenal consciousness, the term 'phenomenal consciousness' loosely refers to subjective experiences of the sort that allow for self-awareness and self-reflexivity, meaning how a subject *feels* when he/she experiences something. There is a raw quality to the experience that uniquely impinges on the subject that is different from other separate experiences where the subject can identify and is aware of each individuated experience and how it qualitatively reveals itself to them. The basic argument for denial of animal phenomenal consciousness can be formulated as follows:

Argument 2:

(1) Whatever lacks phenomenal feel and self-awareness does not have conscious experiences.

(2) Animal lack phenomenal feel and self-awareness.

a: because they lack notions of indexicals (idea of context).

b: because they lack a concept of the self (or "I").

c: because they are unable to disclose their mental states.

d: because they lack the ability of mental monitoring.

e: because they lack episodic memory.

f: because they lack mental time travel.

(3) Therefore, animals do not have conscious experiences.

(4) Therefore, animals do not suffer; from (3).[41]

This discussion raises implications: If animals lack intellection and consciousness (and from a religious perspective, a soul), then this would suggest that (1) they do not feel pain or experience suffering in the way human beings do, (2) they have subordinate moral status to human beings, and (3) they inhabit an anthropocentric environmental regime that defines their value. If this is the case, then there really is no substantive or actual problem of evil in the case of animals because they would neither feel pain nor suffer in a morally significant way. It would also mean that animals have merely biological (consumption), psychological (aesthetic), and religious (ritual slaughter) roles. Thus, their instrumentality is what would define their value because they do not have individual lives defined by a unique and greater purpose. Even if such implications are granted, the fact that animals are acknowledged as feeling pain even if they may not be subjectively aware of that pain would still make that a bad state of affairs for animals and any bad state of affairs would surely be permitted by an Omnipotent, Omniscient, Perfectly Just, and perfectly loving being with some justifiable reasons. Therefore, even if it is granted that animals do not suffer to a measurable extent like humans do, nevertheless they feel pain and the permission for allowing them to feel pain—often repeatedly—requires an explanation.

Animal Pain and Suffering: Stating the Problem

Given the core scriptural and scientific issues outlined above, a working abstract formulation of the evidential argument from the evil of pain and suffering in relation to nonhuman animals as a subspecies of the general theistic problem of evil could be presented as follows (let us call the argument "APS" [Animal, Pain, and Suffering] for short):[42]

APS:

(1) There is a profusion of animal pain and suffering which an omnipotent, omniscient, omnibenevolent, just and wise being could have prevented without thereby losing some greater good or permitting some evil equally bad or worse.

(2) An omnipotent, omniscient, omnibenevolent, just and wise being would prevent the occurrence of profuse animal suffering, unless it could not do so without thereby losing some greater good or permitting some evil equally bad or worse.

(3) Therefore, there does not exist an omnipotent, omniscient, omnibenevolent, just and wise being.

Premise (2) expresses a description of what kind of being God is and what He would do given certain circumstances. Such a description broadly corresponds to that of the Islamic tradition. The premise states God would prevent any pain and suffering toward animals unless there was some overriding reason not to like losing a greater good or some equally or worse evil occurs. In other words, God would not permit gratuitous or pointless pain and suffering toward animals; 'pointless' meaning that which is unnecessary for fulfilling God's own purposes. Premise (1) is the empirical premise that claims there are vast quantities as well as intense amount of pain and suffering of animals that appear gratuitous; that is to say that God could have prevented it without losing some greater good or permitting some equally or worse evil, but He seems not to. The latter claim can be explained through a required inference ('O' = observation, 'C' = conclusion, 'E' = specific case of horrendous evil acts against animals like torturing them to death, exterminating them, and the like):

(O) No good outcome we know of is such that God obtaining it would justify specific cases of animal pain and suffering $(E_1, E_2, \ldots, E_n)$.

(C) It is likely that no good outcome we know of is such that God obtaining it would justify specific cases of animal pain and suffering $(E_1, E_2, \ldots, E_n)$.

The 'good outcome' mentioned in (O) would be something discernible, tangible, or even merely possible (what has not yet occurred but could). It would also include that which brings about happiness, pleasure, love, and virtue—the kinds of outcomes that are not religiously objectionable either. Of course, being an inductive inference, one cannot claim to *know* for certain or prove beyond doubt that cases like E_1, $E_2, \ldots, E_n$ are pointless. There may be a good outweighing an animal being tortured to death unbeknown to us or a good we are not aware of connected to that tortured animal. Even if we do not know for certain, what we do have are rational grounds for accepting (O), which lends strength to the premise. With argument APS thus stated, I want to list eight presuppositions that I take to be crucial in understanding the problem of animal pain and suffering—assumptions in the background that are often presupposed but not stated. I will call these presuppositions Additional Value Theses and will number them T1–T8. The APS Value Theses T1–T8 are:

T1: God ought to prevent the evil of animal harm, pain, and suffering.

T2: God ought only to desire the happiness and pleasure of all creatures—including that of animals.

T3: God ought to recompense any pain and suffering of animals.

T4: God ought not to use evil as a means.

T5: God ought never to allow gratuitous evil.

T6: God ought to justly balance evil and harm of animals with an equal or greater good.

T7: God ought to have justifying reasons for permitting the evil of animal pain and suffering.

T8: God ought to reveal His reasons for justifying and permitting the evil of animal pain and suffering.

A wide range of possible theodicies for the evil of nonhuman animal pain and suffering has been conveniently listed by Peter Harrison under nine general types and is reproduced below:[43]

1. There is no all-powerful and all-good Deity.
2. Animals make wrong moral choices and their suffering is warranted.
3. The suffering of animals contributes in some way to their moral development.
4. Animals suffer as a result of human transgressions.
5. Animals will be compensated for their suffering in some future life.
6. Animals suffer as a result of the transgressions of super-human beings.
7. The suffering of animals contributes in some way to a greater good.
8. Animal pain is not an evil.
9. Animals neither suffer, nor are the subjects of painful experiences.

In the medieval Islamic theological literature, there is unsurprisingly no affirmation of 1 but there are various accounts that establish 2, 3, 4, and 5 with suggestions of 6, 7, 8, and 9. The views discussed below fall into one or more of these categories presented by Harrison in his typology. To these we will now turn.

Mu'tazilite Eschatological Recompense and Ash'arite Skepticism

Early theological debates during the formative period of Islamic thought revealed deep tensions over conceptualizations of God and His relation to the world, and the problem of the evil of pain and suffering is one clear fault line of that conceptualization. The case of animal pain and suffering is no exception. Two broad antagonistic views developed around explaining God's permission of suffering toward animals: the Mu'tazilite stance and the Sunni theological stance *contra* Mu'tazilites. As we shall see in this section, vehement disagreement meant the Value Theses T1–T8 were all points of dispute. Excerpts from four source texts are given in the Appendix as stimuli for the subsequent analysis in the chapter.

Beginning with the Mu'tazilite account first, 'Abd al-Jabbar's response to the problem of animal pain and suffering is framed through his doctrine of "compensation" (*'iwad*) which falls under 5, 7, and 8 on Harrison's typology.[44] To briefly outline the doctrine, God's justice, mercy, and wisdom constrain Him to recompense any harm or suffering that animals experience if God is the direct agent. God's justice, mercy, and wisdom also constrain him to place a system of compensation to victims of pain when the agents are other animals. This expected compensation is the purpose that makes God's permission of their pain and suffering a good. Irrespective of whether animals are aware of any pain they inflict (or whether the victims are aware of the pain they suffer), they are nevertheless obligated to compensate their victims because "the obligation to compensate is not due to possessing an intellect but the occurrence of pain."[45] Thus, every instance of pain must be compensated, regardless. Two further matters were tackled by 'Abd al-Jabbar related to this issue: (1) If animals act according to their natures, like carnivorous animals that possess sharp teeth and claws and so unavoidably inflict pain on other creatures, then is God obligated to compensate for that as such animals do not have a choice in how their natures were created and how their actions are affected by their nature?[46] (2) If God through His omniscience knows that an animal will inflict pain on another animal due to being enabled (*makkana*) with predispositions or potential to inflict pain, would God not be obligated to compensate because He could have intervened to prevent the infliction of pain but does not do so?[47] The two arguments can be put as follows:

Argument 1:
(1) God created animals with certain natures.
(2) Animals did not have a choice in what natures they were created with.
(3) Animals act according to their natures.
(4) Their nature leads them to inflict pain on other creatures.
(5) Therefore, they have no choice in the actions they do.
(6) Absence of choice means they are not obligated to compensate their victims.
(7) Therefore, God must compensate for their actions because He is responsible for creating their nature.

Argument 2:
(1) God enabled animals to inflict pain on other creatures.
(2) God can prevent animals from inflicting pain.
(3) If God does not prevent animals from inflicting pain, He must compensate for that pain for permitting it.
(4) God does not prevent animals from inflicting pain.
(5) Therefore, God must compensate for the pain for permitting it.

'Abd al-Jabbar's maneuver to respond to both arguments is that enabling a creature to inflict pain (*tamkin*), meaning the animal possessing a nature that predisposes it to potential detrimental acts to other creatures, is not equivalent to (1) directly causing the animal to act, (2) compelling the animal to act, and (3) God's approval or willful and active permission (*ibaha*) for the animal to act.[48] Animals, despite their nature and predisposition, are free to choose (*ikhtiyar*), he argues, whether or not to inflict pain on other creatures. This choice is what ultimately makes them liable to compensate.[49] 'Abd al-Jabbar defends God from the liability of compensation with two broad arguments: First, 'Abd al-Jabbar makes an analogy with the divine atemporal realm with the worldly temporal realm to prove his point. If a person lends a knife to another person in order to slaughter a sheep but that person uses it to kill someone else, then this does not imply that the lender is obligated to compensate for the murder. If this logic is followed, then ironsmiths and sword welders will have to compensate everyone who was murdered by weapons they had made. But this would be absurd. Therefore, if human beings are not obligated morally or by law for compensating the victim of this knife crime, then similarly, God is not obligated to make any compensation for the pain suffered by the free choices of animals simply because He created them with a specific nature that gives them the potential to harm.[50] The perpetrator of the crime must compensate, not God. Second, although God in His omniscience knows that a certain animal will inflict pain because they have been enabled to do so, this does not mean He approves of it or even permits it. It does not necessarily follow from God's nonintervention that He either approves or permits such acts.[51] 'Abd al-Jabbar does, however, discuss scenarios when God directly permits or commands inflicting pain and suffering on animals. He is unequivocal in obligating compensation on God if God is the agent of such pain and suffering. It is this very compensation that makes the divine act both good and purposive.[52] As an example, he discusses the case of animal sacrifice or slaughter. Here, God commands the slaughter of animals as a religious rite and such a command is a good because the animals will be granted a compensation for the pain they suffer in being objects for that command to be fulfilled.[53] Their compensation is akin to that of the reward (*thawab*) acquired by humans when they fulfill a command of God.[54]

1.
    (1) All acts of God are good and purposive.
    (2) God commands the slaughter of animals for consumption.

(3) Animal pain and suffering occur through God's command.

(4) Therefore, animal pain and suffering must be good and purposive.

2.

(1) If a living creature suffers pain, it must be compensated.

(2) Nonhuman creatures suffer pain when slaughtered.

(3) Therefore, nonhuman creatures must be compensated.

(4) God commands the slaughter of animals.

(5) Therefore, God must compensate animals for the pain they suffer.

Interestingly, 'Abd al-Jabbar explains the rationale (*'illa*) behind God's goodness in commanding the slaughter of animals for consumption: it enables the slaughterer (*al-dhabih*) to be warned and to reflect in how the command by God contains immense good and benefit (*wa li-anna al-dhabh huwa alladhi yaqa'u bihi al-i'tibar*).[55] This should engender gratitude within a person for God's graces and gifts and motivate them to undertake fulfilling God's commands.[56]

The Ash'arite view, on the other hand, is entirely contrary to this Mu'tazilite account. One set of their arguments attacks T1, T2, and T3 and another argument seeks to challenge T4–T8. Hence, the Ash'arite stance is aggressively sweeping in scope. In the case of the first set of arguments, both al-Ghazali and al-Razi in their formulations on animal pain and suffering reject all Mu'tazilite claims that God is under an obligation to recompense any creature. The standard Ash'arite lines of response to these claims include demonstrating first how it is a category mistake to apply the definitions of 'obligation' and 'injustice' to God. If by 'obligation' it is meant meriting censure for the omission of an act or duty and by 'injustice' it is meant infringing on the rights of another's property, then these are inapplicable to God just like it is inapplicable (and nonsensical) to say a wall is 'ignorant' or the wind is 'frivolous.' God cannot be under any moral obligation to compensate animals simply because He is neither beholden to a moral decree or command nor in debt to any created being. God also cannot be judged as unjust because creation is His dominion and property and thus no violation of property rights occurs. Animals owe their existence to the contingent act of God's benevolence. Second, failing to compensate harm and suffering to animals would not entail God acting contrary to His wisdom if by wisdom is meant knowledge of the order of things and the power to materialize that order (*nizam al-umur wa-l-qudra 'ala tartibiha*). There is nothing inherently contradictory, the Ash'arites claim, between God not compensating animals for their pain and suffering and this definition of wisdom. In other words, it does not logically follow that God is not wise if He does not compensate animals. Finally, the doctrine of compensation would create moral quandaries. If an animal will be compensated with a far greater good G for some evil E it suffers, then it would be morally praiseworthy to cause harm to that animal in order for it to receive G because such an action would maximize the good for it. But this would be contrary to our moral intuitions not to mention being morally paradoxical. Although arguably a caricature, the Ash'arite counterargument is intended to highlight the logical entailment of a view that places the locus of ethical obligations solely on the outcomes.

In addition to the above lines of argument, Ash'arite skepticism can apply to diffuse the force of the Mu'tazilite claims. God would be justified in allowing animal pain and suffering, but that justification is beyond human comprehension (Let "E" stand for "animal pain and suffering"):

(1) At least some E in the world seems to be gratuitous.
(2) Therefore, at least some E in the world are gratuitous.
(3) If God is perfectly Good, Wise, and Just then E would not exist.
(4) E does exist.
(5) Therefore, God is not perfectly Good, Wise, or Just.

The Ash'arite skeptic would argue that the inference from (1) to (2) would be unwarranted due to human cognitive limitations. Our finite and limited epistemic scope—what we are able to know—as well as God's infinite knowledge makes it unsurprising that this should be so. We have no power to fathom how the instances of E suffered by animals due to natural, moral, or anthropogenic causes were necessary or possible to serve some greater purpose or good; we only know from the Qur'an that God's providential governance of the world and its full history is absolutely meticulous. Because it appears to us that there are cases of animals gratuitously suffering, we are led to conclude that in all probability these cases are actually gratuitous. In addition, if what God does is based on His will and His will is ultimately inscrutable, we are not in any epistemic position to posit reasons why God permits E, unless He explicitly discloses that reason.[57] The search for grounding God's actions (whether permissions, omissions, or commissions) is ultimately futile. In this way, no maneuver by the Ash'arite skeptic is made to offer possible explanations why God may have permitted the pain and suffering of animals as is the case in theodicies. However, being epistemically foreclosed from knowing God's reasons why He acts does not diminish the gravity of animal pain and suffering nor does it cause moral paralysis by thinking there is no way for us to know our moral duties toward them. The Qur'an and the teachings of the Prophet are emphatic on treating animals with kindness, compassion, and care, which involves alleviating their suffering. Thus, on the Ash'arite skeptic's view, although we may not know why God allows animals to suffer, we *do* know the set of positive commandments He has issued toward ensuring their well-being. What is also worth pointing out is that this form of Ash'arite skepticism does not extend to skepticism about our abilities to access animal minds. It is not a claim about the human cognitive limitations on the penetrability of animal minds. As the quote from al-Juwayni on animals suggests, Ash'arites do not deny the reality or existence of animal pain and suffering but only that such pain and suffering in no way undermines God's goodness, wisdom, and justice.

The blunt logic of the Ash'arites may seem disconcerting and unsettling, perhaps even chillingly dismissive. The reduction of the discussion to what is logically possible for God regarding His creatures also seems to undermine the experiential and existential sensitivity embedded in the issue. The Ash'arite denial of human beings and God inhabiting "the same moral community"[58] came at the expense of conceding that God's agency in the world was ultimately capricious. On the contrary, the Mu'tazilite insistence of a deity constrained by the very terms of His own justice that compels Him to reserve an eschatological indemnification for animals seems appealing.[59] However, such a deity would be a kind of 'cosmic book keeper,' a being that merely quantitatively tallies the pain of creatures to balance the books. Neither, it may be argued, appears to resonate with any appeal to our intuitive moral sensibilities. Perhaps a Maturidite account offers more attractive insights. To this account we shall now turn.

Maturidite Mystery Theodicy

The strategies discussed above employed by the Ash'arites to diffuse the prima facie force of the Mu'tazilite claims apply generally to the Maturidites. This would mean they too challenge T1, T2, T3, T6, and T8. However, I would argue that the underlying theodicy discernible from an assessment of the Maturidite texts is not skepticism per se but stronger: a *mystery*. Thus, the Maturidite position on animal suffering is ultimately a mystery theodicy. This becomes clear when we synthesize various strands of their theological doctrines. Here, al-Maturidi and Ibn al-Humam are particularly significant in order to provide the overall framework. Before formulating that, I want to suggest two additional theodicies Maturidites can use to explain the existence of animal pain and suffering corresponding to 6, 8, and 9, respectively, on Harrison's typology.

Iblis: one possible cause for the suffering in creation—including that of animals—is Iblis.[60] When Iblis was cast out for arrogantly disobeying God's direct command, God granted his wish to be endowed with supernatural powers with which to lead not only human beings into error and misguidance (al-Hijr, verses 39–40; al-Saba, verses 20-21) but to interfere with the material reality of the created order. That would include animals. The Christian philosopher and open theist Gregory Boyd, for example, has recently argued broadly following C. S. Lewis that much of the natural evil in the world must be attributed to the demonic activities of nonhuman spirits that are attempting to thwart God's will to draw all of His creation into the fold of His love. He says:

> To be sure, according to Scripture the creation was originally created good, and the glory of God is still evident in it (Gen 1; Rom 1:20). But something else—something frightfully wicked—is evident in it as well. Of their own free will, Satan and other spiritual beings rebelled against God in the primordial past and now abuse their God-given authority over aspects of the creation. The one who "holds the power of death—that is, the devil" (Heb. 2:14) exercises a pervasive structural, diabolical influence to the point that the entire creation is in "bondage to decay" (Rom. 8:21). If this scenario is correct, then the pain-ridden, bloodthirsty, sinister hostile character of nature makes perfect sense. If not, then despite the valid contributions of a number of thinkers on "natural" evil, the demonic character of nature must remain largely inexplicable.[61]

Whether a plausible explanation for animal pain and suffering along similar lines suggested by Boyd and Lewis can be extrapolated from Islamic source texts would, I think, be difficult to make but nevertheless quite tempting. We could speculate, for example, that if Iblis as an autonomous being is a necessary part of the created world then one consequence of that is Iblis (and his demonic cohorts) exploiting animals through a misuse of his endowed free will by causing them pain and suffering or causing them to create harm and adverse effects on other creatures. This possibility of demonic activity through animals is suggested by a number of reports from the Prophet. One report is when a small mouse came dragging a burning wick and dropped it before the Prophet, burning a hole in his straw mat. On this, the Prophet remarked: "When you go to sleep, extinguish your lamp because the devil guides a creature like this to burn you."[62] Although there is no concept of the fall within the Islamic narrative of human beginnings, nature is penetrable through supernatural entities that disturb its material reality for evil and not good.

Although this kind of explanation may address certain species of problems (like demonic possession), it seems to afford exclusive and extensive power to Iblis. On a Qur'anic view, it would be hard to accept Iblis's interference on every creaturely level in order to account for their pain and suffering if God is the meticulous vanguard of His creation. Moreover, this kind of explanation does not help the skeptic who does not accept the Qur'anic supernatural worldview.

No suffering: one way to respond to the profusion of gratuitous animal pain and suffering is to reasonably ask whether animals endure anything like intense suffering. If they do not, then we can conclude they do not suffer in a morally significant way. Perhaps animals have been created with this kind of nature. Al-Maturidi clearly upholds the standard theological view in medieval times that animals have been created to be fully subjugated by humans for their total benefit. Causing them pain or disciplining them is permitted if they obstinately refuse to benefit humans. This must mean they are not the same type of creatures with the same threshold of pain as humans. He writes:

> However, the response to them for that is to say God created these beasts and birds and other things besides for human benefit and need. It is allowed to punish and discipline them in order to bring them back to being beneficial if they try and resist, in order to train and teach them.[63]

Michael Murray has argued that there are good scientific and philosophical grounds for doubting that most animals experience pain.[64] One problem with this, however, is that animal pain is epistemically closed off to us because it is "a private experience" not "directly observed, verified or measured" and this generates the "fundamental difficulty in research on pain."[65] Another problem is that different researchers work with different definitions of 'pain.' Zoologist James Rose, for example, distinguishes between "theoretical/explanatory definitions" and "operational definitions."[66] An operational definition explains how pain is measured in a particular experiment. For instance, the presence of shock avoidance learning has often been operationally defined as an indication of pain.[67] This does not, however, give us any insight into what an animal actually experiences.[68] A theoretical/explanatory definition tries to give a meaningful definition of pain. For example, the necessary conditions for pain offered by the International Association for the Study of Pain (IASP) is that it is:

> (i) an unpleasant sensory and emotional experience associated with actual or potential tissue damage, or described in terms of such damage; (ii) pain is always subjective; and (iii) pain is sometimes reported in the absence of tissue damage and the definition of pain should avoid tying pain to an external eliciting stimulus [emphases added].[69]

Following the IASP definitions, Rose argues that we need to distinguish between *nociception* and *pain*. Nociception is the encoding and processing of harmful stimuli in the nervous system, and, therefore, the ability of a body to sense potential harm. Pain is more than a simple sensory experience signaling the existence of damaged tissue: pain is a psychological state. Pain often, but not always, accompanies nociception; pain sometimes occurs without nociception; and the degree of pain is often poorly associated with severity of injury. People can sustain severe injuries and not report pain; sometimes they report variant degrees of pain than the extent of their injuries would suggest. Moreover, pain can be greatly reduced or increased by "psychological" manipulations such as a visual illusion, created or reduced by hypnotic suggestion while nociceptor activation is unmodified. Furthermore, pain has a strong social learning component and depends greatly on prior experience, beliefs about it, and interpersonal interactions rather than the extent of nociceptor activation per se. For example, a child's pain response depends greatly on the behavior of caregivers.[70] So, in Rose's view, animals without a neocortex complex enough to sustain complex psychological states experience only nociception, not pain.[71]

Because phenomenal states are private, and not open to direct observation, it is rather difficult to establish that animals *do not* accompany nociception. Rather than arguing that animals do not suffer pain and only experience nociception, it might be more helpful to distinguish between 'conscious pains' and 'intense, personal suffering.' A more modest argument could then be made that most vertebrates only experience 'conscious pains'—simple, unpleasant phenomenal experiences that signal tissue damage. However, 'intense, personal suffering' requires a higher order state of consciousness than simple, first-order, phenomenal states. Complex psychological states such as 'dread,' 'regret,' or 'sorrow' seem to require a very complex nervous system—at a minimum, first-order brain states must be processed by higher cortical regions to create second-order states about those first-order states. Most animals lack the higher cortical regions capable of such processing of the information to produce such beliefs, propositional attitudes, and emotions. Philosopher Roger Scruton notes that, unlike animals, humans are self-conscious, refer to themselves in the first person, and actively assert and value their own individual desires. One human individual is not replaceable by another.[72] Scruton further observes that deep personal attachments are not possible in the animal kingdom because animals lack our sense of individuality and empathy. Thus, a mare, for example, "does not cherish her foal's life, personality or identity; does not stand vigil over its moral and psychological development; does not feel its pains and joys as her own" and this must mean that there is a lack of "a consciousness of self and other" from the "mental repertoire of the non-human animals."[73] The absence of rational individuality and deep personal attachments and empathy in the mental lives of animals means that they cannot suffer loss in the qualitative manner that humans do. They do not experience the dread of death as humans do, nor regret, repentance, and grief. Moreover, while many kinds of animals might suffer unpleasant phenomenal states that signal tissue damage ('conscious pains'), it is not at all clear that they suffer anything like the human psychological state of intense, personal suffering.

This explanation may seem counterintuitive to how we understand animal experience and behavior to be. It may also seem contrary to the Islamic source texts on animals and their status outlined earlier where a high view of animal psychology was affirmed. Finally, suggesting that animals do not suffer may open the door to their abuse and maltreatment—especially at the hands of those with commercial and entertainment interests. Finally, in light of modern scientific knowledge, it seems that attributing causes for, say, animal diseases or natural disasters to dangerous supernatural entities lacks explanatory power, or, indeed, is not helpful.

Mystery theodicy: Returning to my claim of the Maturidite mystery theodicy, the core statement for this kind of theodicy (call it MT) can be set out as follows (Let '*E*' stand for 'animal pain and suffering'):

(MT) If God is absolutely powerful, under no obligations, and His wisdom is inscrutable, then for any evil E and profusion of E, E is a mystery.

There are four core doctrines for consideration:

(1) Evil is only proximate.
(2) God is absolutely powerful.
(3) God is not under any obligations.
(4) God's wisdom is inscrutable.

If doctrines (1)–(4) are true, it would follow that human beings, as finite cognitive creatures, can never understand the causes behind E although we would trust that if there were any causes, it would be governed by God's wisdom. Regarding doctrine (1), the Maturidites affirm the reality of evil and even affirm God's sponsorship of evil. In the end, however, there is no evil.[74] In order to explain my paradoxical way of stating the doctrine, let me list the core propositions regarding evil within the Maturidite perspective:

1. Evil is a reality—it is not a chimera.
2. Evil is part of God's creation.
3. Evil is not equivalent to whatever causes some tangible harm to creatures.
4. Evil falls within the purview of God's power.
5. Evil is not contrary to divine wisdom.
6. God does not enact certain evils because it would be pointless (*'abath*), meaning it would serve no overarching wise end.
7. Evil can be salutary.
8. Evil is only *proximate*, meaning it is a bad state of affairs *immediately* perceived or judged by humans.
9. Ultimately, there are no evils, only wise purposes to God's acts.

For the Maturidites, evil is real and not metaphorical. There are actually bad states of affairs. However, evil is only *proximate* and not *ultimate*, that is to say, evil is something that God either enacts or permits that is immediately perceived as a bad state of affairs, but in the end, because it is grounded in God's wisdom, it actually serves a wise purpose. The wise purpose may not materialize in the immediate perception of that state of affairs but will unfold such that in the end, it emerges. Even though there is an unbridgeable epistemic gap between human finite cognition and God's omniscience that obviates any possibility of fathoming His wisdom, we can be assured that there is a wise purpose because by His nature He acts with this wisdom. The Maturidites thus shift the focus of what grounds God's acts from their proximate effects to their ultimate effects. In this way, evil relates to teleology (end purpose) and not consequences (effects in the world). Jackson explains the Maturidite position:

> God's acts do not have to be of immediate practical human benefit in order for them to be wise and transcend pointlessness; nor can they be wise and devoid of pointlessness if there is no *ultimate* end that they serve, even if it remains in God's putative "right" to commit such acts. In sum,

by avoiding acts that are ultimately vain, God is exonerated from evil [. . .] divine acts are judged according to their *ultimate* effect, and only those acts that are deemed to be teleologically evil—that is, ultimately devoid of good, just and wise effects—violate God's omnibenevolence.[75]

This would allow the Maturidites to insist that in regard to animal pain and suffering, though it may appear to us in the immediate time-space factor that animal pain and suffering is an evil, in the end it actually is not due to a wise purpose God's permission serves—number 8 on Harrison's typology. For doctrine (2), al-Maturidi is unequivocal in rejecting the Mu'tazilite doctrine of optimal good (*aslah*), which means that God only wills or does what is morally good (*hasan*) and He is necessarily exempt from any act that is morally bad. God acts with a purpose, and justice and compassion inhere in the Divine purpose. Existents by their nature contain both good and evil. God can will only the good and is obliged to accomplish that which is best (*al-aslah*). Therefore, He neither wills nor commands that which is evil. Humans as creators of their own acts act by a contingent power (*qudra*) that God has placed in them. Therefore, they are responsible for their own actions, and when they commit good or evil, God is obliged to reward or punish them accordingly.[76]

al-Maturidi uses as evidence Qur'an chapter al-Anbiya', verse 83, *And Ayyub, when he cried out to his Lord, [saying]: "Indeed, adversity afflicts me, and You are Most Merciful of all who show mercy."* He writes:

> The tribulation [Ayyub] suffered was just. [God] not granting him soundness and health was a mercy from Him and a blessing. He can grant what He wants to whomever He wants and prohibit whatever He wants to whomever He wants. Is it not evident to see that He says at the end of the verse as a response to [Ayyub] removing the tribulation that it is "a mercy from Us." If that was not a right of God, there would have been no point in mentioning it. This refutes the doctrine of the Mu'tazila that God is obligated to do what is optimum for [humans] for their religiosity because Ayyub attributes the affliction he suffered to Satanic forces saying, "*Indeed, Satan has touched me with hardship and torment*" [al-Sad, verse 41]. If this was a good religiously optimal for him, then he would not have attributed this religiously optimal good action to satanic forces. Thus, this shows the matter is contrary to what they hold.[77]

Like his Ash'arite counterparts, al-Maturidi, as suggested by this passage, upholds a strong notion of divine Omnipotence. God does whatever He wills to do without any hindrance in the operation of His powers.

Regarding doctrine (3), al-Maturidi, like al-Ash'ari, negates any ascription of injustice to God. On 'injustice' (*zulm*), he defines it in the familiar way as "putting something in its improper place" and that anything in the created order that does not own the heavens and the earth "will place and misplace the rights of some to others" and so long as they do that, they can be said to be unjust. However, because God is that being to Whom belongs the heavens and the earth, "He is far above such an ascription."[78] al-Maturidi spells out the reasoning elsewhere, stating that "any owner of a thing can destroy what it owns and so one cannot be called unjust for doing that." If, however, "one destroys something that belongs to another, then he would be considered unjust."[79] His reasoning seems to be:

(1) An owner has the right to dispose of his property as he pleases.
(2) God's property is the entire creation.
(3) Therefore, God has the right to dispose of creation as He pleases.

Therefore, God cannot, by definition, be accused of injustice if He disposes of His creation in any manner that pleases Him. Animals fall under God's creation and so He can choose to do whatever He pleases with them. He is under no obligation to prolong or enrich their lives for even a moment or to compensate them for not doing so. He is not under any obligation imposed externally to administer His dominion in a particular way.[80] Finally on (4), related to God's wisdom, al-Maturidi is no less emphatic. He defines God being wise (*al-hakim*), meaning "never committing an error in anything" and adding "neither are His actions divorced from wisdom."[81] In another place, he explains wisdom to be "putting something in its rightful place"[82]—something he equates with justice (*'adl*).[83] Wisdom, for the Maturidites, thus inextricably informs all of God's actions, otherwise they would be pointless (*'abath*), which is a deficiency and a compromise on transcendence.[84] Ibn al-Humam paradoxically clarifies that although this wisdom is inseparably embedded in God's actions,

> this does mean that they have a goal (*gharad*) whose benefit can be explained going back to the doer. His actions (Most High) and creation of the world are not rationalised with discernible goals as that would negate the perfection of His independence from all things "*and God is independent of all creatures*" [Al 'Imran, verse 97]. If the benefit is explained referring back to other than Him, that will negate His willing an act that could be and wisdom is more general than that.[85]

Ibn al-Humam is explicit in desisting the reader from equating divine wisdom as held by the Maturidites with an explicable purpose or goal because that would mean God's action will stand in need of completion (*istikmal*) in that realizing the goal would be preferable than its absence. But this would entail a lack in God's acts, which is a deficiency and deficiencies are impossible for God. This would make divine wisdom in the end inscrutable.[86] Al-Maturidi makes the point in less systematic terms:

> The basis for it is that it is possible for God—Mighty and Exalted is He!— to create things where the wisdom behind it is a secret, unknowable to creation and not within the wisdom of any human to grasp. Thus, tribulations and hardships have wisdom in it that are unknowable to creation. Therefore, it is possible for God to create Iblis as well as disobedient creatures with a wise purpose behind it but unknowable to creatures and not within the wisdom of any human to grasp based on what we just mentioned.[87]

Ibn al-Humam in *al-Musayara* virtually rehearses the arguments for Ash'arite skepticism. This skepticism as I mentioned, in fact, translates into sheer mystery. The gist of the point is that we as human beings cannot fathom the mysterious workings of God's Will and wisdom and so unmerited suffering toward all creatures as something unjust is not attributable to Him. Ibn al-Humam concludes his lengthy discussion on the Eighth Foundation with a complete tone of humility and surrender. He says:

> The Hanafi masters have said that the case of animals in the hereafter is more serious than that of the Muslims much like the case of the non-Muslim citizen of the state (*dhimmi*). We may not grasp everything that happens to animals and their like but we judge it optimistically and have absolute conviction in that there is wisdom behind [the permission of pain and suffering][88] that we cannot grasp. The believer must utterly submit to [God] and believe in His divine right, abandoning all objections [he may hold] towards Him. He has the sole prerogative to judge and command without being questioned on what He does based on His sovereignty and Lordship, perfect knowledge, impenetrable wisdom that cannot be penetrated by any mind. Indeed, "*God knows and you do not know.*" It is they who will be questioned about their worship and servitude.[89]

Ibn al-Humam here clearly proposes a mystery theodicy for animal pain and suffering. This, he claims, is the position of the Hanafite specialists. We cannot hope to always understand the meaning and pur-pose of suffering and impressing on ourselves any attempt to do so will result in failure. The only conviction we have to guide us is that God operates with a pervading and essential wisdom and that this wisdom will unfold when all things will be resolved and restored in the hereafter. The duty of the believer is to maintain an optimistic view of His Creator and keep trust in Him informed by the kind of being He is as disclosed in the Qur'an.

Ibn Qayyim, Animal Suffering, and the Wisdom in Divine Disclosure

Moving on to Ibn Qayyim al-Jawziya, it is clear on his view that ultimately there really is no real or genuine evil.[90] His account for why God permits human pain and suffering is based on what I will call the Criteria Thesis that can apply here to animal suffering. The Criteria Thesis is as follows:

(1) For any evil E, God has the right to permit E.
(2) The good G secured through the permission of E must at least be possible (deducible) scripturally.
(3) Any G secured through the permission of E sufficiently outweighs E.[91]

According to Ibn Qayyim, in the larger perspective of things, every-thing is genuinely good and that on long and deep reflection, this truth bears out. From the perspective of human beings, states of affairs may appear to be evil, but they are only a partial (juz'iy) and relative (idafi) evil and not intrinsically evil because as he repeatedly asserts in Shifa' al-'alil, God does not create pure evil; rather His acts are grounded in wise purposes by virtue of which it is good—denial of T5. Thus, whatever evil may appear to be in some state of affairs, it is actually a greater good. This calculation also applies to the case of animal pain and suffering. The inexplicable nature and profusion of animal pain and suffering are out-weighed by the possible good that will be brought about: an affirmation of T6[92] and type 7 from Harrison's typology. Ibn Qayyim argues that the benefits and good gained by animals are greater on balance than their pain and suffering. He explains why:

> Now, whatever animals, who are not obligated, endure of them is over-whelmingly inundated by their advantage and benefits. Examples include what they endure of the summer's heat, the winter's cold, the lack of rain or snow, the pain of pregnancy or delivery, or their pursuit of sustenance. But the pleasures [of animals] are many times greater than their pains.

What they attain of benefit and goods are many times greater than what they endure of evils and pains [. . .] the pain of animals is much less relative to their pleasures; the same can also be said regarding their illnesses compared to their health, their hunger and thirst relative to their being satiated and feeling quenched, and their fatigue compared to their relaxation.[93]

The outweighing good that animals gain are reduced to their physical and appetitive pleasures. Although animals clearly feel a degree of pain, they do not, he seems to suggest, suffer like human beings do—a proposed defeater for premise (6) in APS and a rejection of T1 and T5. They do not possess intellects in the way human beings do, thus lacking advanced cognition.[94] They only have sensation and understanding commensurate with and the level appropriate for fulfilling their biological functions. This also entails that they can be subdued and controlled for human benefit. Ibn Qayyim states this explicitly elsewhere:

And reflect on the impressive wisdom behind [God] granting animals hearing and sight to go about attaining what benefits them and what benefits humans because if they were blind or deaf, human beings could not have benefited from them. God also negated them from possessing the kind of intellect given to humans [despite their large size] so that they can be subdued and thus controlled and utilised as they wish. If [animals] were given an identical intellect with their large size, they could defy and disobey humans undermining their control over them. [Animals] have been given understanding and perception according to what enables them to realise their interests and the interests of those who control them. They have thus been negated from the type of mind and intellect granted to humans in order to underscore the excellence and distinction of the latter.[95]

Therefore, due to lacking intellects, animals cannot experience and internalize the pain in any existentially meaningful way. Restricted to only lower-order pain sensations would mean that animals are shielded from agony and trauma—something that may even be construed as a possible outweighing good in that it would be one of God's wise purposes in creating them with such a nature that spares them this dimension of suffering. This would fall under type 9 from Harrison's typology.

Another possible outweighing good could be explained within the horizon of Ibn Qayyim's own educational theodicy: (1) knowledge of God for salvation. This would unfold in two ways: (a) knowledge of God's attributes through divine disclosure in nature and (b) knowledge of the purpose of life. Regarding the first way, in *Miftah dar al-sa'ada*, Ibn Qayyim brings a vast catalogue of examples of how marvelous, meticulous, aesthetic, and exacting animal anatomy and physiology is.[96] The way certain animals hunt their prey is fittingly constituted for their survival and operates with clear function appropriate for within their ecosystems—even if that involves a predator feeding on its prey—all that would be part of the providential organization of the created order. This variability among living organisms in terms of their species and ecosystems would thus be a means of manifesting God's attributes such as Creator (*khaliq*), Director (*mudabbir*), and Giver of Form (*musawwir*) as well as God's wise actions for human beings that, as a consequence, would allow them to deeply enrich their knowledge of and awe and humility toward God. In this way, animal pain through predation, although ostensibly brutal and bloody to the observer, has an instrumental function for developing knowledge of specific divine attributes in human beings. This instrumentality would be a possible good that justifies God's permission for animals to suffer pain.

Regarding the second way, Ibn Qayyim insists on the idea of an ordered cosmos. He describes the world as possessing the "most perfect and balanced system" (*ahsan al-nizam*),[97] which proves the handiwork of a most "Perfect Creator" (*ahsan al-khaliqin*).[98] In fact, the exact and elegant workings of nature are enumerated as a clear and direct proof for the existence of a single and unique Creator. Ibn Qayyim's argument for the existence of an intelligent Designer-Creator from complex natural systems is stated as follows:

> In all this is the greatest and clearest indication that the world is created by a Wise, Powerful and Knowing Creator who has perfectly determined everything and perfectly directed everything through a system. It also indicates that creation cannot have co-creators but a single Creator—there is no deity but He who is High above what the transgressors and ignorant say about Him! If there were to be more than any deity of the heavens and the earth other than God, its affairs would have been corrupted, its system in chaos and its good eliminated. It is impossible for the body to be directed by two equal souls (*ruhan mutakafi'an mutasawiyan*). If that is the case, the body would be corrupted and destroyed despite the possibility of both overpowered by a third. How could it then be that the director of this celestial and terrestrial world be two equal co-deities who are not overpowered by a third? This is impossible from primary knowledge and what is innately self-evident.[99]

Creation, therefore, exhibits the properties and wisdom of God. This would allow human beings to understand God and His character in order to come to know Him, increase faith in Him, and draw near to Him. In this regard, Ibn Qayyim remarks:

Some people perceive the wisdom behind the divine commandments more than the wisdom behind creation. Those elite servants of God who deeply understand God's commandments and religion fully recognise what the wisdom behind His commandments is. Their minds and intellect testify that the basis of what they see is profound wisdom and total beneficence including what is of utmost benefit for humans for their worldly and other-worldly matters. The countless number of such elite people is known only to God. Another group of people perceive the wisdom behind God's creation more than the wisdom behind His commandments. Such people are mostly physicians (*al-atibba'*) and biologists (*al-taba'iyin*) who have directed their research to uncovering and extracting the benefits found in plants and animals, their potential and the benefits that they may offer singularly and as a compound. They only have a share in perceiving the wisdom behind God's commandments akin to or less than the degree of the jurists' knowledge of the wisdom behind creation. Another group of people are blessed with the opening to perceive the wisdom behind both God's commandments and His creation according to their potential and ability. They perceive the exceeding wisdom in this or that thing that overwhelms their minds. Whenever they examine [God's] creation, or the wisdom underlying it, they increase in faith, knowledge, conviction, certainty and submission.[100]

If it is the case that humans come to know God through His creation and knowing God is one of the greatest goods (and the raison d'être of creating human beings), then the good of knowing God would clearly outweigh the pain caused to animals as a by-product of the way nature was designed: criterion (c) from the Criterion Thesis and affirmation of T6–T8. On God's purpose for creating human beings, Ibn Qayyim remarks:

As for the truth regarding the ultimate purpose (*ghaya*) for which He created them—meaning the heavens and the earth and everything between them—it is a twofold aim: an aim [God] wants from His servants and an aim for them. What He wants from them is that they should know God (Most High) and the attributes of His perfection (glorified and exalted is He!) and they should worship Him alone and not associate anything with Him, so He alone will be their God, the One Whom they worship and obey and love. God says: "*It is God Who has created seven heavens and of the earth the like thereof. His command descends between them, that you may know that God has power over all things, and that God surrounds all things in (His) knowledge"* (al-Talaq, verse 12). He informed [us] that He created the world so that His servants might know the perfection of His power and the all-encompassing nature of His knowledge, which requires knowing Him and His names and attributes, and affirming His unity. God says: *And I (God) created not the jinn and mankind except that they should worship Me* (al-Dhariyat, verse 56). This purpose is what is wanted from His servants, which is that they should come to know their Lord and worship Him alone. As for the aim for them, it is recompense on the basis of justice (*al-jaza' bi-l-'adl*) and divine grace, reward and punishment. God says: *"And to God belongs all that is in the heavens and all that is in the earth, that He may requite those who do evil with that which they have done and reward those who do good, with what is best"* (al-Najm, verse 31); *"verily, the Hour is coming—and I am almost hiding it—that every person may be rewarded for that for which he strives"* (Ta-Ha, verse 15); *"in order that He may make manifest to them the truth of that in which they differ and that those who disbelieved may know that they were deniers"* (al-Nahl, verse 39); "surely, your Lord is God Who created the heavens and the earth in six Days and then established Himself over the Throne, disposing the affair of all things. No intercessor (can plead with Him) except with His permission. That is God, your Lord; so worship Him (alone). Then, will you not remember? To Him is the return of all of you. The Promise of God is true. It is He Who begins the creation and then will repeat it, that He may reward with justice those who believed and did deeds of righteousness. But those who disbelieved will have a drink of boiling fluids and painful torment because they used to disbelieve." (Yunus, verses 3–4)[101]

Authentic knowledge of God and the correct relationship with Him are essential for human salvation. Nature—although includes predation, pestilence, and death—nevertheless points to an ordered and interconnecting network of systems based on incomparable exquisite craftsmanship and providence and this allows human beings to fully realize the innate belief they have about God and submit to Him freely and lovingly as their Lord—thus fulfilling their purpose. Hence, nature and the architecture of the natural world are means for human beings to realize their purpose of why they were created—knowledge, worship, and love of God. We can therefore present the possible explanations for how the purported evil of animal pain might be justified based on Ibn Qayyim's own theological ideas as follows:

(1) God has the right to permit animal pain because it is for a greater good.
(2) The good achieved by creating animals without experiencing suffering as well as the good of authentic knowledge of God and His attributes for salvation are at least conceivable (deducible) from scriptural evidences.
(3) The good achieved by creating animals without experiencing suffering as well as authentic knowledge of God and His attributes for salvation outweigh the evil of animal pain.

An immediate objection to this formulation of a "Qaymiyan"-type theodicy is that denial of animal suffering while acknowledging animal pain seems too dismissive or simply evades the explanatory burden. Mere denial of any genuine animal suffering absolves the believer from not only any requirement to address the complexity of the issue but appears to contradict our intuitions and experience of animal life courses and the data of the Qur'an about that. Moreover, how much cognitive complexity is required before animals can be properly said to suffer? On Ibn Qayyim's suggested view, it would be difficult to answer that. Another possible objection is that animals on this view have only an *instrumental value* and not *intrinsic value*; put another way, their moral worth is only in relation to how well they serve human salvific purposes and not because of the course and quality of their own individuated lives. In other words, the view is heavily *anthropocentric*. It may also be argued that it appears extremely difficult to justify the quantity and scope of animal pain (even if suffering is excluded) when far less would surely be sufficient to serve the purpose of human awakening toward their salvation. Thus, a purported greater good (knowledge of God and purpose in life) does not appear to balance evil (the profusion of animal pain).

Conclusion

The explanations for animal pain and suffering explored in this chapter are driven by deep assumptions about God (informed by the Qur'an, Hadith, and reason), evil, animal nature as well as the operation of nature. The Mu'tazilite theologians—at the helm al-Qadi 'Abd al-Jabbar—were the only ones who directly and substantively tackled the issue of animal pain and suffering head-on, offering an account for its rationale in God's eschatological scheme. The Ash'arites engaged in the issue only insofar as it sought to redress what was seen as Mu'tazilite excess in imposing duties on God and retreated into a kind of skeptical theism position. The

Maturidites took advantage of the same theological resources and insights as the Ash'arites and afforded a greater role to divine wise purposes but arguably retreated into a form of mystery theodicy. The traditionalist perspective represented in Ibn Qayyim had sufficient theological ideas for tentatively constructing an animal theodicy even though he did not explicitly formulate one himself on the issue.

4
Toward an Islamic Evolutionary Theodicy

In this chapter, I will propose an Islamic evolutionary theodicy model to explain the evil of animal pain and suffering, taking as my cue Charles Darwin's original observation of predation and waste within nature as a result of the evolutionary process. I will appropriate works by contemporary theologians, philosophers, and scientists as sources that inform my own proposal.

The Darwinian Context

Although a thorough treatment of an evolutionary theodicy within the Islamic theological framework is yet to be undertaken by scholars, I want to tentatively propose a broad outline for one here and then assess whether this kind of theodicy is an attractive option for explaining animal pain and suffering. It will be evident that my proposal incorporates different strands of theology already discussed in this chapter and throughout the book. It will also be evident that a Muslim evolutionary theodicist may not necessarily agree or find the arrangement and formulation I present here appealing due to regarding alternative accounts more or equally plausible. However, I do feel that the core tenets would not necessarily be disputed even if the theological and metaphysical details are. Before I outline my brief proposal, three significant works specifically addressing the evil of nonhuman animal pain and suffering within an evolutionary paradigm will be broadly outlined because they have been highly instrumental in shaping the subsequent philosophical and theological literature as well as my own tentative formulations. They are Christopher Southgate's *The Groaning of Creation*, Michael Murray's *Nature Red in Tooth and Claw* and Nicola Hoggard Creegan's *Animal Suffering and the Problem of Evil*.

However, it would be necessary first to briefly sketch what is called the 'Darwinian' problem of evil as this is the context in which such evolutionary theodicies are proposed and explained among contemporary philosophers and scientists. Yet, before this is done, Darwin's anguish and outrage had explicit antecedents within early Islamic theology. The Syrian poet and skeptic Aba al-'Ala' al-Ma'arri (d. 449/1057), for example, raised the problem of God's lack of compassion and mercy in failing to intervene in the predatory acts of stronger animals over weaker ones:

> Since it is stated that the creator is merciful and compassionate, why does the lion spring to attack gentle creatures that are neither harmful nor robust? And how many have perished through snakebite, including many famous people! (Why) do hawk and falcon swoop upon the grain-gleaning bird? The grouse leaves her thirsting chicks and sets out early to reach water which she would carry to them in her craw, but a hawk finds her far from them and devours her. So her chicks perish of thirst.[1]

When Darwin published *The Origin of Species* in 1859, in it he characterized the natural world as replete with the struggle for existence, waste, predation, suffering, death, and even extinction of species. The progressive development from brute man to intelligent creatures occurs in the wake of a long antecedent arc of supposedly meaningless death and suffering. The picture of the natural world drawn up by geologists and biologists of the nineteenth century was increasingly challenging the depiction of a God who designed creation held in the prior two centuries.[2] This emerging shift led Darwin himself to question God as wise Creator. He wrote to a friend, the Harvard botanist Asa Gray, shortly after going public with his theory:

> There seems to me too much misery in the world. I cannot persuade myself that a beneficent and omnipotent God would have designedly created the Ichneumonidae with the express intention of their feeding within the living bodies of caterpillars, or that the cat should play with mice. Not believing this, I see no necessity in the belief that the eye was expressly designed.[3]

Despite retaining some semblance of a belief in God, Darwin still had many quandaries that contradicted the view of the Designer-God upheld in his day such as the problem of hybrid species, the dissimilarity of species, seemingly ill-adapted species (terrestrial animals with webbed feet and marine animals with nonwebbed feet), incalculable waste (for example, of pollen), and many more observable phenomena that pointed to apparent mistakes, flaws, or imperfections in the created order.[4] Darwin's maneuver was to distance God from the evil in nature. His theodicy "had a strong scientific flavour" but had "embedded metaphysical presuppositions." The general approach was that "God was constrained to benevolence and was distanced from the evils of creation through the interposition of natural laws." By "positing natural selection operating in an unguided fashion on natural biological diversity" Darwin sought to absolve God of any cooperation in evil.[5] Given this, committed theists who believe in evolution as a fact about the world (evolutionary theists) are challenged by the Darwinian problem of evil in terms of why a benevolent God would allow so much pain, suffering, and death to nonhuman sentient creatures in nature and whether the biological evolutionary processes were necessary to serve the wise purposes God had for these creatures and indeed human beings when they finally emerged because of the incredible waste and horror that arise from it. If this is the case, then what ultimate restitution is there for this suffering, death, and waste?

Southgate and the Relief of Nature's Groaning:[6] In a unique work of theology that engages science, philosophy, and ecology, Christopher Southgate's *The Groaning of Creation* tackles how the suffering inherent in evolution can be understood as the creation of a good God. Offering interpretations of both Paul's Letter to the Romans (8:22) and the Book of Genesis (1:31), Southgate's summation is that God's creation must somehow be seen as both "groaning in travail" (ἡ κτίσις συνστενάζει) and worthy of the divine declaration that it is "very good" (טוֹב מְאֹד).[7] Southgate focuses his attention exclusively on nonhuman animals, asking how it is that creation can be understood as both 'groaning' and 'good' when we examine the lives of other animals. In the context of theodicy, he highlights two particular challenges that this dual characterization of creation raises for any animal theodicy. The first is species extinction, which Southgate describes as "a loss of value to the biosphere as a whole. A whole strategy of being alive on the planet, a whole quality of living experience is lost when any organism becomes extinct."[8] The second challenge is the problem of "unfulfilled organisms," that is to say individual animals that have no opportunity whatsoever to experience the richness of existence or a consummate biological life based on their evolved nature because they are either abandoned by their parents or victims of the predator–prey cycle—something Southgate terms "selving," which is borrowed from the poet Gerard Manley Hopkins (d. 1889).[9] The process of evolution (which Southgate accepts) depends on the extinction of species and the suffering of creatures. Creation, therefore, is clearly 'groaning in travail.' Although Southgate highlights the suffering of animals (or any creature) to be theologically problematic (and so one can speak of a 'problem of evil' in that sense), nevertheless, being a theistic evolutionist, he does not consider violence or death inherent in the evolutionary process to be itself evil.[10] Thus, predation or natural disasters, for example, are not evil per se or signs of a deeper evil at work in the world through the agency of supernatural (demonic) forces. He gives the example of the tectonic plates, the "processes that have made the Earth the lovely place that it is, and should not be regarded as in any way demonic"; rather, they should be seen as God's gifts.[11] The only consistent way to view such phenomena in the natural world is to believe that it is the 'only way' God could have created it. In other words, the divine creative possibilities were constrained by factors that would be necessary if God wanted physical life or sentient creatures.[12] What this also does is absolve God of any blame as He no longer is the author of evil but evolution is, which would mean "God's hands are so clean because nature's hands are so bloody."[13] Southgate's proposal at root is that the evolutionary struggle of creation "can be read as being the 'travail' to which God subjected creation in hope that the values of complex life, and ultimately freely choosing creatures such as ourselves, would emerge."[14]

This of course means that there is a possibility that unguided Darwinian processes would produce less than the hoped-for outcomes. Before offering his own theologically imaginative approach, Southgate flatly rejects the following strategies for explaining the suffering of creatures (on scientific grounds and their weak explanatory power):

1. Creationism
2. Intelligent design
3. Process theology
4. A cosmic fall pretext[15]

After debunking these four strategies, he surveys other possible or competing evolutionary theodicies that invoke a framework of a 'good-harm-analysis' (GHA) or that describe God as cosuffering with creatures. Following that, Southgate sets out to answer the problems as he has framed them. In short, how would a Christian respond to the question: 'Why would God create a world in which the pain, suffering, and death of natural creatures is a means to some end beyond the creature's own good?' His approach is what he calls a "compound theodicy" that seeks to hold together God's goodness and love as well as the immense pain of creatures.[16] For Southgate, there are four lines of argument for a plausible and cogent account of animal pain and suffering:[17]

(1) God must be seen as originally creating a good world: a good world with constraints that provide values that can come about in no other way.
(2) God must also be seen as responding to, companioning, and suffering with each creature, taking the responsibility for suffering most especially at the cross.
(3) God works redemption in, and for, and through creatures—providing for them either fullness of life here or in a life to come.
(4) Finally, humanity has a particular role in redemption as coredeemers of the world, and so suffering cannot be divided from the work of humans.

Cumulatively, Southgate argues, these lines of argument help the Christian account for nonhuman animal suffering. One reviewer vividly summarized his compound theodicy as follows:

Creation as it now is, remains unfinished; it awaits eschatological consummation. Meanwhile, God suffers with creation. In the event of the cross, God takes responsibility for the pain of creation. In the resurrection of Christ, God inaugurates its transformation [. . .] He makes trinitarian conception of God's kenotic entrance into creation not only as the self-emptying of God but as "self-offering love" central to the argument. The cross and resurrection enable us to see that in Christ God has inaugurated a new phase in creation in which evolutionary processes will be transformed and healed. The Christ event "takes all creaturely experience into the life of God in a new way" and prefigures creation's life with God in the eschaton. Led by the Spirit, Christians are called to participate in God's own healing, redeeming life.[18]

Southgate thus combines a theology of creation and redemption. The triune God, he asserts, always desires the good. He also asserts that the God of Christian theism is also a kenotic God, one who has actually entered into the intricate and tangled web of creation, with all its potential destructive powers, in the life and death of Jesus.[19] He further extends these assertions of theology of creation and redemption with a consideration of eschatology, particularly that of an afterlife involving a recompense for suffering in the world. Thus, not only shall humanity be present in the afterlife but is present in all other entities within the created realm.[20] Given this,

> Southgate fleshes out what it means for humans to be created co-creators with God in a priestly manner with respect to creation . . . and sets forth two interesting proposals as to how humans might decrease the suffering of creation: a move to vegetarianism, and a project to end (or at least strongly curtail) biological extinction. He contends that these proposals model the self-giving creative love that is expressed within the Trinity.[21]

A number of criticisms have been raised against Southgate's account.[22] One of the major planks of Southgate's argument will likely be viewed by those adhering to the traditional tenets of the Christian faith as ultimately failing to achieve its desired ends, due to his total acceptance of and reliance on a thorough-going neo-Darwinism that is disputed among scientists. In addition, his insistence that the world created by God and released through the mechanism of evolution—although not logically impossible—does absolve God of cooperating with or authoring evil in nature. However, it comes at the cost of divine omnipotence. God could not create any other way. Subordinating God's benevolence at the expense of omnipotence may be unpalatable for many Christians. Moreover, inferring that animal suffering is wrong from mere natural facts, as Southgate does, contravenes the Humean ought/is distinction and thus commits a deontic fallacy by deriving an *ought* from an *is*.[23] Furthermore, Southgate's evolutionary theodicy account may be criticized for being highly speculative. In other words, he affords primacy to imaginative theology or formulating theological possibilities consistent with the assumptions of evolutionary creation above and beyond the actual biblical data. He might also be accused in this regard of offering solutions inspired from the Bible such as God's cosuffering with creation that (far from being coherent) have no substantial bearing on or make no difference *explanatorily* as theodicies to addressing the problems he has set out.[24] Finally, his view appears to uphold an instrumentalist view of evil. This might be seen as trivializing suffering and death.[25]

Murray on the Necessity of Nomic Regularity: Michael Murray in his provocative and landmark work *Nature Red in Tooth and Claw* has developed a contemporary version of a kind of regularity argument found with precedence in medieval theology in order to offer a possible explanation for a "Darwinian problem" of animal pain and suffering. In his words, the

Darwinian problem consists in "the vast and unquantifiable array of non-human-animal suffering that is endemic to the evolutionary machinery—machinery which has been winnowing unfit organisms from the planet (often kicking and screaming) for nearly three billion years."[26] After stating what he takes to be the evidential argument from evil, he contends that there are only really three ways a theist can address it. The argument and the three approaches are as follows:

Evidential Argument from Evil (EA):

(1) If there were a God, there would be no gratuitous evils (GEs).
(2) There is at least one GE.
(3) There is no God.[27]

Approach 1 (defences): affirm premise (1) that would imply negation of premise (2) but show there are good reasons to believe God permits evil.
Approach 2 (theodicy): attack premise (2) by offering positive knowledge of why God actually permits evil in the world.
Approach 3 (*causa dei*): demonstrate that atheists have no reason to believe premise (2).[28]

Murray then surveys each approach. He is critical of Approach 1 because although the logical compatibility of God and evil is upheld, the *evidential* weight of evil is not undermined.[29] He rejects Approach 2 because he believes that many of God's actual purposes for permitting evil are inscrutable. His preferred method is Approach 3, which seeks to show how a person cannot be justified in accepting premise (2), meaning a nontheist epistemically has *no good reason* to accept (2). He seeks to do this by offering what he calls "causa dei" ([CD] taken from Leibniz), which are "explanations" on behalf of God's innocence and goodness "in light of the evidence."[30] Thus, in the context of animal pain and suffering, a CD is an attempt to show that in light of our justified acceptances, we are not justified in believing that animal pain and suffering is gratuitous and hence we are not justified in taking such pain and suffering as evidence for the nonexistence of God.[31] There are four CDs Murray sets out to discuss in detail that plausibly demonstrate the compatibility of evil with theism. "Compatibility" with theism here means that each CD must meet the standard Murray proposes:

(1) *The Necessity Condition*: The good secured by the permission of the evil, E, would not have been secured without permitting either E or some other evils morally equivalent to or worse than E.
(2) *The Outweighing Condition*: The good secured by the permission of the evil is sufficiently outweighing.

(3) *The Rights Condition*: It is within the rights of the one permitting the evil to permit it at all.[32]

In addition, Murray sets out a three-condition epistemic standard for a CD to successfully explain God's permission of evil in the face of the evidential argument from evil. They are: (1) the reasons are true *for all the theist knows or justifiably believes*, (2) if true, these reasons would constitute a good explanation for animal suffering (meaning these reasons would be consistent with theism and would explain why permitting animal suffering would be necessary for securing any outweighing goods), and (iii) these reasons need not count as *plausible*, but rather *as plausible as not, overall*.[33] The four possible CDs Murray focuses on then are:

CD1: Neo-Cartesianism = denial of the reality or moral significance of animal pain and suffering.[34]
CD2: The Fall = animal suffering is a consequence of moral evil due to human fallen nature.[35]
CD3: Greater Good = animal pain and suffering are outweighed by a greater good for them whether in the present world or next world.[36]
CD4: Nomic Regularity = a law-like universe that functions as an intrinsic good but has a necessary by-product: the reality of pain and suffering.[37]

Murray's ultimate preference is an appeal to CD4, the *nomic regularity* (NR) category where animal pain in prehuman and posthuman eras is a by-product or concomitant consequence of a physical universe that operates in a law-like manner. For human free choices to be efficacious in the world, NR is necessary, Murray says, because

we must be able to form intentions to bring about states in the world, and we must have reason to believe that by undertaking certain bodily movements we make it likely that those states of the world will come about ... [otherwise] we would never have seen any correlation between what we will to happen in the world and what does happen in the world.[38]

However, NR comes at a cost. The natural laws that allow humans to believe that their actions are efficacious and will achieve their goals also present them with conditions that produce pain and suffering. Animal distress and anguish also seem to be a necessary by-product of NR. Moreover, although NR explains animal suffering in terms of human free will, the point here is not on the consequences of human free choices but on the antecedent conditions necessary for that free will. Murray's claim therefore is that NR is a necessary antecedent condition for free and effective human choice and the natural laws it entails give rise to animal as well as human suffering. In a modification of this NR account, Murray further argues that only out of a certain level of chaos and discord can value emerge: what he calls "chaos to order" (CTO). Murray summarizes this CTO account as follows:

> some theodicies of animal suffering contend that animals with minds capable of experiencing pain and suffering are necessary evolutionary precursors for organisms with the special cognitive skills of human beings—skills that, for example, make possible free choice and moral responsibility. Of course, explanations of this sort seem to make animals mere by-products on the evolutionary step-ladder leading to human beings, making one wonder whether there is some good explanation for why God had to employ such precursors in the first place. One answer might be found in the claim, defended most famously by the French philosopher Nicholas Malebranche, that a world is better insofar as the complexity in that world results from the regular, orderly operation of divinely ordained laws of nature.[39] If one finds such a position plausible, one might argue that the only way to get such beings as us into creation via law-like processes is to allow our universe to unfold in much the way that it did: evolving from an initial singularity to later stages in which there are highly concentrated pockets of privileged order (such as is found on our own planet, and perhaps others as well). Animals would then be necessary stages in the development of this law-like universe, leading to such organisms as us as well as perhaps organisms of even greater complexity and worth in the future [. . .] the sufferings of millions of lower animals throughout almost endless time are apparently irreconcilable with the existence of a creator of "unbounded" goodness.[40]

Murray's argument is that the most persuasive morally sufficient reason for God permitting the evil of animal suffering is that values such as moral freedom and moral goodness require a cosmos that is ordered by the regularity due to the laws of nature, and for all we know such a cosmos could only have had the prehuman history it has had, which includes the painful evolutionary development from chaos to order. This long arc of evolutionary history requires first "the accumulation of complex states (molecular, planetary, galactic, biological)" and second "a long pedigree of pre-human animals capable of experiencing pain and suffering; since these animals will be necessary precursors to descendants capable of ever more complex forms of mental life and moral value."[41] Therefore, in this evolutionary development, the emergence of human beings appears to be the ultimate good reason God had for creating the cosmos.[42] To summarize his version of NR + CTO argument as an explanation for animal suffering: (1) a universe that moves from chaos to order in a law-like way is something intrinsically good, (2) animal pain and suffering is an unavoidable by-product or consequence of creating a NR + CTO universe, and (3) the intrinsic good in a NR + CTO universe outweighs the animal pain and suffering that it inevitably produces.

There are a number of objections raised against Murray's proposal of a CD.[43] One objection is that Murray's account pegs the success of a CD explanation of evil based on whether or not the reasons accord with a person's *justified acceptances*. However, since people differ with respect to what they justifiably accept, pegging a CD's success to its compatibility with one's prior justified acceptances leads Murray's approach into a kind of relativism. Indeed, since theists and nontheists differ with respect to their justified acceptances, a CD for animal suffering that is successful for the theist might not be successful for the nontheist. Thus, Murray's approach appears only to have force for an internal theistic epistemic community.[44] Another objection, directed more at Murray's theological maneuvering, is his use of Gregory of Nyssa and Augustine to argue for a precedence of a CTO universe. For Murray, God making the world with the ability to carry on creative processes of its own, meaning for it to be seeded with developmental possibilities of aesthetic, moral, and religious value that emerge over time, "is of greater value than creation of the finished project by divine fiat."[45] On this kind of argument for precedence, however, Bethany Sollereder notes:

> These church fathers were not arguing for a chaos-to-order universe as a good in its own right, as Murray is trying to do. Instead, they were attempting to harmonise the day-by-day account of creation in Genesis 1 with the (to them) self-evident truth that the only way an eternal God could interact with a world of time is instantaneously. The chaos-to-order element of their argument is simply a spandrel, an unintentional by-product of their discussion on time. To try to argue that Augustine felt a world of unfolding development was inherently better than a world made by divine fiat is a misrepresentation of Augustine's view since he did argue for a creation by divine fiat of the seeds of possibility![46]

Finally (which is more of an overall worry than a direct criticism), some have argued that Murray's caution against dismissing the neo-Cartesian view inclines him toward believing that animals do not suffer pain in any approximate degree to how humans do. This inclination has the implication of downplaying animal pain and suffering, which in turn leads to downplaying their moral significance. Engle in her review concludes with this very point. "If human psychology is such," she states, "that the less bad we think some evil is, the less we're willing to do to prevent it," then this downplays "the moral significance of animal suffering" and make others—particularly theists—"less inclined to take conscious steps to avoid contributing to such suffering" and make then instead "more inclined to contribute to that very suffering."[47]

Creegan on Suffering Explained through Wheats and Tares: Nicola Hoggard Creegan in *Animal Suffering and the Problem of Evil* acutely explores how animal pain and suffering can be explained in the natural world underpinned by Darwinian evolution and does so with a combination of an interpretive religious imagination and a deep empathy for animals. Her core focus is attempting to answer the question why so much suffering preceded the emergence of human beings as a species.[48] Predation, death, and illness, for example, caused countless animal suffering before *Homo sapiens* evolved. Why would a loving God allow His purposes to be achieved in *this* way?[49] Drawing on both theological and scientific resources, Creegan is interested in alternative accounts of a "thin description" of evolution characterized as a "materialist, reductionist, randomly directed evolutionary process"[50] and alternative accounts of animal behavior as lacking proto-moral attitudes.[51] She wants to argue for God's power and beauty discerned in nature and a more enchanted creation. Creegan gives a summary of her arguments advanced in the book which are three:

1. The phenomenon we observe in nature are "a mix of the perfect and the corrupted—the wheat and the tares." We may be able to glimpse good "but never easily or unequivocally."
2. Much of the evil in creation predates human beings although humans have the ability to cooperate in doing evil.
3. Nature reflects the handiwork of God albeit "infinitely subtle and almost infinitely hidden" but "deep in our consciousness as *divinitatis sensum*." This subtlety is what veils us from comprehending evil.[52]

Creegan challenges both the standard theological and existential accounts of evil grounded in the Adamic fall because they not only conflict with Darwinian science but are also hermeneutically inadequate as theodicies.[53] Surveying and critiquing both philosophical (Plantinga, Murray) and theological theodicies (deism, process theology, Russell, Coakley, Haught, and others) for the evil of animal pain and suffering,[54] Creegan then proposes her own interpretive scheme to characterize evolutionary history through using the parable of the "wheat and tares" mentioned in Matthew 13:24–30.[55] In the parable, the sower sows good seed (καλὸν σπέρμα) in the field (ἐν τῷ ἀγρῷ), and the enemy (ὁ ἐχθρὸς) comes in the night and sows weeds (τὰ ζιζάνια) or tares in the same field. When the tares shoot up with the wheat (τὸν σῖτον), the sower's slaves ask the master if they should uproot the weeds. The sower responds that in so doing, the wheat would also be lost. Only in the final harvest (τοῦ θερισμοῦ) will the two be sorted—one bundled and burned and one put in the barn. Historically, this parable was read in the context of the Kingdom of God but following the Jesuit theologian Jacques Maritain (d. 1973)[56] and theologian and ethicist Reinhold Niebuhr (d. 1971)[57] Creegan extends the parable from the spiritual world to the natural world where interplay of good and harmful life-giving forces operate not only in history but also in the entire evolutionary process.[58] Appropriating this wheat and tares paradigm, Creegan argues that God is not the author of evil. She also argues that God is not to be blamed for permitting or failing to remove evil in the world (whether human or animal) because the evil is inseparably bound with the good. It is the tares that are holding up the wheat, as it were. Thus, she differentiates her proposal from those who claim that God allows evil for the sake of securing some greater good. Evil is there embedded from the beginning.

Cautious to avoid an intelligent design perspective in nature, Creegan argues for a more optimistic characterization of evolution that departs from the destructive and "narrow metaphors"[59] available since Darwin. Drawing on authors like Jan Sapp[60] and others, she makes the case that nature reveals "teleology ordered towards life," meaning nature "knows where to go"[61] and works with a strong dynamism on a multiplicity of levels. Thus, biological agents like viruses and phenomena like evolutionary cooperation among species (symbiosis) and emergence in living systems are actually suggestive of symmetry, beauty, and patterns, all important for enriching evolutionary development and enhancing it. This further implies that human beings are not in competition with animals to dominate them for survival purposes; they can actively engage each other as conscious creatures based on "mutual dependence and interconnectedness."[62] Ultimately, she argues, this optimistic characterization of evolution allows more indications and evidence that there is a God and His handiwork is reflected in creation even though it is subtle and seems entirely hidden.[63]

One broad limitation with Creegan's overall account is how it simplifies the Darwinian picture. Not all evolutionary biologists reject the values of species cooperation and species altruism among other social traits. Despite her insistence on the serious implications her recharacterization of evolution has on Christian theology and ethics, she skirts the question of the origins of evil. Relying neither on traditional fall narratives nor on Satan as causes, she admits the limitations of her wheat and tares paradigm in that it does not tell us the whole story. It does not tell us who or what is evil: the ontology of evil will always be inscrutable. Images and metaphors and scenarios from the past—Satan or the Evil one or prehuman fall—do not serve us well today, but the reality behind and beyond them persists. We find ourselves at the edge of the historical and the narrative, in the era of what Barth calls saga or myth.[64]

This lands Creegan in a kind of skepticism toward fully understanding the source and detail of evil. On her view then, evil and the machinations of evil are in the end, it seems, inscrutable to humans. Moreover, there seems to be a heavy reliance on faith—a trust that things are as they are due to God's love and that a final redemption will arrive to set all things right. In Creegan's account then, theodicy is ultimately eschatological and not ontological. This may be seen as diminishing its explanatory power.

An Islamic Evolutionary Theodicy

Having surveyed the above works, I now turn to the account of an evolutionary theodicy from within the Islamic theological framework. The steps I will take are: I will first state without elaboration what theistic evolution (TE) is.[65] Second, I will sketch the core tenets of a formulation of an Islamic theistic evolution (ITE). Third, given ITE, it will form the key rubric from which I then propose an Islamic version of an evolutionary theodicy (IET) and possible objections to it. Let me first state what the term TE broadly means. In brief, it is the notion that "classical religious teachings about God are compatible with modern scientific understanding about biological evolution." According to theistic evolution, "God is the creator of the universe and all life within and that biological evolution is a natural process within that creation." Evolution on this kind of view is conceived as "a tool God has used to develop human life."[66]

In the context of the Islamic tradition, TE would mean data from the primary sources of Islam—The Qur'an and Hadith—is compatible with established facts within the scientific fields of inquiry related to cosmology and biology. Evolution being an established empirical fact would be best explained as the process by which God enabled all life to emerge. The model adopted to explain the relation between God and evolution may vary based on the different interpretations of the Qur'an, Hadith, theological tradition, and even scientific data. Three major models, however, are: (1) *nonteleological* evolution where evolution is random, unguided, and indeterminate and has no ultimate purpose or goal with total absence of supernatural intervention;[67] (2) *planned* evolution where God has set evolution toward an ultimate goal and purpose—a *telos*—but not with continual intervention; and (3) *directed* evolution where God guides or directs evolution toward its *telos* through direct action and intervention.[68] In order to avoid digression and my desire for extreme concision, I will not here argue for the justifiability[69] of ITE but will assume its core tenets are validly admissible as constitutive of Islamic theology and compatible with core Islamic doctrines. The core tenets of ITE I suggest then are:

1. God is absolutely powerful, knowledgeable, just, and compassionate and created everything besides Himself.
2. God has an overall purpose for why He created the world (the "cosmic teleology" thesis).
3. The present world with its physical and natural laws and processes is the only way the world could optimally be (the "best possible world" thesis).
4. All organisms today descend ultimately from a single common ancestor (the "universal common ancestry" thesis).
5. Evolution is a mechanism of change that specifically involves an impersonal biological process by which organisms change (the Darwinian "natural selection" thesis).[70]
6. God acts in the world but no special supernatural intervention is involved to guide the process of creation through time (the "noninterventionist" thesis).
7. God must not be inserted to explain any gaps in the natural causal order as described by science. Theology must not be grafted in to explain whatever is in the methodological domain of science (no "God-of-the-gaps" thesis).
8. God chose evolution as the mechanism to allow special creatures to finally emerge who would have intelligence, moral knowledge, free will, and a capacity to seek Him out.

Given these core tenets of ITE above, the key claims within my proposed IET can be stated. They relate to three theological areas: (1) God's actions, (2) an account of the world, and (3) the notion of evil. Each of these will be outlined in a short and synthesized way as I give the account of IET. In general terms, I understand an evolutionary theodicy to be an attempt to explain how the enormous amounts of suffering, predation, premature death, pestilence, and extinction inherent in the evolutionary process can be satisfactorily reconciled with belief in a perfect, holy, loving, just omniscient, and absolutely powerful God. A defining strategy (but by no means the only one) of this kind of theodicy is to argue that certain highly positive and valuable creaturely attributes could only be exemplified by creatures that are produced via a partly random, unguided, and uncontrolled process of evolution. In other words, evolution on this kind of theodicy was the only possible way for God to create these kinds of creatures. In the more specific case of an adapted Islamic version of evolutionary theodicy, it could perhaps be described as follows:

(IET): how a Muslim explains the possible reasons behind why—given God's selection of evolution—there is so much inescapable suffering, pain, predation, death, pestilence, and extinction inherent in nature and how these facts are reconciled with the characterization of a transcendent, absolutely powerful, knowledgeable, loving, just, and compassionate Being inferred from the revealed data of the Qur'an and Hadith.

I will state the core tenets of IET and then outline how an account of animal pain and suffering is explained.

IET—*core tenets*:

1. There is no human primordial fall event in creation that corrupted it. Thus, human agency through sin is not the exclusive cause of animal pain and suffering because not only is fallen nature an alien notion to the Qur'anic worldview,[71] but before the emergence of human beings (or supernatural demonic entities) endowed with free will, natural phenomena like predation, parasitism, and pestilence caused many animal species to die.

2. The world according to the Qur'an is a place of disvalues such as pain, death, extinction, geological evil, suffering, distress, trials, tribulations, hardship, and difficulty. These disvalues in the world are not attributed to God directly but the inevitable consequences of unguided natural processes of evolution operating in the world.

3. The evil of pain, suffering, and death through the evolutionary process of nonhuman animals in the prehuman and posthuman eras serves a greater good whether that is having a value-seeded world, free will, biodiversity, a biologically consummate life, or interspecies connection (or any other reason).

4. There is a commensurate eschatological indemnification for the pain and suffering of all nonhuman animals whether caused by sin through human agency or caused by the natural phenomenon of predation.

5. God has a compassionate presence through all creaturely pain and suffering and is intimately aware of the experience of every creature and its fate.

I will now elaborate IET with all the above data within a broad Islamic theological framework addressing the theological areas (1)–(3). There may have been a number of reasons why God has created the world and chosen for it the organic evolutionary process that gives rise to outward evils. This reason or divine *purpose* will also determine the kind of action God undertakes in the world. One possible reason could be that God desired to be hidden and concealed from human beings. This hiddenness generates a "gap" between God and humans. Moreover, this gap or "epistemic distance"[72] between Creator and created enables a degree of personal autonomy for human beings over their lives to the extent that they can approach or draw near to their Creator *voluntarily* and appropriate His commandments *freely*. God being al-Batin ("The Hidden One")[73] would suggest that He desires to avoid any coercive impression on human consciousness and self-realization. Muslim scholars have recognized this aspect of divine hiddenness. Al-Alusi explains this under his discussion of the often-cited statement attributed to the Prophet that God remarked: "I was a hidden treasure and desired to be known so I created creation."[74] He comments that

> The structure of God's saying "I desired to be known . . ." must be considered in light of the fact that if something strongly manifests itself, it necessitates ignorance of the condition of the one who is manifest. Hence, God created all creation so that they would be like veils by which He is come to be known. Do you not see that due to the blazing light of the sun, most eyes cannot look upon it except if there is a barrier placed between it and the eyes?[75]

This 'veiling' generates a degree of ambiguity over human origins that is sufficient for motivating them to seek and uncover their origins. This distance or gap and this ambiguity are made possible by a slow evolution of organic life in the biosphere rather than an immediate, total, direct, and miraculous fiat. In this way, evolution is a more optimal way than spontaneous creation.

Another possible reason could be that for a world evolving by natural selection—which necessitates disvalues (like pain and suffering of sentient creatures)—it would be the only type of world where values (like beauty, ingenuity, and biodiversity) represented by complex and diverse life could

arise. God would thus be constrained by what is feasible given certain ob-
jectives driving His eschatological program (such as reward for humans
and compensation of nonhuman animals). This is akin to a "package deal"
idea where values cannot be without disvalues. Thus, if evolution through
natural selection is the optimum mechanism feasible for God, then the
collateral (pain and suffering) from such a mechanism would be a necessary corollary. In short, the kind of world required for human beings to
populate heaven is only feasible through an evolutionary mode.[76]

A third possible reason for why God has set in motion the evolutionary process is that in the end it is actually a good and thus not an evil. The
good is that the pain and death of animals are enablers for fulfilling their
lives based on the kind of biological creatures they had evolved to become
and adapted for their respective environments. They have evolved to be
driven by survival (such as defense, protection, camouflage, and pursuit of
prey) and reproduction (like attracting mates, caring for the young, and
defending territory). These are fundamental for the fulfilment of their
life-course as animals, that is, for the full consummation of their term of
biological existence. For this fulfilment to be possible, death and pain are
the necessary natural fixtures within the furniture of evolution. It would
be difficult to imagine a biological system or process that did not have
death.

A final possibility could be that the evolutionary process allows for
a deeper interspecies and intraspecies connection. Humans feel a deep-
seated affinity and bond with not only other human entities but their
surrounding earth and animals as well such that they consider it as constituting a part of their self-hood and identity as human beings. Their
relations with nonhuman entities thus form a significant part of what they
determine as being human. If human beings share a common ancestor,
then they are organically connected to that ancestral origin. They are part
of a material continuity with the rest of living creation. The emergence
of Adam from organic substance (*adamat al-ard*, 'the surface of the earth')
informed by God in the Qur'an in al-Baqara, verses 30–32, is defined as
God's temporal "representative" (*khalifa*).[77] Another rendering is "successor,"[78] which may suggest that the Adamic human is the final and emer-
gent species to steward God's creation toward its ultimate purposes. Part
of this stewardship (*ri'aya*) involves safeguarding all life and life-enabling
environments as well as maintaining the interspecies connection through
freely implementing God's commands based on reflecting the kinds of attributes God discloses of Himself in creation (Creator, Sustainer, Protec-
tor, Compassionate, Merciful, Nourisher). Adam's organic origin and his
renewed consciousness through witnessing God's disclosure in creation

sharpen his duty to maintain environments for not only human flourishing but also nonhuman living and fulfilment—he must not upset the balance in nature that has been delivered by God through natural selection.[79] He, as a human animal, evolved to possess a high degree of free will and self-transcendence that vastly exceeds that of other creatures and thus he can assume his role and become the noble representative/successor or ignoble one. God has permitted Adam out of love and greater purpose to assume this role as divine representative or evolutionary successor without thwarting his use of free will and without directly intervening in his management of his duties. Thus, through the material evolutionary process, Adam—that is, humanity—emerges as a being that will establish a rich and interconnected earth (not a subjugation of it) based on God's revealed system of commandments and imbibing and embodying the kinds of divine attributes he witnesses in creation in order to enable human and nonhuman flourishing that would otherwise not be possible. God therefore desired Adam to emerge and freely embody His own attributes in order to bring humanity and indeed creation back to Him.[80]

In the broader scheme, God will fully redeem any pain (ilam), injustice, or wrong (zulm) suffered by animals—whether biophysical or anthropogenic. The universe will be brought to a total end through an extraordinary final act of God[81] (circumventing the physical laws) even though His ordinary providential engagement with the world is noninterventionist. Animal redemption (if not acquired in this world) will be in the hereafter where they will be reconciled to God in heaven with everlasting life. Thus, postresurrection, a concluded cosmos with a new existence in heaven, is more than an environment for resurrected humanity—it includes God's residence with all living creatures.

Conclusion

An Islamic evolutionary theodicy seeks to explain incalculable death, predation, waste, and pestilence in nature over the arc of natural history. I have tried to show how Qur'anic axiological principles and cosmological precepts may be utilized to formulate such an Islamic theistic evolutionary account that goes some way to explain these problems.

5

Flames of Love and Wrath: Hell and the Problem of Everlasting Punishment

I n this chapter, I address one of the most serious species of the problem of evil, which is the problem of hell. The chapter is divided into
four sections. In section one, I briefly set out the doctrine of hell as
presented within classical Islamic Sunni theology, which I have called
the "Mainstream View." In section two, I highlight three core challenges
lodged against this Mainstream View, which are: (1) how hell on the
Mainstream View can be theologically justified, (2) if hell is justified,
what reasons could there be for hell's punishment to be eternal, and
(3) why God would allow some to be damned forever in hell. Section
three contains the responses to the three core challenges and in it I will
survey different theological positions and arguments that I have called
"modified views" of hell ranging from annihilationism, universalism, and
the naturalization model, highlighting the serious problems each has.
The final section briefly explores a related problem with the doctrine
of hell and that is the soteriological problem of evil, namely why the
fate of those who neither heard of nor accept the message of Prophet
Muhammad are damned in hell forever. In doing this, I examine Muslim scholarly opinions on the issue and attempt to show how the scope
of damnation is extremely narrow—reduced only to those who willfully
and deliberately reject God and the Prophet Muhammad. The overall
attempt in the chapter is to establish the logical compatibility between
God's core attributes and the set of theses constituting the Mainstream
View of hell.

The Islamic Doctrine of Hell

The doctrine of hell is one of the most difficult and challenging for the
Abrahamic religions. To modern sensibilities, the existence of a bounded

location in which unending chastisement occurs on human beings on account of their worldly transgressions seems unpalatable and abhorrent. The doctrine is argued to be a thorough indictment of not only the philosophically conceived omniperfect Deity of classical theism but also the unique personal being characterized in the scriptures of the Abrahamic faiths. The philosopher and logician David Lewis (d. 2001), for example, expresses outrage at the doctrine of hell and formulates an argument reminiscent of that presented by the Scottish metaphysician John McTaggart (d. 1925) at the turn of the twentieth century,[1] calling into question the very moral goodness of God because of the existence of hell:

> God has prescribed torment for insubordination. The torment is to go on forever, and the agonies to be endured by the damned intensify, in unimaginable ways, the sufferings we undergo in our earthly lives. In both dimensions, time and intensity, the torment is infinitely worse than all the suffering and sin that will have occurred during the history of life in the universe. What God does is thus worse than what the worst of tyrants have done ... Appearances notwithstanding, are those who worship the perpetrator of divine evil themselves evil?[2]

In recent years, the theological and philosophical debate around the existence, nature, duration, and justification of hell has been intense—particularly within Christian theology—and the insights from that have broadly shaped the contours of the discourse within the philosophy of religion. In contemporary Islamic theology and philosophy, however, the matter has been somewhat less ferocious, perhaps even academically sanguine. This is all the more puzzling given the Qur'an's unparalleled vividness and detail as a Scripture on the rationale, function, horrors, and topography of hell that evoke powerful feelings as well as strong and provocative images in the reader and listener.[3] The volume of hadiths no doubt amplify the Qur'anic data and raise their own particular theological issues.[4] The evolution, geology, and historically internalized imaginations of hell by the Muslim community have been examined thoroughly by Christian Lange and Nerina Rustomji[5] so their rich analyses and pertinent conclusions will not be reiterated here. The focus in this chapter rather is only on those aspects of hell's nature and description relevant for a philosophical and theological treatment related to possible defenses or theodicies.

The problem of hell is generally set in the context of what can be called the "strong view" or "punishment view" of hell, which consists of a number of core doctrines or theses which are as follows:[6]

(H1) Some persons are consigned to hell (anti-universalism thesis).

(H2) Hell is a place of real existence if consigned there (existence thesis).

(H3) It is not possible for some to exit hell, and there is nothing they can do, change, or become in order to exit hell, once they are consigned there (no escape thesis) and

(H4) The justification for and purpose of hell is retributive in nature because it is constituted so as to mete out punishment to those whose earthly lives and behaviour warrant it (retribution thesis).

(H5) Hell will continue to exist without end (infinite duration thesis).[7]

An historical Islamic perspective of hell broadly identifiable with the Sunni tradition is also captured by these five theses and I will subsequently refer to it as the "Mainstream View" of hell. In short, on this Islamic Mainstream View, there is a postmortem binary division of human destiny: either paradise or hell; there is no third eschatological alternative. This destination of either hell or paradise is real and not figurative or imaginary.[8] There is also a finality in that there is a total separation of those who attain eternal life in paradise from those who receive eternal punishment in hell. This finality entails that after a divine judgment has been passed on every person based on the religious quality of their deeds in this world, those sentenced to hell will eternally remain in it without any opportunity to escape. The divine judgment is argued to be retributive in its nature as a just desert for those who merit it. The punishment meted out on the inhabitants involves a demonstrable affliction of suffering and agony through subjecting the body to a comprehensive set of tortures. This Mainstream View of hell generates at least two unique problems very different to the general problem of evil discussed in previous chapters. First, the Qur'an and the Hadith literature clearly mention a doctrine of hell that states the rationale for its creation as well as details of its physical geography and inhabitants. However, as already examined in earlier chapters, neither sources specify exact reasons why evils occur and how these evils serve God's greater purposes. Second, in attempting to defend God's goodness, thinkers such as Ibn Sina and al-Ghazali, for example, did offer possible overriding goods or justifiable reasons that make evil necessary. That is to say, God in His knowledge, wisdom, mercy, and goodness has in store a greater good for humanity that is served by His permission of evil in the world. In the case of hell, no such greater good can be hoped for because if punishment in hell is eternal then the future possibility of any redeeming quality to evil is entirely lost. There is nothing more to gain once in hell. This is why, as noted by

Kvanvig, "hell is apparently paradigmatic as an example of truly pointless, gratuitous evil."[9]

Core Challenges to the Doctrine of Hell

The problem of hell as outlined above is framed in many different ways. Each way it is framed constitutes a separate strand or challenge. In this section and the next, I set out three challenges to the Mainstream View of hell and assess various responses that might be given based on the views of Muslim scholars as well as my own speculations on these challenges drawing on Islamic sources, theological precepts as well as discussions from contemporary philosophical theology. The possible responses examined here lead to the Mainstream View of hell being considerably modified.[10] I will elaborate on the three challenges in general logical form with their family of assumptions that attempt to make explicit alleged contradictions between the propositions about God's nature and the existence, duration, justification, and finality of hell.

Argument 1

Justification of Hell—This challenge is directed at what reasons God may have for creating hell as a sanction for human beings. The inconsistency is said to reside in the following two propositions:

1. God is absolutely powerful, knowing, merciful, loving, just, and wise.
2. Hell exists.

This argument derives its force from a number of subclaims including:

(a) God would not want to create a place like hell;
(b) the notion of indefinitely tormenting and chastising people is incompatible with God's compassionate and merciful character, and the stronger claim that
(c) God would have no justifiable reason for creating a place like hell.

Argument 2

Eternal Torment—This challenge aims at raising an inconsistency between God's compassion, fairness, justice, and wise purposes with the idea of unending conscious torment. The two propositions argued to be in tension are:

1. God is absolutely powerful, knowing, merciful, loving, just, and wise.
2. At least one person will be eternally tormented in hell.

Some subclaims here in the argument include:

(a) God's wise purposes can be served by punishing a person for a limited duration;

(b) unending conscious torment of a person in hell is incompatible with God's compassionate and merciful character, and the stronger claim that

(c) God would have no justifiable reason for punishing someone eternally for committing a finite crime.

Argument 3

Allowing damnation—This challenge is directed at what reasons God may have for allowing some persons to suffer in hell forever. The two propositions apparently in tension are:

1. God is absolutely powerful, knowing, merciful, loving, just, and wise.
2. At least one person will be damned in Hell forever.

Some subclaims in this argument that attempt to make explicit the alleged tension include:

(a) God would not want any person to suffer in hell forever;

(b) eternal damnation in hell is incompatible with God's compassionate and merciful character, and the stronger claim that

(c) God would have no justifiable reason for allowing any person to suffer in hell forever.

Each of these logical arguments will now be addressed by offering possible reasons that justify hell as the ultimate destination for the reprobate, why eternal conscious torment is not logically inconsistent with God's mercy and justice, why it is possible some people will be damned forever, and whether salvation is exclusively procured through Islam.

Responses to the Challenges

Response to Argument 1

A number of possible justifications are given below for why God might create hell. These justifications are based on the Islamic primary sources and other Islamic theological doctrines. Each justification—broadly outlined—is compatible with the Mainstream View of hell as well as any modified view. Thus, none of these justifications necessarily assumes a particular model or account of hell's nature, description, or duration.

Sovereignty Thesis: The Qur'an emphatically establishes God's sovereignty, power, and control over all aspects of creation.[11] Nothing in creation can stall or obstruct God's will (*mashi'a*) from being accomplished. God is also utterly independent of any created entity and undertakes any action He pleases with perfect power. Al-Ghazali, for example, highlights this in his description of the divine names "al-malik" ('The King')[12] and then "malik al-mulk" ('The Absolute Sovereign').[13] Another aspect the Qur'an emphatically establishes is the utter dissimilarity and division between Truth and falsehood, Good and evil,[14] and everything that either represents or entails them. There is an uncompromising disassociation that governs the interaction between these two ultimate camps. God actively works in the world to ensure that all that is good is elevated and all that is evil is demoted. Al-Qurtubi writes regarding the divine names "al-Khafid" ('The Abaser') and "al-Rafi'" ('The Exalter') that "these two names[15] of God undoubtedly refer to his actions. [God] elevates whoever He wants with grace and debases whoever He wants with His punishment" and then proceeds to list many examples of who or what God elevates and debases.[16] Al-Ghazali explicitly links God's act of elevating and debasing to salvation and damnation. "The Abaser, the Exalter," he writes, "is one who abases infidels with damnation, and raises up the faithful by salvation. He exalts His holy people by bringing them closer, and abases His enemies by sending them far away."[17] If there is no hell, then the two ultimately excluding positions of Truth and falsehood or Good and evil cannot be kept separate. If Good and evil cannot be separate, then God does not have control over evil because He is not able to conquer it and triumph over it. The argument can be stated as follows:

(1) The nonexistence of Hell would mean God is neither sovereign nor in full control of His creation.

(2) If God is neither sovereign nor in full control of His creation, then Good cannot triumph over evil.

(3) God is sovereign.

(4) God is in full control of His creation.

(5) Therefore, if God is sovereign and in full control of His creation, then hell is necessary.

It would be necessary for God—in order to achieve His aims—that He ensures permanent separation between those who have chosen Good and those who have chosen evil. Making sure this occurs would require God manifest His power over evil and falsehood beyond the temporal spectacle. Hell is that manifestation of God's triumph over evil and falsehood.

Justice Thesis: On this position, hell is justified through God's prerogative to punish as a means of implementing justice (*'adl*).[18] The Qur'an, on the one hand, affirms God's love, mercy, kindness, beneficence, and care, but on the other hand it equally affirms His choice to exact vengeance and retribution. God in some context can be swift to punish (*sari' al-'iqab*) and warns as being severe in chastisement (*shadid al-'iqab*).[19] Among a Prophetic report that lists the ninety-nine chosen names of God, one of them includes "al-Muntaqim" ('The Avenger')[20] which is defined as "the one who rightfully punishes the abominable acts committed by sinners."[21] Al-Ghazali explains it as "the one who breaks the back of the recalcitrant" and the one who "punishes criminals, and intensifies the punishment of the oppressors" but "only after excusing and warning them, and after giving them the opportunity and time to change."[22] God's retribution is not arbitrary nor wanton but works through a disclosed process: offering sufficient time and circumstances for sinners, transgressors, and oppressors to change and rectify their situation. Deliberately failing this, God is warranted to punish such perpetrators. This is how His justice is enacted.[23] In addition, God can only remain just if sin in all forms is directly punished—the desert for iniquity. This retributive punishment of sin by God is based on His absolute wisdom, fairness, and authority in a decisive and exacting way. The place sinners are sent to after receiving just sentencing for these sins is hell.

Sin thesis: Sin is considered to be the persistent obstacle between humans and God. The Qur'an contains a wide variety of terms to designate sin and they each range over a set of contextual nuances:

1. *fahisha* (depravity, obscenity, and its derivatives from the root *f / H / sh /*),
2. *haraj* (blame, sin),
3. *ithm* (sin), *junah* (blame),
4. *jurm* (crime, and its derivatives from the root *j / r / m /*),
5. *khati'a* (error, mistake, and terms derived from the same root, *kh / t / '/*),
6. *lamam* (faults),
7. *ma'siya* (disobedience, pl. *ma'asi*), and
8. *sayyi'a* (bad, evils, wrongs, pl. *sayyi'at*).[24]

However, one of the broadest terms in the Qur'anic vocabulary designating sin is "dhanb" (pl. *dhunub*).[25] The fundamental dichotomy of human actions is between, on the one hand, those that accord with God's commands and, on the other, those that transgress them. This transgression of divine commands was assessed to be of varying degrees and as a result, the majority of Muslim theologians had drawn a general distinction between "major" (*kabira*, pl. *kaba'ir*) and "minor" (*saghira*, pl. *sagha'ir*) sins.[26] The former was differentiated from the latter by accompanying indications. For example, early figures like Ibn 'Abbas and al-Hasan al-Basri, respectively, defined major sins narrowly as those connected to otherworldly sanctions: "every sin that God has stamped with fire, [his] displeasure, [his] curse, or with [the threat of His] punishment"[27] and "every wrong action that results in God punishing with the hellfire, [His] wrath, curse or chastisement is considered a major sin."[28] Later scholars would widen the indications of major sins to include those connected to worldly sanctions as well. Al-Qurtubi, for example, writes that a major sin is "any wrong action that the divine law designates as being something major, or an enormity or informs of it being met by a serious punishment or connects it to a capital (*hudud*) ordinance or sternly opposes it," with the condition that it is based on textual evidence and consensus.[29] However, senior theologians—especially those from the Ash'arite School—considered all sins to be an enormity and rejected the distinction:

> Know that a group of the scholars rejected the notion that there can be minor sins arguing rather that all sins are major ones. This included Abu Ishaq al-Isfarayini, the judge Abu Bakr al-Baqillani, the Imam of the two Holy Sanctuaries al-Juwayni in his book *al-Irshad* and Ibn al-Qushayri in *al-Murshid*. Ibn al-Furak in fact relates this from the Ash'arites and preferred this view in his commentary saying: acts of disobedience to God according to us are all enormities. The reason why some [sins] are called "small" or "big" is in relation to one being greater than the other.[30]

In Islamic theology, there is arguably no redemptive story. There was no fall of humanity that resulted in a contaminated nature. The Qur'anic account is that Adam fell into error and committed a mistake in failing to heed God's command, being instead misled by Satan. The result was a demotion from God's proximity, not a species-specific transferral of sin.[31] Despite there being no fall of humanity, the Qur'an nevertheless is at times clearly pessimistic in its depiction of human creaturehood and capability. The Qur'an notes, for example, that Satan tempts Adam's progeny (al-A'raf, verses 26–27) and describes them as feeble (al-Nisa', verse 28), despairing (Hud, verse 9), unjust (Ibrahim, verse 34), quarrelsome (al-Nahl, verse 4), tyrannical (al-'Alaq, verse 6), and lost (al-Fil, verse 2). The Qur'an also mentions that every human community was sent an apostle (al-Nahl,

verse 36) reminding them to adhere to divine guidance, but one after another they were rejected—often in the most deplorable manner (al-Hijr,
verses 10–11; Qaf, verses 12–14).[32] Hence, The Qur'an concludes in one
place that *most people are not believers* (Yusuf, verse 103) and *if God were to
punish humans for their wrongdoing, He would not leave a single creature* (al-
Nahl, verse 61).[33] This pessimism portrays the depth to which humans can
plummet into sin and indeed the seriousness of sin. Thus, although there
is no sinful human nature, there is a frequency of sinful human behavior.
This sin and the desire and attraction for it are what distances one from
God and His proximity. The ultimate outcome of separating or desiring
other than God by remaining attracted to and perpetrating sin is Hell.

God's Holiness Thesis: On this view, the existence of hell and eternal chastisement is justified through God's name "al-quddus." Linguistically, the
meaning of the Arabic root *q / d / s /* ranges from (1) going far in the land;
(2) making something holy; (3) to bless; (4) to purify; and (5) to vener-
ate.[34] The intensive form 'al-quddus' is mentioned twice in the Qur'an
(al-Hashr, verse 23 and al-Jumu'a, verse 1) as one of the special names
of God, and Muslim scholars and lexicographers have expanded on its
signification. Primarily, the term applied to God is understood to refer
to "exalting God above any evil, imperfection and fault."[35] Exalting God
involves negating any mental conceptualization of Him such that "He is
above anything the senses may perceive, or what the imagination may
conceive or what supposition may turn to, or what moves the conscience
or what thinking demands."[36] In this way, God "possesses perfection in
all His qualities and cannot be defined nor conceptualised."[37] God's holiness (*qudsiya*) has also been equated with what is "blessed" (*mubarak*),
a term "that denotes all things good such that only what is good pours
forth from [God]."[38] Thus, God's holiness has immediate and strong con-
notations with His transcendence, perfection, and goodness. Rejection
of God's transcendence and the guidance He revealed for human beings
through Prophets and Messengers is the ultimate act of denial that de-
fies this holiness. Hell as (eternal) chastisement is a vivid display of the
absolute and infinite value of God's holiness. The severity of everlasting
chastisement for denying God's holiness reflects the infinite value of the
holiness that is denied. Drawing on the proportionality principle, this
argument states that the rejection of God's holiness must be merited with
a proportional sanction. The argument can be stated as follows:

(1) God is not indifferent to anything that affronts the worth of His
holiness.

(2) Anything that affronts the worth of God's holiness merits a commensurate sanction.

(3) Chastisement in hell is a commensurate sanction for an affront on God's holiness.

(4) Denial of God's transcendence, goodness, and perfection is an affront on God's holiness.

(5) Therefore, denial of God's transcendence, goodness, and perfection must be met with a commensurate sanction (from (2), (3), and (4)).

(6) Therefore, denial of God's transcendence, goodness, and perfection merits chastisement in hell.

Hell then is a consequence of God vindicating in the strongest terms His own transcendence, perfection, and goodness. God's wrath is not arbitrary or wanton; rather, it is directed at those who violate this holiness. Some ways this violation occurs is to willingly exchange God's transcendence for finite idols, for example, or to exchange goodness and purity for evil and depravity. This violation is in reality a subordination of God's greatness and glory. God is justified, therefore, in upholding His holiness, perfection, and goodness by sanctioning those who undermine it. Hell is that sanction.

Covenant Thesis: On this model, the justification for hell is based on humanity breaching its covenant *mithaq* with God when they agreed to it in their disembodied state.[39] The Qur'an recounts this covenant dialogue in al-A'raf, verses 172–73:

> And [mention] when your Lord took from the children of Adam—from their loins—their descendants and made them testify of themselves, [saying to them], "Am I not your Lord?" They replied, "Yes, indeed we have testified to it." [This]—in case you say on the day of Resurrection, "Indeed, we were unaware of this." Or [in case] you say, "It was only that our fathers associated [others in worship] with God before, and we were but descendants after them. Then would You destroy us for what the falsifiers have done?"

As an etiological account, the covenant event expressly captures, on the one hand, humanity's collective acknowledgment of its own finite and dependent nature and lack of real autonomy and, on the other, its affirmation of God's total sovereignty and unity (*tawhid*). The entire primordial pact constitutes the general framework or organizing principle for understanding God's motivations for acting in history and how that relates to human destiny either in salvation or in damnation. In this way, the degree of fidelity to the covenant becomes the measure for judging whether individuals or communities merit salvation.[40] The covenant thesis can be set out in the following argument, which will then be elaborated:

(1) All humans entered into a primordial covenant with God.
(2) God provides sufficient opportunities to recollect this primordial covenant.
(3) Rejection of God merits chastisement in hell.
(4) Breaching the primordial covenant is tantamount to rejection of God.
(5) Therefore, breach of the primordial covenant merits chastisement in hell.

God's covenantal engagement with humanity is not out of any necessity, need, or lack but an act of choice and mercy based on terms that are set down by the divine will alone. Humanity in its entirety was invoked to affirm and witness God's exclusive divinity, transcendence, and total worthiness of worship. Their affirmation and profession of this monotheism concluded the primordial pact instantiating the first collective conscious recognition of human contingent metaphysical origins and status, resulting in an implanted (dispositional) awareness of God ab initio. While embodied persons in terrestrial life, human beings were provided by God with sufficient reminders of this primordial covenant through dispatching prophets and messengers bearing a program of conduct and admonition for failure to adhere to this program. If the covenant defines being with God, returning to Him, and acknowledging the real finite status of humanity, then renouncing or reneging on that covenant means rejecting God, separating from Him, and rebelling against Him. To do this is to reject the logic of the covenant—monotheism and divine sovereignty—and that necessarily results in chastisement. Hell is that chastisement.

Best Possible World Thesis: This argument incorporates the theological and metaphysical ideas of al-Ghazali—especially his best possible world thesis discussed earlier in Chapter 2. Hell on this account is justified based on the doctrine that the way the world is providentially ordered and inherently structured by God is optimal—the best (possible) way it could be. The argument may be set out as follows:

(1) The actual world W is the best world.
(2) Rejecting the order and decree of things in W is tantamount to rejecting God.

(3) Rejecting God warrants a commensurate sanction.

(4) A commensurate sanction for rejecting God is chastisement in hell.

(5) Therefore, rejecting the order and decree of things in W warrants chastisement in hell.

It may not seem entirely clear how the conclusion directly follows from the premises without some elaboration. Here, it is necessary for the elaboration to mention two types of dissenting people: (a) those who deny revelatory truths and guidance and (b) those who are dissatisfied with God's comprehensive and totalizing decrees. In the case of the first group who deny religious truth and divine guidance, they reject the best way God has determined the actual world and they do this by adopting their own codes, regulations, and frameworks; they eschew any notion of subservience and submission ('ubudiya) to the mercy and wisdom of God and elevate confidence in their own powers as well as moral predilections and legal deliberations above that of God's commands and prohibitions. They arrogate lordship to themselves and determine what they think is best based on the measure of self-actualizing sensual pleasure and desire (hawa).[41] This rejection of what God has determined to be the best is what warrants punishment in hell. In regard to the second group, malcontents express extreme dissatisfaction and lodge scornful complaint against the way things in the world have been decreed, determined, and directed by God's mercy and wise purposes. They desire and demand that it be another way, different and conducive to their rationalizations and invented criteria. This hostile attitude toward God stems from a flawed psychology, one that fails to incorporate contentment with God's decree, belief in the efficacy of those decrees, and complete trust in the way He has organized the nature, goal, purpose, and direction of the created order.[42] The result of this denial, rejection, and malcontent is a sanction. This sanction is hell.

Free Will Thesis: One aspect of Islamic theology related to free will is eschatology. The Qur'an is vivid in its account of death, judgment, and the final destiny of individuals (as well as creation as a whole).[43] In numerous places it asserts how human beings and jinn possess the power of choice and as a consequence are morally accountable beings. Due to this, a person's choices in premortem temporal life play some important role in one's postmortem destination, that is, whether or not that person ends up in either paradise or hell. People end up in hell simply because they choose to go there, and these choices are a result of an individual developed into a type of person with a specific cognitive outlook and psychology antithetical to what God approves of that then necessitates they remain in hell. That which would justify hell on this account, that is, the reason why it would be created in the first place, is a natural consequence of choices made from such a cognitive outlook and psychology. God from eternity knows who will exist and who will freely choose to deny Him, defy the revelation He dispatches with His prophets and messengers, and who will act contrary to their own created primordial nature (*fitra*). Despite this foreknowledge, God allows such persons to ultimately live by the consequences of those choices, and the consequence inevitably means exclusion and separation from God. Thus, hell is a place of suffering, anguish, and pain because it is primarily one of loss, ultimate impoverishment, and distance from the goodness, mercy, and proximity of God. Ibn Rajab al-Hanbali (d. 795/1393) states unequivocally how the most severe form of punishment is considered to be this separation, closure, and distance from God. He writes:

> The worst punishment of hell's inhabitants is their being veiled from God (High and Exalted), distant from Him, His turning away from them and His displeasure towards them just like how God's pleasure over the inhabitants of paradise is the most favourable form of their bliss and how in fact God's theophany and their vision of Him is the highest of all forms of bliss in paradise.[44]

Responses to Argument 2

Muslim theology is emphatic on the everlasting nature of heaven and hell, which entails the inhabitants will also remain in either one without end. The Islamic theological manuals document early orthodox consensus on this. Ibn Hazm, for example, states in *Maratib al-ijma'* that "hell is real and it is an abode of chastisement that will never cease to exist, and its inhabitants will never cease to exist, they will remain in it without end."[45] He also mentions in his heresiographical work *al-Fasl fi al-milal* that "all the sects of the Muslim community are in agreement that Paradise will never cease to exist nor will its bliss ever end, and that Hell will not cease to exist and neither will its torments ever end."[46]

Some Muslim theologians were aware of the concerns raised by the proportionality problem, which is the apparent injustice of endlessly punishing human beings for a finite number of deeds. Ironically, this very acknowledgment is set within the context of denying the Mu'tazilite pessimistic doctrine that unrepentant grave sinners would be consigned to hell forever based on a combination of strong libertarian freedom as well as divine justice and retribution. On the Mu'tazilite view, there is no scheme for a believer of a temporary sentence in hell followed by an exit to paradise. Their insistence on eternal damnation also precluded the possibility of intercession (*shafa'a*) mitigating this damnation and so they generally denied it for the grave sinner in the hereafter. This view would thus appear to deny a posthumous salvation as held by major Sunni denominations, meaning that an opportunity beyond the grave for procuring salvation was fully eliminated. Death then is a firm boundary between being saved and damned.[47] Al-Ash'ari records in his *Maqalat al-islamiyyin* the Sunni and Mu'tazilite disagreement over the fate of believing sinners:

> And they differed over the whether the reprobate is punished eternally in hell. The Mu'tazilites and the Kharijites held that they will be in hell forever in that whoever enters hell cannot exit it. The Sunni folk (*ahl al-sunna*) and the upright ones (*ahl al-istiqama*) held that God will deliver all believing people of the *qibla* from hell and hence they will not be in it forever.[48]

Early consensus emerged among the Muslim community toward a salvific optimism: God will eventually bring all believing sinners (*muwahhidun*) out of hell.[49] (No such consensus, however, formed regarding the fate of those outside of the believing community.) As the debate evolved, a number of arguments were marshalled directly by Traditionalists, Ash'arite and Maturidite scholars, to attack the Mu'tazilite position. One of the arguments included how it could be wise, fair, or just for God to punish believers endlessly due to a finite quantum of bad actions. Al-Taftazani in *Sharh al-maqasid* gives two connected arguments in this regard:

> The third angle based on a Mu'tazilite principle is that whoever remains on belief and does good actions for say a hundred years and within that time or beyond it commits one wrongful act such as drinking a drop of wine, it would not be fair for the All-Wise to eternally punish the perpetrator for that. If that is not considered injustice then nothing is and if that is not worthy of censure then what is? The fourth angle is that if sin is finite in duration, which is obvious, and finite in gravity—because some sins are more serious than others—then the punishment for it ought also to be finite in order for it to be just which is different from disbelief (*al-kufr*) which is infinite in gravity even though it is finite in duration. If eternal punishment in hell is the most serious punishment reserved for the most serious crime—disbelief—it would not be correct to apply it to what is less severe than it like acts of disobedience.[50]

Muslim scholars did not afford the same latitude or (reasoning) mentioned here in favor of the believers for the eschatological future of nonbelievers. My aim here is not to survey the factors that led to the formation of this doctrine within the community but to present possible arguments that establish the logical compatibility between the propositions brought into tension in Argument 2. The Qur'an alludes to possible reasons why eternal chastisement in hell for the nonbeliever is justified. Two of them will be mentioned here in addition to several other arguments. Cumulatively, they offer defenses that establish the compatibility between God's absolute power, knowledge, mercy, love, justice, and wisdom with some people suffering eternal conscious torment. Before that, however, it is important to clarify the term "infinite" that is often used in the literature. Nowhere does the Qur'an or Hadith state individuals will suffer punishment infinitely, whether that is infinite *intensity* (the qualitative degree of pain experienced) or infinite *duration* (meaning the length of time). In the first sense of infinite, it would seem impossible for a finite conscious creature to be the *loci* of infinite psychosomatic torment. The Qur'an or Hadith clearly teaches that hell's punishment is in degrees; it is not *maximal* (the greatest amount of punishment there can be).[51] If it were maximal, then there could not be comparative degrees of punishment. The second sense of infinity is even more remote and implausible. Again, no finite conscious creature can traverse (suffer) an infinite duration of punishment simply because an actual infinite punishment is not even possible. In fact, an actual infinite of anything is not possible in reality. Hell's punishment is in each instance finite but everlasting or unending, meaning it continues without cessation.[52] The exact modality of how this occurs may vary. One possible way could be through God renewing the very bodily sites of torment of each person in hell after they are destroyed by each execution or affliction of punishment. Al-Taftazani argues for this kind of possibility:

> Muslims are in complete agreement that the inhabitants of Paradise will be in it forever and the non-believers will be in the fire forever. If it is argued that bodily power is finite and therefore cannot accept everlasting life in that moisture, which is an element of life, will evaporate due to the heat (especially the intense heat of hellfire) then that will lead to necessary destruction and that perpetual burning simultaneously with perpetual life is something beyond reason, we will reply as follows: this is a philosophical principle not accepted by religious believers nor considered sound by proponents who attribute the creation of all contingent entities to an All-Powerful being. Regarding the proposition of finite power and perpetual

life, it is possible that God create a substitute [body] such that reward and punishment remains perpetual. God (Most High) says, *"every time their skins are roasted through, We will replace them with other skins so that they may taste the punishment."*[53]

Al-Taftazani's argument suggests that it is logically possible that God maintain—either by recreating or renewing—the required properties of a person (including their entire body) in hell to receive chastisement. This recreation or renewal can continue indefinitely without respite. If this is the case, then the force of the argument that hell's inhabitants will suffer infinite punishment loses some of its force because for every interval of punishment t_1, t_2, t_3, the intensity of the punishment is finite and not maximal.

We turn now to the two direct Qur'anic arguments. The first of them is what I shall call the *absolute seriousness argument*. In a dramatic dialogue, the Qur'an retells how after creating Adam, God commanded the angelic host to prostrate before him with all obeying the command except Iblis who spurned the command and retorted against God with his own logic of defiance arguing by analogy that he was created from fire whereas Adam was created from clay and the latter in his estimation is a superior substance than the former. This resulted in Iblis being condemned from God's sight and damned forever.[54] Iblis's disobedience was against God Who is the Most Honorable, Holy, High, and Exalted. The one being offended is totally unlike any being in kind, that is, the ontological status of God is incomparable as it is infinitely greater. The implicit suggestion is that the higher the status of the offended party, the more serious the sin. Because God is an infinitely greater being—in fact the greatest being—then sinning against Him is infinitely grave meriting infinite sanction. This is what is known as the "status principle" (SP). Oliver Crisp captures SP succinctly when he writes that "the value of a deity outweighs the value of a human to an infinite degree, such that crimes against a member of that ontological kind carry significantly greater (in fact, infinite) consequences."[55] Thus, Iblis's singular act (refusing to obey God's command to prostrate to Adam) resulted in eternal damnation due to its gravity, which is determined by the being against whom the offence was directed. In this way, finite sins merit infinite (meaning unending) punishment because the being offended is the greatest being. This argument from the Qur'an clearly assumes that a punishment does not have to be equal to or proportionate to the duration of a fault or offense. Iblis's act was singular, an instance. Therefore, the measure of punishment decreed (unending damnation) was not the *duration* but the *gravity* (disobeying God's direct command).

The second Qur'anic argument is what I have labeled simply as the *divine foreknowledge argument*. In al-An'am, verse 28, the Qur'an mentions about those who after being shown the reality of hell's punishment still resolve to deny God and remain on their associationism (*shirk*): *but what they concealed before will be apparent to them. Even if they were returned, they would revert to what they were prohibited from. Indeed, they are liars.*[56] The meaning of the verse according to al-Razi is that "if God were to return [these non-believers] to the world, they would never abandon their rejection and would never commit to belief but will remain on their initial path of disbelief and rejection."[57] He then quotes the explanation of al-Wahidi:

> This verse on its most apparent indications shows how the Mu'tazilite view is incorrect because God has informed about a people He has passed judgment on from eternity (*qada'uhu min al-azal*) for their polytheism. Then God explained how if they were shown the reality of the hellfire and its punishment and then asked to be returned to the world again, they would still revert to their polytheism. This is because of the prior decree on them because a rational person would never doubt what he sees.[58]

Hence, the punishment is unending because if the nonbelievers were to return to this world for another opportunity, they would still reject belief in God and accept associationism. Thus, the Qur'an is informing about God's decision from eternity based on His counterfactual knowledge of what these nonbelievers *would have done* if they *were to* return to the world every time. The perpetual chastisement is a result of the recurring cause: the irrevocable nature of their disbelief. Their rejection of God therefore is total and this leaves no other option but separation from Him and the destination for that separation is hell. This is corroborated in the hadith that states:

> The Messenger God, the truthful and truly inspired one, told us that: "The creation of one of you is put together in his mother's womb for forty days, then it becomes a clot for a similar length of time, then it becomes a chewed lump of flesh for a similar length of time. Then God sends the angel to him and commands him to write down four things. He says: 'Write down his deeds, his life span, his provision, and whether he is doomed or blessed.' By the One in Whose Hand is my soul! One of you may do the deeds of the people of paradise until there is no more than a

forearm's length between him and it, then the decree overtakes him and he does the deeds of the people of hell until there is no more than a forearm's length between him and it, then the decree overtakes him and he does the deeds of the people of Paradise until he enters therein."[59]

'Ali al-Qari on this narration comments:

They will be entered into hell based on justice and the varying levels of action. The duration of being in hell forever is because of [their] intention and overreaching desire [to commit sin]. Thus, it cannot be replied that manifest justice applies to someone who disbelieves for seventy years cannot be punished more than that length because the intention of a non-believer is that if he were to live forever, he would insist on his disbelief either based on ignorance or obstinacy.[60]

Another argument, related to the everlasting nature of chastisement, is that mentioned briefly by al-Maturidi in his *Kitab al-tawhid*. The eighth/fourteenth-century Hanafite jurist and theologian Akmal al-Din al-Babarti (d. 786/1384) helpfully paraphrases the argument in an expansive way in the closing part of his commentary on the text *Kitab al-wasiya* attributed to Abu Hanifa. I will cite both al-Maturidi's argument and then al-Babarti's paraphrase:

al-Maturidi: disbelief is the most extreme type of disobedience against God and so its punishment is proportionate. Belief is to have utter conviction *(tasdiq)* in that which is infinite and without end and disbelief is to deny that which is infinite and without end. The recompense for both is according to this [acceptance and rejection]. For this reason, anything other than disbelief can be pardoned because it does not involve willful rejection of that which is infinite.[61]

al-Babarti: The shaykh Abu Mansur al-Maturidi (God have mercy on him) mentioned in *al-Tawhid* while discussing the difference between disbelief and any sin less than it that may be pardoned or what prevents its pardon saying: disbelief is a doctrine that is believed with conviction. Doctrines are believed with conviction forever and its punishment likewise is on this basis. All other major sins are not committed forever but in finite moments of overpowering desires. Hence, they are punished for that very basis. Moreover, disbelief is intrinsically something repugnant that cannot be excused nor its offense lifted and so similarly, according to wisdom, its punishment cannot be excused or pardoned. Rationally, all other sins can be pardoned and so can their respective punishments but a disbeliever being pardoned would not be pardon in its proper place because he rejects The Benefactor (*al-mun'im*) and sees that as true.[62]

A number of different points converge on this argument. First, al-Maturidi clearly frames the discussion within the divine attribute of wisdom. As already mentioned in Chapter 3, for him wisdom is to place something in its proper place. Failing to punish disbelief proportionately by pardoning it would be irregular and a misplaced pardon because disbelief involves a total rejection of God, a willful refusal of what is the only True Reality and hence inexcusable. Second, al-Maturidi employs some type of equivalence principle: finite sins merit finite punishment. If this is the case, a permanent sin merits permanent punishment. That which is a permanent, lasting, or absolute sin, one that is definitive, irrevocable, and cannot be modified, amended, or terminated, is disbelief (*kufr*). No other sin has this entrenched nature with serious eschatological ramifications. Disbelief involves committing to other than God in a binding way, that is, forever. The entailment of this commitment is exclusion from God and the place of this exclusion, as well as separation, is hell. Third, al-Maturidi appears to also invoke the Status Principle (SP). Disbelief involves rejecting an infinite being that merits infinite punishment because of the incomparable status of the one being rejected. Al-Maturidi's argument therefore is not that finite sins demand eternal punishment, but disbelief demands eternal punishment because its entailment is irrevocable denunciation of God. Al-Razi's variation of this argument helps identify this key point:

> A group of people argued that God's punishment is finite meaning it will end and they used the verse, "*they will tarry in [hell] for ages.*" This is because the injustice of sins is finite and so its punishment with something infinite is injustice. The reply to that [objection] is that the word "ages" (*ahqab*) does not denote a finite duration because the Arabs use this term and others to denote perpetuity. There is no injustice in this because a non-believer is resolute, entrenched and bound in his disbelief as long as he is alive and hence, he is perpetually punished. No punishment is perpetual except on something that is perpetual. In this way, "*the recompense is fitting.*"[63]

The generic form of both arguments is as follows:

(1) Perpetual punishment is fair if what it applies to is something perpetual.

(2) Disbelief is something perpetual.

(3) Therefore, perpetual punishment of disbelief is fair.

Premise (1) is reasonable. The Qur'an in al-Naba', verse 26 describes the unending punishment for nonbelievers as a "fitting recompense" (*jaza'an wifaqan*)—appropriate, deserving, commensurate, and proper. Severe acts of sin ought to be met with severe punishment that is not disproportionate or excessive.[64] Premise (2) states that the only candidate for perpetuity is the most severe act of sin, one that is permanent, and that is the sin of disbelief. Disbelief is fixed as it were at the moment of death through a set of convictions that involve total rejection of God. There is then a psychological determination that necessitates a person to remain in rejection of God from the moment of death. Remaining in this rejection of God is the abiding demerit that occasions unending punishment. So long as this is even possible, endless punishment would be fair.

Another argument for unending chastisement would be a contrastive one. If it is reasonable that eternal bliss in paradise is the reward for a finite set of good actions then its counterpart seems reasonable as well: unending punishment for a finite set of sins. Finally, eternal conscious torment is just and compatible with God's attributes because its theological alternatives—annihilationism, universalism, and naturalization (all discussed below)—do not properly or adequately capture God's justice, sovereignty, and mercy based on the overall weight of the scriptural references as well as compatibility with other divine attributes and core Islamic theological doctrines.

Responses to Argument 3

The responses outlined here attempt to address the specific problem of why, on the Mainstream View, some people will be damned forever. Each of these responses is a modified version of the Mainstream View and share core assumptions about divine justice, fairness, and mercy.

Annihilationism—One possible response to the challenge in Argument 3 is to hold that the condemned in hell do not suffer unending conscious torment but will be annihilated by God in hell and will therefore cease to exist forever. This suffering of hell's inhabitants therefore will be cut short by means of extinction. This view is based on a punitive temporary theory of hell and is known as "annihilationism." Other preferred terms by proponents include "conditional immortality" and "conditionalism" (although there are some nuanced differences).[65] Annihilationists would generally uphold (H1), (H3), (H4), and even (H5) but deny (H2). This view of hell is nonexistent in the Islamic theological literature, so critical assessments of actual reasons motivating it or arguments in favor of it are not possible. In what follows then, I aim to sketch a proposal drawing on some of the relatively recent philosophical and theological literature followed by an examination of some of the difficulties such a view may hold for its proponents.[66]

One possible motivation for adopting annihilationism is what Brown and Walls call a "natural consequence" reason where "certain facts about the essence of sin and its natural consequences either entail or make probable annihilation as the ultimate fate of the wicked."[67] These "facts" about sin rest on the idea that sin is evil and evils are a privation, that is, they have no positive ontology; they lack real existence. According to Avicennan metaphysics within the Islamic tradition (and within Christianity the Thomistic tradition), only existence/being (*wujud*) has goodness (*khayr*), which is why God is pure goodness (*khayr mahd*) because He has full and perfect existence/being making Him pure perfection (*kamal mahd*).[68] Evil, on the other hand, would be the opposite of goodness because it lacks being (*'adam*). For Ibn Sina, the fuller a thing is in its being, the more goodness it has. The less being something has, the worse it is or the more evil it is—insofar as evil is a privation.[69] Thus, the degree to which something has goodness is measured by how much being or existence it has. Being then is convertible with or coextensive with goodness.[70] Moreover, anything that correctly actualizes its proper nature (*tab'*) would be considered good. The nature of a knife, for example, is to cut. To be a good knife, therefore, is to be able to fulfill its nature: cutting.[71] If this is the case, then the annihilationist could argue that if a person S becomes increasingly evil, he will diminish in his being, meaning he will exist less and less in degree. The degree of S's diminished being is proportionate to his descent into evil. If the trajectory of descent continues such that S is completely saturated in evil, S will eventually cease to exist. This nonexistence "is the fate of the wicked in hell: they become increasingly depraved until they finally become so evil that they become extinct."[72]

Although Ibn Sina considered goodness and being as convertible, it is not altogether clear that he would equate a person being sufficiently evil with nonexistence. For him evil is broadly divided into two metaphysical categories: essential evil (*al-sharr bi-l-dhat*) and accidental evil (*al-sharr bi-l-'arad*). The former type of evil is any lack or privation in some entity that leads to (1) its total annihilation, (2) its diminished well-being but not cessation, or (3) its unnatural state.[73] The latter type of evil is something that (1) actively compromises what is good or (2) is a lack in an entity of some nonessential quality that does not diminish its well-being. Given this, unless sinful actions are argued to be essential evils, it would be difficult to see how they would lead to the destruction or annihilation of an individual.

Another possible motivation for annihilationism would be to vindicate God's moral perfection and justice.[74] Hence, (H3) from the Mainstream View of hell is argued to undermine God's goodness and justice because in the case of the former, He would be condemning people to a type of punishment they cannot possible deserve, which is unending, relentless psychosomatic misery, agony, and pain and in the case of the latter, He would be meting out a duration of infinite punishment for a finite set of crimes. Pinnock writes how "everlasting torment is intolerable from a moral point of view" because it makes out God to be a "bloodthirsty monster who maintains an everlasting Auschwitz for victims whom He does not even allow to die." Such a "cruel and merciless" God would be unthinkable to worship. On this kind of view, "idea of everlasting torment (especially if it is linked to soteriological predestination) raises the problem of evil to impossible dimensions."[75] Pinnock objects that "unending torture of the wicked" would be nothing but "sheer vengeance and vindictiveness" on God's part because there would be no point in "endless and totally unredemptive suffering" through punishment just for its own sake. It would also amount to "inflicting infinite suffering upon those who have committed finite sins" going far beyond "an eye for an eye and a tooth for a tooth," resulting in a serious "disproportion between sins committed in time and the suffering experienced forever." Therefore, "the fact that sin has been committed against an infinite God does not make the sin infinite."[76]

It is to be noted that Muslim scholars tacitly acknowledge that annihilation is less severe than any kind of psychosomatic torment. Certain hadiths, for example, do allude to how some sinful believers will be annihilated (literally burned to ashes) in hell and then—drawing on botanical imagery of regrowth—will have their ashes scattered in paradise, watered by its inhabitants to then sprout a new human life from the remains. These individuals (known from various reports as "jahannamiyun" or "hellfire dwellers") would have been ransomed through an act of intercession (*shafa'a*) of a pious person or the super intercessory power endowed to the Prophet Muhammad.[77] One report from the companion Abu Sa'id al-Khudri states:

> The Prophet said: "The dwellers of hell, who are destined to stay there forever, will neither die nor live. As for those believers who enter the fire as a punishment for their sins or faults, God will cause them to die a real

death until they are burned to ashes. Then He will allow intercession for them. Their remains will be scattered over the rivers of paradise. Thereafter, it will be said: 'O dwellers of paradise, pour water over them.' Thus, their bodies will sprout like a plant when it is carried away by the flood."[78]

Al-Qurtubi interestingly comments on the rationale for annihilating these believers. "The death of these wrongdoers," he writes, "is a real and actual death because the verbal noun was mentioned for emphasis and this is out of deference for them because they will not have any sensation of pain after being annihilated like its inhabitants feel who are in [hell] forever."[79] Thus, God spares certain believers the pain and humiliation of prolonged or perpetual postmortem suffering by annihilating them and then recreating them from their scattered ashes in Paradise. Therefore, a form of selected annihilation seems to be affirmed. On the basis of this rationale, if it is better to annihilate a person because it is less severe in its consequences on the patient, then God ought to annihilate hell's inhabitants rather than relinquishing them to an eternal punishment.

However, it is not clear in what way on the annihilationism account it is exactly more just for God to totally extinguish from existence those consigned to hell than either a sentence of eternal conscious torment or even a temporary chastisement as argued by the universalist. The annihilationist in fact is faced with a similar problem that confronts those who hold the Mainstream View in how the damned are given an infinite punishment (annihilation) for a finite set of sins. As Brown and Walls explain, "everlasting punishment is, in fact, annihilation." The reason why the punishment of annihilation is everlasting is "not because the recipients will consciously experience it forever but because its consequences, while not experienced, nonetheless last forever." Hence, on an annihilationist view "no less than defenders of DH [doctrine of hell], hold that some humans will face everlasting punishment, punishment that is all the more poignant since it involves the loss of the infinite good of eternal life with God."[80] In fact, a universalist critique of annihilationism would be that it entails loss of salvation through extinction. This is because loss of being altogether would deprive one of possible eternal bliss through reconciliation with God. In this way, annihilationism would rule out any possibility of exiting hell.

A final motivation for adopting annihilationism could be that such a view better upholds the notion of divine sovereignty and in that makes better use of the Qur'anic text.[81] If God alone possesses ultimate authority and power over His creation and proactively governs creation according to a determined providential plan as the Qur'an emphatically asserts, then He must be able to exercise it without any independent and external constraints. God rules over creation and accomplishes His will. He has neither competitors nor rivals. Nothing of the created order must constrain God's absolute power and sovereignty—not even evil like sin. Yet, on the Mainstream View, God must cede His absolute sovereignty in a sense to the created order because He cannot adequately repay sin. If hell is perpetual conscious torment, it is never really eradicated. This means that ultimately God's sovereignty is not efficacious because there will be "a realm in which evil is relegated to a small dimension to continue in perpetuity in its own right." Therefore, "the traditional theology of hell does not go *far enough* in maintaining the fullness of God."[82]

Hell is God's instrument of wrath but by purposefully allowing hell's inhabitants to remain as sentient beings locked in an eternal cycle of repeated punishment that expresses and exposes this wrath, it is difficult to see how this manifests God's absolute power because there is never any resolution nor redemptive outcome. Murrell offers a vivid analogy by asking whether "human sovereignty or justice be served if the hangman's noose never broke the subject's neck, the electricity surging through the body never killed the condemned prisoner, or the lethal injection never properly resulted in the condemned organs failing?" His answer is "a resounding *no*." He continues: "when the neck does not break, when the electricity does not kill or when the toxins do not destroy, it is considered by any measurable standard to be a failure and additional processes must be implemented to produce the desired result of death."[83]

Finally, if an eternal punishment idea is maintained, this would have the undesired implication of the problem of an infinite dualism where alongside God and heaven, evil and hell would continue to exist forever. Pinnock explains how nonannihilationist views imply this metaphysical and theological problem of an "unending cosmic dualism" where "Heaven and hell just go on existing alongside each other forever." This "disloyal opposition would eternally exist alongside God in a corner of unredeemed reality in the new creation." This would not be the case if "the destruction and the wicked were no more."[84] In order to allow God's sovereignty, power, and justice to fully manifest and avoid the implication of a metaphysical dualism, He must exercise His full authority over hell and its inhabitants by making them cease to exist, that is, by annihilating them. To address the implication of a metaphysical dualism raised by Pinnock, al-Maturidi's reply to the Jahmiya[85] who upheld the annihilation of heaven and hell is, I believe, apt. Al-Maturidi writes in his commentary of the creed manual *Fiqh al-Akbar* attributed to Abu Hanifa:

If they argue that the position of the eternality of both heaven and hell lead to a form of associationism (*shirka*) with God's eternality [bearing in mind] "*everything will perish except the Face of God*," we will reply that this is another one of your aberrations (*turrahatikum*). Heaven and hell at one point did not exist and were then created by God's act of creation (*takwin*). Both are sustained in perpetuity by God.[86]

Thus, the dualism that Pinnock raises is not in reality an independent, active opposition or adversary to God; it is a kind of derived dualism for lack of a better phrasing in that the continuation of chastisement and conditions of hell (and paradise) depend on God's active conservation of it. There is, therefore, no threat to God in terms of there existing a rival and independent and self-perpetuating power as both abodes owe their very being to God.

A final and perhaps more serious objection to annihilationism is that, ultimately, it appears to oppose the Qur'an. The literal reading of the verses reveals an emphatic denial of death by destruction or extinction in the eschaton.[87] The Qur'an upholds death that marks the end of temporal life but does not uphold any notion of final destruction.[88] A few verses will suffice to prove the point. First, in al-Inshiqaq, verse 11, it reads, *he will cry out for destruction* and in al-Furqan, verses 13–14, it has, *And when they are thrown into a narrow place in [hellfire] bound in chains, they will then cry out for destruction. / [They will be told], "Do not cry this Day for one destruction but cry for much destruction."* In both chapters, the word "thubur" is used from the root *th / b / r /*, meaning to vanquish, to perish, and to ruin.[89] In this context, it refers to death and destruction. The unbearable agony of hell's punishment will cause the inhabitants to beg for death or destruction but will be denied it.[90] Other verses that deny annihilation to the damned include al-Zukhruf, verse 77, *And they will call out: "O Malik,*[91] *let your Lord annihilate us!" He will say, "Indeed, you will remain,";* al-Haqqa, verse 27, *I wish my death had been annihilation;* and al-Fatir, verse 36, *And for those who disbelieve [for them] will be the fire of Hell. Annihilation will not be their lot so they may die, nor will its torment be lightened for them. Thus do we recompense every ungrateful one.* Here, the variations on the verb *qaDa* from the root *q / D / y /* with the preposition *'ala* denote extermination, annihilation, destruction, and death.[92] Again, the inhabitants of hell would desire that they be utterly extinguished than endure unmitigated punishment, but God will not grant that.[93]

Universalism—Another response to the challenge of eternal damnation is to argue that there is a finality to hell and, subsequently, there will be no persons inhabiting hell forever. This is the view known as "universalism." Other names include "universal restoration," "universal reconciliation," and "universal restitution."[94] Universalist type of views within the Islamic theological tradition insist on grounding salvation for all primarily in God's love, mercy, and compassion and not God's wrath or retributive motives. I take all forms of Islamic universalism to uphold the following components:

(1) Annihilation thesis: there is an end or finality to hell, that is, it will cease to exist.
(2) No residence thesis: eventually hell will not be populated by any free creature.
(3) Mercy thesis: God's mercy governs His motives and relations with His creatures.
(4) No choice thesis: inhabitants of hell have no choice in ultimately being reconciled with God.
(5) Therapeutic thesis: punishment in hell rids the inhabitants of unwanted traits and qualities, restoring them to their *fitra*.

Two articulations of universalism will be analyzed: the first by Ibn Taymiya and the second by his student Ibn Qayyim al-Jawzya. Turning first to Ibn Taymiya, from the set of theses that make up the Mainstream View of hell, he would accept both (H1) and (H2) but reject (H3) and (H5). It may even plausibly be argued he would contest (H4) based on his understanding of God's mercy as well as his theodicy model. Regarding (H1) and (H2), Ibn Taymiya is clear that hell is real and that there will be inhabitants of hell. These are undeniable Qur'anic statements and ones that he affirms in his numerous creed manuals and works. However, the possibility of exiting hell—the denial of (H3)—and rejection of (H5) is where Ibn Taymiya's originality and boldness is evident. The view of the majority of Muslim theologians prior to him held to the eternality of hell as orthodox doctrine. This can be summarized in the following argument:

(1) The inhabitants of hell will remain in it for as long as hell exists.
(2) Hell is eternal.
(3) Therefore, the inhabitants of hell will remain in it forever.

Ibn Taymiya's response is that premise (2) is not a definitive doctrine, denial of which cannot amount to heresy. Hence, his counterargument could be put as:

(1′) The inhabitants of hell will remain in it for as long as hell exists.

(2′) Hell is not eternal.

(3′) Therefore, the inhabitants of hell will not remain in it forever.

His defense of (2′) relies on subtle Qur'anic exegesis, appeal to re-ligious authority as well as assumptions about divine love, justice, and fairness. So long as (2′) is even possible (3) does not logically follow. In summary, (2′) is possible because of the following reasons:[95] (i) *Qur'anic ambiguity*: for Ibn Taymiya, a number of Qur'anic verses have sufficient ambiguity in them to make inconclusive the claim that hell's punishment and duration are both unending. For example, the word "ahqab" (sing. *huqb*) in al-Naba', verse 23 that reads *tarrying in [hell] for ages* does not necessarily mean forever but a long stretch of time or a finite and defined duration.[96] Another verse he cites is from Hud, verses 107–108, which reads, *[the wretched shall be] abiding [in Hell] so long as the heavens and earth endure, except what your Lord wills. Your Lord does indeed what He wants.* Ibn Taymiya cites a number of early exegetical authorities that suggest hell's punishment is finite in duration. He cites al-Tabari who recorded an interpretation from Ibn 'Abbas that the verse "... 'they will abide in it forever so long as the heavens and earth endure, except as your Lord pleases' means: God made an exception [in this verse] ordering hell to fully consume them," thus terminating the duration of the punishment.[97] Moreover, Qur'anic references to the inhabitants of hell remaining per-petually in it (*abadan*) with the decreed punishment (al-Baqara, verses 161–62, al-An'am, verses 27–28, al-Mu'minun, verses 107–108, al-Fatir, verses 36–37, al-Ghafir, verses 49–50, al-Zukhruf, verses 74–78, al-Haqqa, verses 25–27) does not necessarily mean eternal punishment but condi-tional punishment, that is, the inhabitants cannot escape hell *so long as hell exists*.[98] (ii) *Authoritative views*: Ibn Taymiya appeals to authority citing some of the most senior companions of the Prophet like 'Amr ibn al-'As,[99] Abu Hurayra, Ibn Mas'ud,[100] and Abu Sa'id al-Khudri that interpret there being a cessation of hell's punishment.[101] One particular statement is that of the second Caliph of Islam 'Umar b. al-Khattab suggesting the temporary duration of punishment in hell. The report is as follows: "if the 'People of the Fire' (*ahl al-nar*) were to remain [in the Fire] to the extent of (the number of) stones in a mountain, then theirs would be a day in which they would leave it."[102] (iii) *No consensus*: the view that punishment in hell is everlasting lacks scholarly consensus according to Ibn Taymiya. Absence of consensus must mean that the matter was differed over among the early community.[103] This would imply that neither hell's eternality nor its unending punishment constitutes a cardinal Islamic doctrine. (iv) *Divine mercy*: Here, Ibn Taymiya makes a few arguments. First, God's mercy is an intrinsic property, meaning "an essential part of His essence." Heaven is grounded in God's mercy and compassion and therefore arises out of an intrinsic quality of God. What grounds divine punishment of hell is a contingent act of God, more specifically, "His created act and something He creates has an end like the example of the world. This holds especially in the case of something created for a wise purpose connected to something else." The next argument he gives is a direct textual one: that God's mercy "prevails over everything" citing the narrations "I have obligated mercy on Myself," "My mercy precedes by wrath," and "My Mercy dominates by wrath." Unending punishment would undermine this sense of a dominating and absolute mercy.[104] For his final argument that problematizes the Mainstream View of hell, Ibn Taymiya alludes to the proportionality problem, in other words, why finite beings are deserving of infinite punishment and what wise purpose that would serve. God for him is neither capricious, arbitrary nor a being who acts aimlessly. His actions have motivations that serve an end for humans— whether that is generally for a greater good within an overall providential plan or specifically for soul building in preparation for the hereafter. His analogy is that just as within the Shari'a legal sanctions serve a general intelligible purpose (such as deterrence) in this world, in the same way, punishment in hell must serve some intelligible purpose—there must be some wisdom grounding it—otherwise it brings into question the kind of being God is and the kind of judgments He makes. Ibn Taymiya wants to assert that there is a pattern to divine actions, but ultimately, divine mercy must have a restorative purpose—it must redeem and renew. He argues that the Mainstream View led many theologians like Jahm b. Safwan and the Ash'arites after him to depict God as an impersonal Creator where His mercy is subordinate to His attributes of power, knowledge, and will. He writes:

> For that reason, when Jahm saw this contradiction, he denied [in effect] that God is the Most Merciful saying God does whatever he wants. Those who later followed him like al-Ash'ari and others did not emphasise [God's] wisdom and mercy but His knowledge, power and will without preferring either one of them. This is why when it was insisted from them that they affirm He is All-Wise, they explained Him as Omniscient, Omnipotent and the Helper and that none of these three attributes required wisdom.[105]

Ibn Taymiya's most illustrious student Ibn Qayyim al-Jawziya builds on his teacher's core theses and substantiates it with additional arguments that also oppose (H3), (H4), and (H5). The treatment by Ibn Qayyim is more extensive and bolder in its claim than his teacher's,[106] but in summary, he takes two approaches: hermeneutical and philosophical. In the case of the first approach, Ibn Qayyim argues—like Ibn 'Arabi before him—that the Qur'an indicates that paradise is fundamentally dissimilar to hell:

1. Those without merit may be admitted into paradise, whereas those who deserve punishment will land in hell.
2. Paradise is a categorically "unending gift" from God (Hud, verse 108), whereas hell is conditionally unending (al-An'am, verse 6; Hud, verse 107 and al-Naba', verse 23).
3. Hell is finite in duration as suggested by the word "day" (*yawm*) in al-An'am, verse 15 and Hud, verse 26 but the felicity in paradise is never described as such.[107]

Like Ibn Taymiya, Ibn Qayyim insists that Qur'anic words such as *khalidin* and *abadan* although ostensibly mean "forever," "unending," and "everlasting" can also suggest the contrary. The latter term does not have to denote ontological perpetuity but uninterrupted and unending realities within a given context like this world.[108] In the case of the second approach, Ibn Qayyim's position is that punishment in hell is not an end in itself but a means. The purpose of hell is not gratuitous retribution but overall restoration of its inhabitants. Once the restorative aims have been achieved, the means no longer become necessary:[109] Ibn Qayyim, like Ibn Taymiya, invokes the mercy maxim found in the hadith, "My mercy prevails over my wrath." If God is essentially loving, compassionate, and merciful, and if His mercy dominates His wrath—as Ibn Qayyim categorically insists it does—He would ensure the salvation of all and annihilate hell. This is his core logic of salvation. In *Hadi al-arwah*, for example, he writes, "forgiveness is more beloved to [God]—praise be to him—than vengeance, mercy is more beloved to Him than punishment, acceptance is more beloved to Him than wrath, and grace is more beloved to Him than justice."[110] God is neither vengeful nor vindictive. He does not benefit from nor is in need of retributive justice. Ibn Qayyim writes that God does not "quench his thirst for revenge" nor does he "harrow His servant with this purpose"; rather, He does it "with the aim of redeeming him." The punishment "is, in fact, a benefit (*maslaha*) to him, despite the infliction of great pain" much like how applications of Shari'a penal penalties (*hudud*) in reality are of benefit to the recipient.[111] In addition, Ibn Qayyim's reasoning for the rationale of divine punishment is similar to Ibn Taymiya in how he argues that "God's attributes of mercy and good pleasure are essential but anger and wrath are not," allowing him to state that "the chastisement that flows from God's anger and wrath need not be eternal" and that the source of chastisement is located in God's justice and wisdom that is governed by wise ends and purposes.[112] In *al-Sawa'iq al-mursala* Ibn Qayyim warns that unending chastisement lacks any sense and cognizable benefit.[113] Ibn Qayyim eschews the status argument that defends the eternality of punishment on the basis of God's status as infinite. He agrees that divine sanction is warranted and is motivated by—like with all things—God's mercy and compassion. This divine sanction, however, is remedial and restorative in power. He writes:

> The wise purpose [of God]—Glory be to Him—required that He make a remedy (*dawa'*) appropriate to each malady (*da'*) and that the remedy for the malady be among the most toilsome of remedies. The Compassionate Physician cauterizes one who is ill with the Fire, cauterization after cauterization, to remove the vile matter besmirching the upright nature.[114]

In the same way as a physician must resort to cauterization with fire when confronted with a difficult harm in a patient and in the same way divinely ordained temporal penal codes are a merciful means to resolve one's affairs with God prior to meeting Him in the hereafter, likewise finite chastisement in hell is a means to meaningfully restore individuals to their original created disposition—their *fitra*.[115] Hell will quarantine them from all the qualities and attributes that led them away from God in the first place after which the rationale for their chastisement falls away and at which time God will admit them into Paradise and fold up hell.[116]

The universalist stance was attacked since its formulation and the bulk of the effort was directed at the exegetical arguments to support it. Four key texts composed in this regard are extant. The first is a text written by Ibn Taymiya's vehement detractor Taqi al-Din al-Subki (d. 756/1355) called *al-I'tibar bi-baqa' al-janna wa-l-nar* composed explicitly to rebut his views in *Fana' al-nar* as heretical and legitimate grounds for excommunication (*takfir*).[117] The second is a small tract written by Ibn Yusuf al-Mar'i al-Karmi called *Tawqif al-fariqayn 'ala khulud ahl al-darayn* that is a summary discussion of the whole topic rebutting the core universalist claims.[118] The final two texts are by Yemeni scholars: the first by the eighteenth-century *hadith* specialist Ibn al-Amir al-San'ani (d. 1182/1768) called *Raf' al-astar li-ibtal adillat al-qa'ilin bi-Fana' al-Nar* that is a meticulous rebuttal of Ibn Taymiya and Ibn Qayyim and the second by the sunnifying figure of Zaydism Muhammad b. 'Ali al-Shawkani (d. 1250/1834) entitled *Kashf al-astar fi ibtal qawl man qala bi-Fana' al-Nar* that is an exegetical analysis of the view of hell's finitude rather than a direct refutation of a particular author.[119] All four texts focus on undermining the universalist position on primarily textual grounds and hermeneutical principles.[120] Al-Subki, for example, marshals a catalogue of Qur'anic verses to establish the following points as incontrovertible based on the language:

1. the eternality of hell,
2. the eternality of paradise,
3. no cessation of punishment in hell, and
4. no escape for the unbelieving inhabitants of hell.

These verses, he argues, are to be taken on their literal reading (*zahir*) and do not admit of any (need for) figurative interpretation (*ta'wil*) because they are unambiguous.[121] Al-San'ani through verbatim quotes of Ibn Taymiya and Ibn Qayyim dismantles the exegetical endeavors of both authors to demonstrate how they fail to conclusively establish hell's annihilation from scripture and speculative reasoning (*nazar*). Al-Shawkani discusses all the exegetical positions on the conditionality thesis doubtfully attributed to the Prophet's companions and the two generations that immediately followed them and concludes that none of them are authoritative (*hujja*) because they are tantamount to eisegesis and thus not binding on anyone to follow. The truth, rather, is in exegetically harmonizing the various verses (*jam'*) without resorting to two mutually exclusive views on the matter of hell's duration.[122]

Another problem with the universalism of Ibn Taymiya and Ibn Qayyim in addition to the exegetical weakness as pointed out by their opponents is that it rests on a second chance view of hell that is contrary to the finality thesis purportedly stated by the Qur'an whereby death is the demarcation that ends any chances for postmortem recovery or redemption. Al-Subki argues that the Qur'an emphatically states the irrevocable finality of damnation and that the notion that hell will restore the *fitra* of its inhabitants such that they become "Muslims" again is contrary to scripture and the rationale of hell itself:

> If it is asked that perhaps souls are purified from all evil with this chastisement such that through it [the inhabitants] enter into full submission to God, I will reply: God protect us from such a view! Regarding their

becoming Muslims in the hereafter, this is of no benefit to them according to the consensus of all Muslims and God's statement *"no soul will benefit from its faith as long as it had not believed before"* (al-An'am, verse 158). Regarding their being purified [by hell] then this is also invalid because of God's statement *"God has set a seal on their hearts"* (al-Baqara, verse 7) and *"their hearts were sealed over"* (al-Munafiqun, verse 3) which makes it impossible for evil to be purged from their hearts or for good to enter it.[123]

The universalist position also appears to generate an asymmetry between God's attributes in how it purports to assert God's mercy over His other attributes. This leads to a misplaced and imbalanced understanding of divine actions and motives. It does not explicitly follow from God enabling some to suffer unending punishment in hell that it undermines His love and mercy because these two attributes come into full expression through granting eternal bliss in paradise as a reward for those who willingly sought God and were fully conscious of Him through their earthly life. This was the point raised by al-Subki.[124] By way of an analogy, it would not be accurate to conclude that just because a school followed up on its reward and sanction policy by excluding one pupil from school due to s/he consistently breaching behavior guidelines that the program of rewards given to all other students is somehow undermined or that the school is not serious about the educational future of all its pupils or even the fairness of the school is in some way brought into disrepute. Yet it seems mistaken to think that the school ought never ultimately to exclude any pupil because that results in denial of access to education—even if the behavior of the pupil had escalated to the extreme. Similarly, on a universalist logic, God ought never to sanction with an unending chastisement—even if the person willfully and knowingly rejects God and His commandments. Related to this problem is yet another one, which is that ultimately on a universalist theological position like that of Ibn Taymiya and Ibn al-Qayyim, God's salvation is by compulsion. It is a coerced imposition of divine mercy. This mercy trumps human autonomy, that is, human free choice, that may involve irrevocably rejecting God. By making chastisement in hell curative, its inhabitants are expunged of all reprehensible accretions accumulated during worldly existence to be restored to their primordial state of nature to be then finally admitted into the company of God. This kind of determinism would seem to genuinely defeat human free will because it is not the choice that determines the ultimate destiny of a person but God. This coercive power of divine mercy, for example, is presented in a theosophically ingenious way by the foremost medieval Andalusian mystic and spiritual master (*shaykh al-akbar*) Muhyiddin Ibn 'Arabi discussed in just a moment.

Finally, on universalism any notion of exclusive salvation through Islam is in the end non-efficacious. If Islam is salvifically non-efficacious, then the Prophet Muhammad is obsolete, no longer necessary, and there would be no unique power of the "Great News" (*al-naba' al-'azim*) that is the Qur'an as a final dispensation. A person's own antemortem chosen path whether that of a particular established religious tradition like Christianity, Judaism, Hinduism, Buddhism, or a newly devised cult like Satanism or even fictional worldviews like Scientology and Jediism would not be eschatologically momentous postmortem because such a person will in the end attain reconciliation with God. This would also entail that the paradigmatic enemies of God whether Iblis in his fall from the precreation event or Pharaoh's claimant to be lord or Abu Jahl's oppressive opposition to the mission of the Prophet will also be enveloped in God's mercy and taken out of hell. It seems to follow then that on universalism, the future of the most heinous criminals and ardent adversaries of God's prophets, messengers, saints (*awliya'*), and upright believers has an identical future with God—an identically *deserved* future it would seem. Such entailments run contrary not only to the plain verses of the Qur'an that point strongly toward salvific exclusivism through Islam but undermine justice as evil is not overcome. The former issue will be assessed further under responses to Argument 4 so I shall leave it for then. The importance of God's justice and indeed His triumph over sin and evil was already discussed under responses to Argument 1.

Naturalization: A third possible response to Argument 3 could be what I have called the "naturalisation" view of hell.[125] A type of this view is attributed to the Mu'tazilite Abu 'Uthman 'Amr b. Bahr al-Jahiz (d. 255/868–69)[126] by Abu al-Fath al-Shahrastani (d. 548/1153). It is explicitly found in Ibn 'Arabi and later extensively developed by Mulla Sadra.[127] On this naturalization view, the inhabitants of hell will perpetually remain in it but their chastisement will not remain painful forever because the fire of hell will eventually transform the natures of its inhabitants such that they will be naturalized to the pain, finding it in reality sweet and agreeable. Similar to this view without any attribution of transmutation of natures is that held by a heretical group called the Battikhiya named after Isma'il al-Battikhi as mentioned by al-Ash'ari:

> One group held the view that the inhabitants of paradise will delight in its
> bliss and the inhabitants of hellfire will also delight in its punishment just

like a vinegar maggot enjoys feeding off the vinegar and honey maggot enjoys feeding off the honey. This group is the Battikhiya.[128]

Turning first to al-Jahiz for the naturalization view,[129] al-Shahrastani writes:

Among his views is that regarding the inhabitants of hell, they will not endure eternal punishment but they will become like the fire itself (yasiruna ila tabi'at al-nar). He would also say that hellfire itself would attract people to it without anyone being made to enter it [by God].[130]

'Abd al-Qahir al-Baghdadi (d. 429/1037) mentions al-Jahiz's view that hell attracts people to enter it and not God who enters them into it but does not mention the view that its inhabitants transmute into fire:

One of the many infamies that al-Jahiz held include that God does not enter anyone in the fire. Rather, it is hell that attracts people into it by its nature and withholds them in it forever. This view will lead him to also hold that paradise attracts its inhabitants too due to its nature and hence, God does not admit anyone into paradise either. If that is what he would say, any desire to do good actions for the sake of God will be obviated and any petitionary prayers will be meaningless. If he says that God enters the people of paradise into paradise, then he would have to say He enters them into hell as well.[131]

As far as we can gather, al-Jahiz did not explicitly doubt the morality of divine punishment, that is, he was not challenging its justification manifested through hell. He also did not ascribe to any form of annihilation of hell either. Rather, he reconceptualized its eternity. The duration of hell does not involve unending conscious torment because its inhabitants will over time transmute into the very substance of hell—fire. A fuller account of this kind of view is presented by Ibn 'Arabi.[132] Ibn Qayyim in *Hadi al-arwah* surveys seven opinions (aqwal) on hell and describes Ibn 'Arabi's position as follows:

The second [view] is that [hell's] inhabitants will be punished in it for a period of time. They will then be transmuted by it such that their natures become like fire and begin to enjoy it because it agrees with their [new] nature. This is the position of the leader of the monists (imam al-ittihadiya) Ibn 'Arabi al-Ta'i.[133]

Chittick summarizes Ibn 'Arabi's view as follows:

> Ibn Arabi tells us that God does not keep people in hell forever in order to punish them, but rather to have mercy on them. They will eventually become accustomed to the torments and even begin to enjoy them, but if they were taken to paradise, they would be embarrassed before God and the prophets, and that would be a much more painful torment than the fires of hell.[134]

Ibn 'Arabi as we shall see upholds (H1) of the Mainstream View but modifies (H2), (H3), and (H4). He does not deny that hell is a place of punishment for those whose earthly life deserves it. He, like most of the scholars before him, accepts that hell will be populated by believers, but nevertheless they will attain either postmortem pardon or posthumous salvation. Any person other than believers, however, will remain in hell. This unending residence in hell, though, is qualified. He interprets Qur'anic passages in a way that suggests that punishment in hell is a finite phenomenon. On the exegetical points, Ibn 'Arabi to give one example comments that in the expression *khalidina fiha*, the feminine pronoun *ha* always refers back to the word *nar* (fire) and not to *'adhab* (chastisement), which is grammatically masculine. Another example is his combined reading of al-Baqara, verse 162, which refers to the punishment of nonbelievers as *never to be lightened* with Yunus, verse 52, that reads *then it will be said to those who had committed injustice, "taste the punishment of eternity! Are you not being recompensed for all that you did?"* He understands that the inhabitants of hell "tasting" its punishment is a bounded unit of duration and within that finite unit of duration the punishment will not be lightened. For him, it does not mean the punishment will never be lightened for an infinite duration.[135] Ibn 'Arabi's conclusion is that although there will be people who may be in hell forever, they nevertheless will not abide in their state of punishment forever.[136] He affirms this conclusion elsewhere by invoking the mercy maxim. In Yusuf, verse 64 it is stated that God is *the most merciful of the merciful.* Ibn 'Arabi eschews the status principle (SP) and upholds the proportionality principle (PP) objection by denying how finite and temporal acts of transgression can merit infinite duration of punishment. He ruminates:

> I have found in myself—who am among those whom God has innately disposed toward mercy—that I have mercy toward all God's servants, even if God has decreed in His creating them that the attribute of chastisement

will remain forever with them in the cosmos. This is because the ruling property of mercy has taken possession of my heart. The possessors of this attribute are I and my peers, and we are creatures, possessors of fancy and personal desire. God has said about Himself that He is "the Most Merciful of the merciful," and we have no doubt that He is more merciful than we are toward His creatures. Yet we have known from ourselves this extravagant mercy. How could chastisement be everlasting for them, when He has this attribute of all-pervading mercy? God is more noble than that![137]

Elsewhere, he echoes this same reflection:

How could there be everlasting wretchedness? Far be it from God that His wrath should take precedence over His mercy—for He is the truthful—or that He should make the embrace of His mercy specific after He had called it general![138]

In regard to divine mercy, this is his metaphysical foundation for the rationale of hell and the nature of its punishment for its inhabitants. Everything is brought under the essential property of God's mercy—a mercy that is totalizing and even governs other expressive qualities like wrath:

God says, *"My mercy embraces everything"* [7: 156], and His wrath is a thing. Hence His mercy embraces His wrath, confines it, and rules over it. Therefore wrath disposes itself only through mercy's ruling property. Mercy sends out wrath as it will.[139]

God's wrath Ibn 'Arabi here argues is not an essential attribute of God but a nonessential expressive quality, a nondefining contingent and temporary enactment of divine anger. What is essential and permanent is God's mercy and it is foregrounded prominently over all other attributes. This also means that mercy extends to the very abode of hell. God's aim is not to perpetually punish those in it—because for him punishment is not retributive but curative; rather, it is to show mercy toward them. This mercy manifests by making hell agreeable to the constitutions of its inhabitants, transforming their experience into pleasure and not suffering. Highlighting the terms "people" (*ashab*) and "folk" (*ahl*) referred to by the Qur'an in al-A'raf, verse 36 and the Prophet in a narration,[140] respectively, for those who ultimately inhabit hell, Ibn 'Arabi understands these references to mean such people or folk *belong* in hell; that is, hell is their rightful abode. If hell is their rightful abode, the chastisement in it ought to be commensurate with its inhabitants. In order to make this chastisement commensurate or agreeable with its inhabitants, God grants them a specific constitution at the conclusion of the Day of Judgment so that the chastisement eventually becomes pleasurable and not painful. Ibn 'Arabi comments:

> Then the chastisement is removed from their inwardness and they achieve ease in their abode. They find an enjoyment known by none but God, for they have chosen what God has chosen for them, and at that point they come to know that their chastisement had been only from themselves.[141]

Belonging to hell would mean that its inhabitants would be out of place, estranged, or "foreign" to the equilibrium of Paradise due to their sinful nature, and hence it would be an inappropriate abode for them.[142] Ibn 'Arabi writes how different natures or constitutions require their appropriate abodes:

> So, wisdom is not inoperative, for God keeps the bitter cold of Gehenna for those with hot constitutions and the fire for those with cold constitutions. They enjoy themselves in Gehenna. If they were to enter the Garden with the constitutions that they have, they would suffer chastisement, because of the Garden's equilibrium.[143]

Elsewhere he writes:

> When they give up the thought of leaving, they become happy, so they enjoy bliss in this measure. This is the first bliss they find . . . Thereby they find that the chastisement is sweet, for the pains disappear, even though the chastisement remains.[144]

On Ibn 'Arabi's view then, God overcomes the evil of eternal conscious torment of those who have through their choices and self-arrogation ended up in hell by exercising the totalizing power of His mercy. This exercise of totalizing mercy manifests in granting hell's inhabitants a "citizenship" for that abode by naturalizing them in it after a short period of direct chastisement. This naturalization process involves transmuting their natures or constitutions such that it agrees with the environment of their abode. Thus, the psychosomatic torment becomes something agreeable and sweet. Divine mercy therefore manifests neither in annihilation of hell nor in eternal conscious torment but alteration of hell's inhabitants to make experience of punishment ultimately pleasurable.

Ibn 'Arabi's view of hell no doubt caused controversy with those, on the one hand, absolving him of holding such a view and, on the other, those who responded with widespread condemnation branding him a heretic.[145] One immediate problem raised by his view is that it appears to squarely contradict the numerous verses of the Qur'an listed and discussed by, for example, al-Subki, al-San'ani, and al-Shawkani on the perpetual nature of chastisement in hell. The plain language of so many of these verses does not readily admit of figurative or imaginative theosophical interpretation. Therefore, exegetical strength does not seem to favor the naturalization account. Second, Ibn 'Arabi's model of hell comes at a metaphysical cost. His views as can be seen amount to a strong modification of (H2) and (H3), and although he affirms (H5), the result is something like the following:

> (a) Hell is eternal but from the perspective of its inhabitants, it is not endless conscious torment but endless delight.

For (a) to be possible, God effectively reconstitutes the very nature of its inhabitants. For a creature to be transmuted in a way that internalizes or is receptive to the fire of hell with a modality of enjoyment and twisted sort of delight would be to create a different type of creature. The divinely engineered alteration of creaturely constitution is too radical. It would undermine, for example, personal identity over time. The person admitted into hell although may still be similar in some respects to the person who was on earth nevertheless could not be *numerically* the same person because of the new constitution. In God granting a new and different constitution, He effectively is replacing the person's mental, psychological, and bodily properties with their counterparts that find metaphysical punishment experientially delightful. Third, the depiction of hell in the revealed Islamic sources strongly indicates a place of unimaginable torment that constitutes eternal misery. This eternal misery is not intermittent, in cyclical periods, nor is it moderate discomfort. It must be unending existence of which each moment or interval of chastisement is a bad state of affairs where the state of affairs is defined by the entire gambit of severe psychosomatic pain described in the Qur'an and Hadith. Ibn 'Arabi's account would render this notion of hell meaningless or otiose. Hell would not be the very abode it is if it involves delight of any kind. Last, as already pointed out with universalism, Ibn 'Arabi's view also undermines any notion of human autonomy but this time with the added complexity of his own views of the inefficacious reality of human actions and (thereby) human responsibility because such actions take place through God's interactions of His own names and attributes because, ultimately, there is only God and the created is merely the contingent site that plays out this Divine internal expressive dialogue. In the end, choice does not determine afterlife destiny; "creatures have no role at all in the acts that they ostensibly create and perform" and are therefore thoroughly determined.[146]

The Soteriological Problem of Evil

Muslim scholars extensively discussed the fate of nonbelievers who either lived their lives having never heard of the Prophet Muhammad and the message of Islam or have been reached with the message but for various reasons do not embrace the faith. If Islam is the exclusive culmination of earlier revelations and the Prophet Muhammad the seal of a long line of prophets and messengers through whom salvation alone is attained, then what would be the afterlife destiny of those who never receive his message? Would this mean large swathes of humanity will pass away without access to or understanding of God's mercy sent to humankind? Such status of being unreached would result in eternal damnation in hell, if we assume they are nonbelievers and have a rational obligation to know and seek out God. If this is the case, surely God would not want anyone to be unreached with the message of Islam and thereby deprive them of His mercy and means to salvation. To do so would be unjust because it would be setting them up for damnation due to circumstances beyond their control and choice. This serious challenge has been labeled the "soteriological problem of evil."[147] The argument can be stated with the following two allegedly inconsistent propositions (let us call it "SP" [the soteriological problem]):

SP:
(1) God is absolutely powerful, knowing, merciful, loving, just, and wise.
(2) All nonbelievers will be damned in hell forever.

Additional subclaims driving the force of SP include:

(a) God would want all persons to receive the final message of Islam,
(b) the unreached who are damned eternally in hell is incompatible with God's justice, love, and mercy,
(c) restricting salvation exclusively through the Prophet Muhammad would also be incompatible with God's justice and mercy, and the stronger claim that
(d) God would have no justifiable reason for creating nonbelieving persons who will end up in hell forever.

Efforts in this section to address this soteriological problem from an Islamic theological perspective will inevitably be partial and general as there is little space to unpack the entire gambit of related issues. I will first argue for a restrictive scope of damnation to only those who knowingly and willfully reject the message of Prophet Muhammad. This is one account evident in the theological tradition and assumes (or is compatible with) an exclusivist and inclusivist positioning on salvation. Thus, SP is a substantial problem for both the Muslim exclusivist and inclusivist and not arguably the Muslim annihilationist, pluralist,[148] and universalist view.[149] After outlining the argument for the inclusivist and exclusivist view, I will conclude why, if there is creaturely free will and God's right of self-vindication, some people will inescapably remain in hell forever.

Let me first outline the Islamic soteriological exclusivist and inclusivist views. The Islamic soteriological exclusivist (ISE) position is that Islam is the only valid salvific structure and that salvation is effectually and particularly found in the person of the Prophet Muhammad, meaning he is ontologically necessary for salvation.[150] On this view, Islam has arrived to set right the gradual entry of errors in all of its religious precursors, and the Prophet Muhammad has been sent as the final emissary of God and the temporal *loci* of His Mercy and vehicle of His message. However, on ISE, the beneficiaries may not necessarily and exclusively be Muslims. As will be shown below, other non-Muslims too can be beneficiaries of salvation without any formal profession of the faith. On similar terms with the exclusivists, the Islamic soteriological inclusivist (ISI) view upholds the finality of the Prophet Muhammad and the Islamic path as well as God's encompassing mercy but is receptive to the possibility that salvation may be gifted to other religious individuals or through alternative routes. That is to say, God's salvific will (His desire to want all to be saved from moral and spiritual destruction) can operate outside of religious persons who are not Muslims. I take ISI to be minimally claiming the following:[151]

(1) There is only one way of salvation and that is through belief in the Prophet Muhammad and belief in everything he brought.

(2) Some who do not explicitly/consciously/actively/intentionally have belief in the Prophet Muhammad and belief in everything he brought are saved.[152]

The proponents of ISI argue for the compatibility between both propositions through a number of ways of which two are: (i) a person being the beneficiary of the Prophet Muhammad's global intercession on the Day of Judgment even if one did not know him as the benefactor or was not a direct follower of his faith and (ii) by believing in the core tenets of Islam based on the evidence from natural reason when one did not have an actual encounter with Islam. Thus, on both ways, Prophet Muhammad would not be epistemically necessary for a person's salvation but will nevertheless be saved.[153]

Given this, there are two broad and relevant categories of people that require outlining before addressing SP. The first category includes those who were present within a particular historical time and as a result were the direct audience or recipients of an accurately and reliably communicated divine message brought by a prophet or messenger. In this category, such persons were informed and conscious recipients without any impediments beyond their control. If they embraced the message, they were believers and if they denounced the message, they were unbelievers. I shall use the term "reached" for this category. The second category consists of those who were not informed recipients of a divine message. They either had an unreliable and inaccurately communicated divine message or had no access to one for however long they lived due to impediments beyond their control (whether cognitive, physical, or other). I shall use the term "unreached" for this category. Based on this division, it will be argued how proposition (2) in SP is too strong. It is not the case in fact that all non-believing persons will be damned forever. There are exceptions and they include the following categories of excused persons from the unreached:

1. the 'people of the gap' (*ahl al-fatra*),
2. children of non-believing families,
3. the mentally and cognitively challenged (*majnun, al-ma'tuh*), and
4. the old and infirm (*shaykh al-fani, shaykh al-kharaf, harim*).

None is an informed or conscious recipient of a revelation from God. From the category of the reached who are excused we have:

5. those who are recipients of an entirely unreliable and inaccurately communicated divine message and
6. those who are recipients of a reliable and accurately communicated divine message with a religious disposition (they 'believe in God and the Last Day') but decline it based on sincere and earnest searching and investigation.

These six categories therefore include a diverse spectrum of people and as a result considerably reduce the scope of (2). Perhaps then (2) ought to be revised to give a weaker damnation proposition:

(2) Some nonbelievers will be damned in hell forever.

This revision of SP would relieve some of the force and power of the problem. Beginning with the reached categories first, the relevant matter that is of concern is what exactly constitutes culpable disbelief, that is, the kind of disbelief resulting in damnation. The word "belief" (*iman*) is generally defined as "conviction in the Prophet and whatever is proven decisively and unequivocally from him."[154] The word 'disbelief' (*kufr*) is defined oppositionally to mean absence of conviction. The Ash'arite jurist and exegete al-Baghawi (d. 516/1122) presents the definition of disbelief as follows:

> "Disbelief" means rejection (*juhud*). Its original [lexical] meaning is from the word "kufr" which means to cover something. This is why the night has been called a *kafir* because it covers everything with its darkness. The farmer has also been called a *kafir* because he covers the seed with the soil. Thus, a disbeliever (*kafir*) is someone who covers up the truth due to his rejection of it.[155]

Al-Ghazali, for example, tersely delineates the dividing line between belief and disbelief in a reductive way: which is acceptance or denial of what a prophet or messenger of God brings to the people.[156] Hence, belief is to accept what a prophet or messenger of God delivers and disbelief is to reject what they deliver. In the case of Islam, belief is to accept everything that the Prophet Muhammad brought and disbelief is to reject what he brought. The details of what exactly constitutes affirmation of (*tasdiq*) as well denial of (*takdhib*) what the Prophet brought is a matter of theological dispute that led to extreme schisms and polemical interchanges within Muslim theological denominations. Al-Ghazali's composition of a treatise entitled *Faysal al-tafriqa bayn al-Islam wa-l-zandaqa* ("The Decisive Criterion for Distinguishing between Islam and Heresy") was an attempt to articulate a cogent case for a more accommodating paradigm through an applicable set of theological and hermeneutical parameters and rubrics.[157] The aim was to widen the range of admissible theological perspectives where certain individuals within the Sunni fold were truncating that range. An aspect of that treatise addresses the fate of those who reject the message of Islam and the motivations behind that rejection. Al-Ghazali like many Muslim scholars before and after him were emphatic on the damned fate of any individual who willfully, arrogantly, deliberately, and subversively rejected the message of Islam.[158] This meant discussing at length the different types of culpable disbelief (often found in the exegetical literature).[159] Of relevance for the present discussion on soteriology are the following seven types of disbelief:

1. *kufr al-'inad* (disbelief through obstinacy), which involves a person knowing the truth but deliberately and stubbornly refusing to accept it;
2. *kufr al-inkar* (disbelief based on denial), which is to outright deny truth and belief inwardly and outwardly;
3. *kufr al-juhud* (disbelief out of rejection), which involves inwardly accepting truth and belief but outwardly manifesting something contrary;
4. *kufr al-nifaq* (disbelief out of hypocrisy), which is to inwardly reject belief and the truth but outwardly display its contrary;[160]
5. *kufr al-kibr* (disbelief due to arrogance), which is refusing to accept truth and belief out of one's unpleasant pride and crabbed ego;
6. *kufr al-i'rad* (disbelief through avoidance), meaning to turn away from and deflect from belief and truth; and
7. *kufr al-jahl* (disbelief based on ignorance), which involves rejecting truth and belief due to a severe lack of knowledge or learned facts.[161]

All these categories of disbelief are grounds for eternal punishment in hell because they constitute disbelief proper. Al-Ghazali too is in broad agreement with these types. The two exceptions that are excusable are those whose disbelief is due to an unreliable communication of the Prophet's message and sincere rejection of it. What governs these exceptions are epistemological. A person cannot make an informed and meaningful choice if there are no compelling reasons or arguments to do so. This is suggested in al-Nisa', verse 115 that reads, *If anyone opposes the Messenger after guidance has been <u>made plain and clear to him</u>, and follows a path other than that of the believers, We shall leave him on his chosen path—We shall burn him in hell; an evil destination indeed*. Ibn 'Arabi suggests that the presentation of the message of Islam must be accepted by each individual recipient in an unequivocal way so far as it is relevant for them, one in which it no longer becomes inculpable disbelief. He writes:

Note that [God] did not say, "[We do not punish] until We [have sent] a person." Hence the message of the one who is sent must be established for the one to whom it is directed. There must be clear and manifest proofs established for each person to whom the messenger is sent, for many a sign has within it obscurity or equivocality such that some people do not perceive what it proves. The clarity of the proof must be such that it establishes the person's [messengership] for each person to whom he is sent. Only then, if the person refuses it, will [he/she] be taken to account. Hence, this verse has within it a tremendous mercy, because of the diversity of human dispositions that lead to a diversity of views. He who knows the all-inclusiveness of the divine mercy, which God reports, [encompasses] all things [Qur'an 7:156], knows that God did this only because of mercy toward His servants.[162]

Ibn al-Qayyim is more explicit in this regard:

The third principle: establishing the indisputable [intellectual] proof varies from time, place and person to time. The proofs may be established against the non-believer at one time than another or one place than another or in one respect than another just like it may be established for one person and not another.[163]

Thus, the necessary epistemic conditions for inculpable disbelief (ID) regarding the message of Islam M would include:

(ID): a person S would not be culpable for disbelief in M so long as: (a) S fails to properly comprehend the core claims of M, (b) there are no defeaters for S's believing in the core claims of M.

The account of both Ibn 'Arabi and Ibn al-Qayyim shifts the emphasis from an external and formal set of markers that would automatically signify a willful rejection of the Islamic message to internal and subjective markers that consider how the recipient actually epistemically engages with the evidences.[164] I want to now outline each of the four unreached categories in order to give a little detail in addition to linking it to the description of disbelief outlined above. Regarding the first of the excused category, the *ahl al-fatra*, they are

people who've had no true access to God's religion . . . roughly translatable as "People of Times of Weakened Prophecy." They are those people who live in a time and place that the message of God's prophets has not reliably reached. The notion of the *Ahl al-Fatra* is based on the wording of Qur'an 5:19 and the principle laid out in Qur'an 17:15, namely that, "No bearer of burdens will bear the burden of another," and "We would not punish [a people] until We had sent a messenger."[165]

There are three major theological views regarding the status of *ahl al-fatra* and they are:[166]

1. The *ahl al-fatra* are from the excused and therefore automatically saved because technically they are not nonbelievers as they did not have the opportunity to either affirm or reject a message brought by a Prophet or Messenger and are not obligated by reason to either know God or act virtuously based on reason prior to the advent of a Prophet or Messenger.[167]
2. The *ahl al-fatra* are not from the excused and therefore are not automatically saved because they lack belief. For this reason, their default destination is hell. They are obligated by reason to arrive at knowledge of God and to act virtuously based on moral reasoning prior to the advent of a Prophet or Messenger.[168]
3. The *ahl al-fatra* are not from the excused and therefore are not automatically saved because they are obligated by reason to act virtuously failing which they will incur censure and blame in this world. However, their afterlife fate will depend on a postresurrection test—if they pass it, they will enter paradise and if they fail it, they will enter hell.[169]

The first position for the purposes of my argument will be taken as it appears to be evidentially more favorable.[170] The esteemed seventeenth-century scholar Muhammad b. 'Abd al-Rasul al-Barzanji (d. 1103/1691) argues for the saved status of the *ahl al-fatra* and by extension all unreached persons with a general argument that he presents in a syllogism. He writes:

We have stronger and much clearer evidence than that which is the following: Every non-believer will be in hell. Whoever does not receive the summons to Islam will not be in hell. From this conjunctive syllogism of the first figure in the first mood we have the conclusion: whoever does not receive the summons to Islam is not a non-believer.[171]

He then justifies each premise with textual evidence:

Explaining premise one: God (Most High) informed in many verses that all the non-believers will be in hell. He said for example, "*We have made hell for the non-believers as a prison-bed*"[172] where the letter *lam* is for generality giving the strong modifier: for every non-believer. God also said, "*Indeed, those who disbelieved among the People of the Scripture and the polytheists will be in the fire of hell, abiding forever in it*"[173] and the relative pronoun denotes generality. There are many other such verses. The [Messenger of God]—God bless him and grant him peace—said in an authentic report related by al-Bazzar in his *Musnad*, and al-Tabarani in *al-Mu'jam* with a channel of transmission all with upright transmitters from Sa'd b. Abi Waqqas (God be well pleased with him) and Ibn Majah relating from Ibn 'Umar (God be pleased with them both): "whenever I pass by the grave of a non-believer I give him the tidings of hellfire." Explaining premise two: God (Most High) says, *"We do not punish unless We have sent a Messenger."*[174] Ibn Jarir narrates as well as Ibn Abi Hatim from Qatada regarding this verse that: God does not punish anyone unless news has first come from God or some proof from [Him]. God also says, *"that is because your Lord would not destroy the cities for wrongdoing while their people were unaware."*[175] Al-Zarkashi mentions in *Sharh jam' al-jawami'* evidence for the view that showing gratitude to the benefactor is not obligatory rationally but textually.[176] God also says, *"And if not that a disaster should strike them for what their hands put forth [of sins] and they would say, "'Our Lord, why did You not send us a messenger so we could have followed Your verses and been among the believers?'"*[177] Al-Zarkashi also mentioned it. Ibn Abi Hatim mentions the explanation of the verse through a report with a good channel of transmission from Abu Sa'id al-Khudri attributed to the Prophet that he said: "the one who died in the period of *fatra* will say, 'my Lord; neither a book nor Messenger came to me' and then he recited this very verse. God says, *'And if We had destroyed them with a punishment before him, they would have said, 'Our Lord, why did You not send to us a messenger so we could have followed Your verses before we were humiliated and disgraced?'"*[178] Ibn Abi Hatim relates its explanation from 'Atiya al-'Awfi from Ibn 'Abbas and Qatada who both commented that: God does not punish a community until He has sent them a Prophet. When they reject and oppress him, they are destroyed for that reason. God says, *"And We do not destroy any city unless it had warners as a reminder. And never have We been unjust."*[179] 'Abd b. Humayd, Ibn al-Mundhir and Ibn Abi Hatim relate from Qatada that he said regarding this verse: God does not destroy a town except after the proof, clarification and excuse has been established or until messengers are sent or books revealed as a reminder for them, an admonition, proof, and remembrance. Regarding, *"and never have We been unjust,"* he commented that it means: We do not punish them except after the clarification and proof has been established. And God further says, *"And they will cry out therein, 'Our Lord, remove us; we will do righteousness—other than what we were doing!' But did We not grant you life enough for whoever would remember therein to remember, and the warner had come to you? So taste [the punishment], for there is not for the wrongdoers any helper.*"[180] The commentators mention that God is justified in punishing them because he sent a prophet. And this is what the word "warner" refers to in the verse. All these verses are clearer in their indications than the earlier ones because one may claim against them that the punishment refers to worldly destruction[181] but these verses are explicit that the cause for eternal punishment in hell and the inability to exit it is the advent of a messenger. And for God is all praise for the bounties He has given.[182]

What excuses the unreached then is that the very rationale or antecedent condition for damnation in hell—the advent of divinely dispatched prophets and messengers—is absent. Al-Barzanji summarizes the logic as follows:

It was known from the definition of disbelief (*kufr*) that the people of the interval (*ahl al-fatra*) before any summons to Islam reaches them are not considered non-believers according to the meaning that necessitates that they be in hellfire. This is because there can be no disbelief *per se* prior to a refusal and denial of that summons and their can neither be refusal nor denial unless it is after the summons has reached them, and there can be no summons except after a messenger has been sent by God.[183]

Regarding the second category of the unreached, the children of non-believers,[184] there are six general views held by Muslim scholars regarding their fate as discussed by the Egyptian jurist and hadith expert Badr al-Din al-'Ayni (d. 855/1453) and they are:

1. The children will be subject to the divine mercy and will (*mashi'a*). God will ultimately decide their fate.[185]
2. The children will follow the fate of their parents. If the parents are damned, so too will they.[186]
3. The children will remain in a type of intermediate state between heaven and hell (*barzakh*).[187]
4. The children will be made attendants for those in paradise.[188]
5. The children will be tested on the Day of Judgment—if they pass it, they are saved and if they fail, they are damned.[189]
6. The children will all be in paradise.[190]

Al-'Ayni lists this last position as the preferred theological one by specialists citing the statement of the Shafi'ite legal authority Yahya ibn Sharaf al-Nawawi (d. 676/1277):

This is the most correct position and the preferred one by the exacting scholars because of the verse, "*We do not punish a people until we send a Messenger.*" If a person who has reason and discernment is not punished because the summons of a divine message had not reached him, then *a fortiori* the one who does not yet have reason and discernment will also not be punished.[191]

The third category of the unreached are the cognitively impaired or those with mental disorders such that they lack *compos mentis* and hence cannot be the subject of legal accountability (*taklif*).[192] There are three general cases discussed. The first case is a person born with severe cognitive impairment but later in life is restored to normality or a threshold of normality by which they can make decisions and discern rights and obligations.[193] The second case is someone who lived a life without any mental disorders or impairments but in later life was afflicted by it.[194] The third case is a person born with severe cognitive impairment and dies in that state.[195] The first two cases have little disagreement among scholars as such a person will be judged according to what they did while in their functioning mental state. It is the third case that gives rise to three major differing positions which are:

1. The mentally impaired from birth to death will be tested on the day of Judgment just like the *ahl al-fatra*, the children of nonbelievers, and the old and infirm based on several narrations that inform how they protest their innocence before God on the Day of Judgment because they did not have any opportunity to access or were not audience to a revelation.[196]
2. The mentally impaired person will be among the saved as they are considered to be monotheists (*hunafa'*). Ibn Hazm states this position:

Regarding the mentally impaired (*majnun*) who have no mental faculties until they die, as we have already mentioned, they are born as monotheists (*millat hunafa'*), as believers, and they do not change or revert from that [innate belief], so they die as believers and thus will be in Paradise.[197]

3. The mentally impaired will be judged according to the belief of their parents based on al-Tur, verse 21, *And those who believed and whose descendants followed them in faith—We will join with them their descendants, and We will not deprive them of anything of their deeds. Every person, for what he earned, is retained.* Because they have no capacity to reason nor any actions based on free and moral decisions, they are automatically subsumed under their parents' beliefs.[198]

Ibn Taymiyà, Ibn Qayyim, and Ibn Kathir, however, all suggest a view that would anchor the destiny of each of the excused or unreached in a divine foreknowledge model of salvation. Ibn Taymiya, for example, argues that

> those who have not been given a decisive proof in this world through a divine message like children, the mentally ill, and the people of the gap (*fatra*), then there are a number of opinions regarding them where the most clear one is what has come in the various reports that they will be tested on the day of Judgment by God dispatching to them someone who will command them to obey or disobey God. Those who obey will merit salvation and those who disobey will deserve damnation.[199]

One of the evidences among others used by Ibn Taymiya is the following hadith by Abu Hurayra:

> Four kinds of people will be brought forth on the Day of Resurrection: the infant, the insane, the one who died during the *fatra* [the period between two prophets] and the old and infirm man. All of them will speak in their own defence. Then the Lord will say to a neck of Hell: "Come forth!" and He will say to them: "I used to send Messengers to My servants from among themselves. Now I am the Messenger of Myself to you. Enter this [the Fire]." Those who are decreed to be among the doomed will say, "O Lord, how could we enter it when we are trying to escape it?" And those who are decreed to be among the blessed will rush to enter it. And Allah will say: "<u>You would have been more disobedient towards My Messengers.</u>" So those will enter Paradise and those will enter Hell.[200]

Here, an afterlife test will be offered to those unreached in the temporal world. Their success or failure is based on how they would have been if they were to be in a circumstance in which they were to be reached by a divine message. Ibn al-Qayyim is more explicit in his proposal of a divine foreknowledge of counterfactuals applied to the fate of the children of nonbelievers. He comments on the hadith by Ibn 'Abbas that the Messenger of God was asked about the fate of the children of polytheists and he replied: "God alone knows what they would be doing because He created them":[201]

> This is the most balanced of the opinions, which reconciles all the evidences and brings all the narrations on this topic into harmony. On this basis, some of them will be in Paradise, as in the narration of Samura

whereas others will be in hell, as indicated by the narration of 'A'isha. The Prophet's reply also indicates this: "God knows best what they would have done, because He created them." It is known that God does not punish them on the basis of what He knows regarding them unless what He knows actually comes to pass. He only punishes whoever deserves it based on His foreknowledge of it and not because it is a new knowledge for Him. The object of His knowledge will manifest itself in the Hereafter. The phrase: "God knows best what they would have done" indicates that God knows what they would have done if they had lived. The ones who obey Him at the time of the test are the ones who would have obeyed Him if they had lived in this world and the ones who disobey Him at that time are the ones who would have disobeyed Him if they had lived in this world. This indicates that He knows about what does not happen and how it would have been if it did or had happened.[202]

Ibn Kathir reports this foreknowledge of counterfactuals as the strongest position held by early figures of Islamic theology:

Some held the view that [the *ahl al-fatra*] will be tested on the plains of the day of rising. Whoever from among them completes it successfully, they will enter paradise revealing the eternally prior knowledge of God regarding that success and whoever fails, they will enter hellfire revealing the eternally prior knowledge of God regarding that failure. This is the view that combines all the evidences . . . this was the opinion related by *shaykh* Abu al-Hasan 'Ali b. Isma'il al-Ash'ari from the orthodox group, it was the position defended by al-Hafiz Abu Bakr al-Bayhaqi in his book *al-I'tiqad* and other exacting scholars and specialists.[203]

Based on the above, God through His foreknowledge knows how a child *would have* responded to the revealed message or summons of a Prophet or Messenger during his life if he *were to* live it and the afterlife test is a demonstrative representation of what would have been the case. Hence, Ibn al-Qayyim's remark that "the ones who obey Him at the time of the test are the ones who would have obeyed Him if they had lived in this world and the ones who disobey Him at that time are the ones who would have disobeyed Him if they had lived in this world."[204] Therefore, those who would have freely accepted the revealed message merit salvation and those who would have freely rejected the message would be deserving of damnation. Given this view of foreknowledge, the unreached categories (i)–(iv) are not informed and conscious recipients of a revealed message and therefore are pardoned on the basis of God's knowledge of counterfactuals regarding their life course if they were to live it. They will enter paradise if they pass the test, otherwise they will be entered into hell. We could state this as follows:

> God knows that for any individual S under what complete circumstances S would freely accept or reject the revealed message of a prophet or messenger.[205]

The final category of the unreached includes the extremely old and infirm. The reason for their excuse is the inability to physically respond to the summons or due to the weakened powers of reasoning or intellectual undertaking. The narration mentions how the senile will protest their innocence against God arguing, "my Lord! Islam came to me but I was unable to understanding a thing! (*ya rabb, atani al-islam wa ana la a'qil*)."[206] Such a condition of senility does not enable informed acceptance or rejection of knowledge and belief claims. Hence, they are excused on the reasoning that if God does not punish anyone given the summons to Islam whose noetic structure is fully functioning, then a fortiori He will not punish those whose noetic structure is not fully or properly functioning.[207]

Even with this restricted scope of damnation, there still remains the fact that some people will be irrevocably hell-bound based on the revised proposition (2′) mentioned above. This must mean God cannot or does not desire to save everyone from eternal damnation. Indeed, (2′) entails that regardless of how restricted the scope of damnation is, some persons will nevertheless be consigned to eternal flames in hell. Why is it that all cannot be saved? To briefly answer this question, I will draw on what I have discussed previously throughout the chapter as well as offer additional points in order to thread them together into a closing set of claims.

First, it may be that some persons are in hell forever because regardless of whatever possible world God creates them in, they still choose to reject God's revelation revealed to the Prophet Muhammad. That is to say, no matter what circumstances they are in, whatever way things may be or could have been, their choices in either case will always involve willful and conscious rejection of belief in the Prophet Muhammad after a proper and informed delivery of the message of Islam. Second, those persons who willfully and consciously reject belief in the Prophet Muhammad are allowed to exercise that choice because they have free will. God will not coerce them into belief as that would be tantamount to forcing individuals to gain divine mercy and approval, which seems like a contradictory notion. What both these general points entail is that there cannot be a world where there are creatures with free will and no possibility of hell. All are not saved because that possibility is removed due to free will. The event mentioned in the Qur'an of Iblis's contempt in the divine presence is textual evidence that there is an option, a choice between alternatives: accepting God or rejecting God. This also shows how there are two outcomes from the two options: being included *with* God (heaven) and being excluded *from* God (hell). If either options or alternatives are removed, then it leaves only one option—God—but that would mean there can never be a way to actualize the consequences of rejecting God, no hell-bound person. Such persons would have no option *other* than God. Again, in the example of Iblis, if there was only one option, and that is to be with God, then his rejection of God would have meant he still had to *remain* with God despite defying God's command and becoming accursed. It would also entail God would have to tolerate or accept Iblis's defiance and rejection of Him. This would further entail that God would have no self-vindication of His glory, majesty, and greatness. Thus, if there is free will, it would not be possible for there to be a world in which all are saved and none are damned because given free will as a factor, there would be no guarantee that it will be used to only and ever accept God and the message of Islam. By way of an example, when a school drafts a behavior policy, included in it are procedures for rewards and sanctions. If it was a school where there were no human pupils but only robots that have no intelligence (not even machine intelligence), then it might not be all that meaningful to have a reward and sanction section in the policy because there would not be any grounds for the robots to merit reward and face sanctions because they would lack moral properties due to lacking moral freedom. Only a world in which there is no free will would there be no possibility of anyone going to hell because hell is necessitated by free decisions by some to consciously and willfully reject God through rejecting the message of Islam.

Conclusion

In this chapter, a number of issues were discussed related to the Mainstream View of hell demonstrating how that is compatible with the core attributes of God. The possible justifications for the existence of hell as well as its nature were also examined according to technical, theological, and philosophical views espousing a modification of the Mainstream View. Finally, the soteriological problem of evil was explored with a general suggestion why it is that given free will and God's right of self-vindication, it is unavoidable that some persons will reject and defy God and hence end up in hell. In the specific case of the Islamic message, the argument proposed was for a restrictive scope of damnation, one that excluded the category of those persons who never hear of nor receive a disambiguated version of the message of Islam. In the end, the only categories of persons who are included in the scope of damnation in hell forever are those who deliberately, consciously, and antagonistically reject the message of Islam.

6

Concluding Remarks

I have presented in this book possible reasons Muslim thinkers have given or can give for why it is that God either creates or permits evil. These reasons form theodicies and defenses that attempt to demonstrate the logical compatibility between God's attributes of power, knowledge, mercy, justice, and wisdom with various versions of the problem of evil. One of my aims was to unearth some strands of an enormously rich spectrum of intellectual engagement with these problems that may help the general non-Muslim reader gain insight into how specifically Muslims in the past thought about and responded to the different types and iterations of the problem. Another of my aims was to enable Muslims access to theological and philosophical arguments from within their own tradition as a resource to help them grapple with and think through the very same complex problems. In doing this, I have at times reproduced verbatim certain arguments and explanations presented by theologians and philosophers. Other times, I have reformulated their arguments in a systematic and methodical way. Yet other times I have embarked on my own speculative reconstructions and proposals based on certain precepts and ideas that wherever possible arguably comply with valid scriptural readings. Furthermore, I have tried to situate this book as a small but different contribution to an existing body of academic studies that have broadly established Islamic theodicy as a topic or field of inquiry.

In Chapter 1, I outlined the meaning of evil from the Qur'an and thereafter mentioned, in addition to Ibn Sina's account of evil, its conceptualization within mainstream Sunni theological denominations. In addition, I sketched the notion of theodicy and those motivated by an anti-theodicy position. This laid out the broad theological intuitions on the issue constituting the overall framework governing my analyses and discussions in the subsequent chapters.

In Chapter 2, I discussed the problem of evil as it relates to persons with disabilities based on how disability is (or can be) broadly conceived within Islamic teachings. The various theodicies I examined in the chapter were extracted from indications in the Qur'an and Hadith as well as internalized interpretations of the early Muslim community. My final proposed disability theodicy involved defeating a species of disability labeled "horrendous-difference disabilities"—those that utterly inhibit any meaningful mode of a person's living based on his or her wishes and desires and thus appear to defy any conceivable justification for their existence. My proposed maneuver to defeat these species of disability consisted in centering the subject of experience—the person with disability—as the primary unit of importance. Hence, the disability must enable the subject to unlock access to a meaning-making framework that is subjectively empowering. I then appropriated the notion of hospitality within the Islamic tradition as that meaning-making framework whereby through a shared acknowledgment of vulnerability, duty of care, and reciprocal enrichment, persons suffering horrendous-difference disability can come to internalize a sense of restored self-worth and generative value not only before a welcoming host community that embraces them but before God, who waits with an incalculable reward.

Chapter 3 was where I examined how the rich resources within medieval Islamic theology could be utilized to offer different ways in which animal theodicies can be constructed. After outlining the key ideas shaping the position, value, and importance of animals within Islam, I presented the Mu'tazilite theodicy as one that obligated God to indemnify or compensate the pain and suffering caused to animals with something greater. I contrasted this greater-good type theodicy with the Ash'arite and Maturidite positions. I framed the former as a skeptical theism variety that challenges a version of the evidential argument for evil that attempts to establish how pointless animal pain and suffering undermines belief in the God of Islamic theism. For the latter, I argued for a mystery theodicy where, ultimately, why animals feel pain or are made to suffer escape any cogent explanation needing the stance of a retreat into surrendering to God's infinite knowledge and wisdom and how He governs His creation. As a separate position, I argued for an animal theodicy based on the theological ideas of Ibn Qayyim al-Jawziya. At core, the theodicy is an educative theodicy model whereby human beings are made to deepen their reason for being created on earth in addition to enriching their appreciation and knowledge of specific attributes of God.

Chapter 4 extended my exploration from specifically nonhuman animal suffering to the wider problem of why the natural world based on natural selection embeds disvalues such as predation, pestilence, diseases, and species extinction and why God might permit such phenomena to occur. For possible theodicy models for this "Darwinian" or evolutionary problem of evil, I proposed a set of postulates for an Islamic theistic evolution and then derived possible theodicies based on those postulates as well as Qur'anic scriptural evidences.

In the final chapter, I attempted to tackle the problem of hell, which is one of the most serious challenges posed to belief in God and the core divine attributes that Muslims consider necessary for Him to possess. Here, I sought to address, on the one hand, how the creation of hell could be justified both textually and rationally using familiar Islamic precepts and notions found within the scriptural source texts of Islam and how on the other God could arguably chastise morally culpable beings for eternity. Thus, my aim in the chapter was to demonstrate how God is ultimately justified by creating hell as an everlasting destination of unimaginable torment and to also present the different ways Muslim theologians addressed the issue and the presuppositions guiding their respective accounts. In the final section of the chapter, I attempted to present a small discussion on the Islamic soteriological problem of evil and argued for a restricted scope of damnation in that only those who willfully defy and reject the message of Islam after a nonambiguous articulation of it is presented for consideration. In other words, any person who did not receive the message of Islam (or the message of any divinely dispatched prophet or messenger) is counted as saved and not damned. However, some persons will inescapably be damned because if there is genuine human free will and God's right of self-vindication, then there will always be some persons—irrespective of how many or few, where, when, and what circumstances they may be in—who will always willfully and antagonistically reject God and the message of Islam.

Undoubtedly, there is much this book does not cover and much that it may have failed to address. This is inevitable given the limited space and restricted scope and focus. Even so, I want to lay out one further avenue of exploration that I feel the field of Islamic theodicy could well take and indeed may require to take in order to reflect broader shifting attitudes and outlooks toward suffering and the human condition. Muslim theologians and philosophers ought to take note of the anti-theodicists' claim that there are serious limits to theodicies as explanatory models or accounts. Instead of focusing exclusively on theoretical arguments within a dominantly apologetic framework that characterizes much of

Muslim discourse on evil, a different direction for theodicy may be more pressing, which is one that uses the resources of the accumulated theological tradition (by which I also mean the spiritual dimension) to help anchor those who suffer and/or witness horrendous evils with constructive frames of reference rather than be moved to accept it as a primarily discursive puzzle to be solved. Sollereder has called this kind of approach "compassionate theodicy," which involves using theology "as part of the toolkit for people to reappraise their situations" with "sensitivity, appropriate timing" and as "tentative pieces of meaning making rather than as a done-and-dusted solution." Thus, theodicy is akin to a "meaningmaking endeavour." What this enables or helps facilitate is believers to "interpret their situation in ways that diminish emotional isolation and distress, and thus lower the overall perception of suffering."[1] This approach was attempted in Chapter 2 with my disability theodicy, albeit in a tentative and explorative manner. As Sollereder notes, adopting a compassionate theodicy would entail changes in (1) the audience and (2) methodology. Regarding (1), a shift *inward* toward the believing community and their condition should be made and not *outward* toward an adversarial community where epistemological concerns about disarming theoretical arguments against the existence or core attributes of God are the major preoccupation.[2] As for (2), a compassionate theodicy will sensitively concretize suffering and evil by disengaging it from "abstract data points in a debate" or avoiding reducing its functionality and significance to a set of propositions structured in a dialectical or formal argument. The aim, rather, is to engage evil and suffering with an array of practical and transformative tools, that is, to make it a phenomenological concern by operationalizing theology in life.[3] For specifically the Muslim community, primacy ought to be given to how the Islamic faith—its value categories, precepts, and practices—will play a role in the coping and meaning-making process for various contexts and situations the believer finds him/herself in. As Sollereder remarks, the approach of the compassionate theodicy is to "provide intellectual resources and not finished answers."[4] Hence, it places emphasis on a person's journey of growth, contextualization of adverse experiences, and reappraisal of suffering in order to ultimately draw closer to understanding God and His purposes for creation.

Appendix: Four Texts on the Problem of Animal Pain and Suffering

T ext One is a segment from al-Ash'ari's *al-Maqalat* outlining some early positions on the afterlife destinies of animals. Text Two is al-Ghazali's terse statements rejecting the doctrine of animal compensation in *al-Iqtisad*. Text Three is from al-Razi's brief exegetical discussion on animal compensation followed by his counter-points in *Mafatih al-ghayb* under al-An'am, verse 38, and Text Four is a segment from Ibn al-Humam's *al-Musayara*, which is a commentary on al-Ghazali's *al-Risala al-qudsiya*.

Text One—al-Ash'ari, *al-Maqalat*

On Their Disagreement Over Animal Compensation: They have differed over animal compensation giving rise to five views: (1) a group held that God will compensate [animals] in the Hereafter and will grant them bliss in Paradise and will give them the most beautiful form. Their bliss will not end. (2) Another group held that it is possible for He (glorified is He!) to compensate them in this world as well as the next. It is also possible that He compensate them in Paradise based on what we already related regarding the earlier proponents. (3) Ja'far b. Harb as well as al-Iskafi were of the view that it may even be possible that snakes and scorpions and similar dangerous and poisonous creatures are compensated in this world and the next. Then they will be entered into Hell as a punishment for the nonbelievers and the iniquitous. [The] animals will not suffer any of Hell's torment just like the Keepers of Hell (*khazana jahannam*). (4) Another group stated that we know that [animals] will be compensated but we do not exactly know how. (5) 'Abbad[1] was of the view that they will be raised and then annihilated. Those who held that [animal] compensation is everlasting differed, resulting in two views: one group held the view that God will perfect their intellects such that they will be given everlasting compensation where one will not cause pain to another. Another group disagreed, arguing that they will be compensated based on their condition in the world.[2]

Text Two—al-Ghazali, *al-Iqtisad*

We claim that God is able to bring suffering upon an animal that is innocent of any crime and that He is not required to reward it. The Mu'tazilites say that this is impossible because it is bad. Hence, they are necessarily led to assert that if a bug or a flea is harmed by being smashed or swatted, then God (Exalted is He) is obligated to resurrect it and compensate it for it. Others affirm that their spirits would return through incarnation into other bodies and would attain pleasure that is equivalent to their previous pain. This is a doctrine whose corruption is clear. We, however, say that bringing suffering upon those who are innocent of crimes, such as animals, children, and the insane, is feasible; indeed, it has been witnessed and perceived.

> There remains our opponent's statement, which is that God is obligated to resurrect the creature that is harmed and compensate it after that harm. We return to the meaning of "obligatory." It has been shown that being obligated is impossible with respect to God (Exalted is He). If they explain this by intending a fourth sense of "obligatory," then it is incomprehensible.
>
> If they claim that refraining from [this compensatory act] is contrary to His being wise, then we say that if by "wisdom" it is intended, as previously stated, the knowledge of the order of things and the power to produce this order, then there is nothing in [refraining from this act] that is contrary to wisdom. If another sense is intended, then the only form of wisdom that is due to God is what we mentioned; anything other than that is a meaningless expression.
>
> It might be said that this leads to His being unjust, whereas God says: *"Your Lord is never unjust to His servants."* We say that injustice is inapplicable to God due to pure negation, just as being oblivious is inapplicable to a wall and being frivolous to the wind. For injustice is imaginable on the part of someone whose act might affect what belongs to another, yet this is unimaginable with respect to God (Exalted is He), or on the part of someone who is under the command of another and acts in a way that is to contrary to this command. A man is not imagined to be unjust in whatever he does regarding his own property, so long as he does not contradict the commands of the revelation; [if he did], he would be unjust in this

sense. Thus injustice is inapplicable to someone who cannot be imagined to infringe upon the property of another or to be under the command of another. This is because the necessary condition for injustice is absent; it is not because such a one lacks something in himself.

Let this subtle point be understood, because it is the cause of the mis-understanding. If injustice is given a meaning other than this, then it is incomprehensible; and hence no affirmation or negation applies to it.[3]

Text Three—al-Razi, *Mafatih al-ghayb*

The rational ones (*'uqala'*) have two views regarding this. The first view states that God (Most High) will resurrect the beasts and the birds to compensate them; this is the position of the Mu'tazila. This is because causing them pain for a previous crime without compensating them is bad and because compensating them is obligatory. Thus, God will resurrect them in order to give them that compensation. The second view is the position of our companions, which is that God compensating them is absurd. Rather, He resurrects them based on His desire, will, and His divine prerogative. They adduce a number of proofs against the invalidity of the view that it is obligatory for God to compensate them. One of the proofs is that the term "obligation" refers to that which necessitates blame for omission of something, and God being necessitated with blame is absurd because God is perfect in His essence and it is inconceivable for that which is perfect in its essence to be necessitated with blame by an external command because that which has an essence cannot be frustrated by being subject to an external command. The second proof is that He Most High has absolute ownership over all created things and such a being can do anything in His possession without any need to compensate another. The third proof is that if it is good to cause pain to another in order to compensate them, then it would make it good for us to cause harm to another without his approval in order to compensate him, but that would be absurd. Therefore, the doctrine of compensation is invalid. And God alone knows best.

> Now that the [key] issue is known, we will mention some subsidiary discussions that Qadi 'Abd al-Jabbar mentioned in his book.[4] The first discussion: every animal must be compensated by God (Most High) for the pain they suffered. This compensation will not be granted in this world as it is rationally obligatory on God to resurrect them in order to grant that compensation; if that is not the case, then it would not rationally be obligatory for God to resurrect them. Moreover, He (Most High) informed about resurrecting all [animals] and that is established decisively from scripture.

What we only say is that there are animals that are not compensated at all because it may be that a part of their life remains that is shielded from any pain. After which He (Most High) causes them to painlessly die. There is no evidence to suggest that death is necessary and that pain always arises from it. Thus, according to such a view, no compensation is necessary whatsoever. The second discussion: every animal permitted by God (Most High) to be slaughtered must be compensated by God. [Those slaughtered or killed] are of different types: one type includes those [animals] permitted to be slaughtered for consumption. Another type includes killing those [creatures] that are dangerous like common predatory animals or harmful insects. Yet another type is those inflicted by pain and suffering [and are put to death] and another type includes those God has allowed to be ridden with a heavy load on them as well as used for strenuous work. As for if human beings wrong [these animals], then the compensation is obligatory on that wrongdoer. If, however, they harm each other, then the compensation will be on that wrongdoing [animal]. If it is asked on whom compensation is obligated regarding a person who slaughters an animal ritually (tadhkiyatan) but does not consume it, it will be answered that the wrongdoing will be attributed to the one who undertook the slaughter (al-dhabih) and he will be obligated to compensate. This is why the Prophet (God's bless him and grant him peace) forbade slaughtering animals except for consumption. The third discussion: what is meant by compensation is something with enormous benefit to such an extent that if the animal was intelligent and knew that the only way for it to secure this benefit was through being slaughtered, it would approve of it. This is the kind of compensation that makes causing [them] pain and harm a good. The fourth discussion: the position of al-Qadi ['Abd al-Jabbar] and that of most of the Mu'tazila of Basra is that compensation ceases. al-Qadi says: this is the position of most of the exegetes because they say that [God] (Most High) after compensating them, turns them to dust. At that time, the disbeliever will cry, "*I wish that I were dust!*" [al-Naba', verse 40]. Abu 'l-Qasim al-Balkhi argued that it is obligatory for the compensation to be perpetual (da'iman). al-Qadi's proof against this argument is that if it is considered good that a person from among us who commits to undertaking strenuous work is paid exclusively [for that work], then we know that causing pain to another is not a condition for perpetual payment. Al-Balkhi argues that the only way the compensation can cease is if the animal is caused to die but causing it to die necessitates pain and that pain itself must then be compensated and so on *ad infinitum*. The response to him is that there is no evidence to establish that death can only be realised with pain. And God knows best. The fifth discussion: if one animal is entitled to compensation from another animal, then if the wrongdoing animal (*al-zalima*) is in receipt of compensation from God (Most High), then God will transfer that compensation to the wronged animal (*al-mazlum*). If the matter is not as described, then God will complete that compensation directly. This is in brief some of the rulings on the Mu'tazilite doctrine of compensation. And God alone knows best.[5]

Text Four—Ibn al-Humam, *al-Musayara*

Another subsidiary discussion—which falls under the Sixth Foundation—is that God has the right to cause pain and punish any creature that did not commit a prior crime and has the right to deny a requisite reward. This is contrary to the Mu'tazila who did not permit this unless [He] compensates for it; otherwise He would be unjust and acting contrary to His own wisdom. This is why they obligated some animals to compensate other animals. However, we hold that injustice is disposing of something without ownership or entitlement. The evidence for that occurring is seen in the various trials animals are put through such as ritual slaughter or castration and similar acts without any prior crimes committed. If they argue that He (Most High) will resurrect the [animals] and reward them either at the time of the resurrection or in Paradise by entering them into it in the most beautiful form such that the inhabitants of paradise delight in beholding them or [reward] them in paradise distinguishing them according to their respective doctrines in that, we will reply saying that reason does not necessitate this. If reason does permit it but no text exists for it, it would not be permitted to definitively believe in it. Regarding what is reported about the hornless sheep attaining its right from the horned sheep, then if it is an established report, it refers to God including retaliation for creatures. That is not rationally objectionable according to us but is not obligatory on God (Most High) to do it. If the report is not established, we suffice with what is said.[6]

Notes

Introduction

1. At the time this book was being revised, the entire world was in the grip of one of the most serious pandemics in recorded history—the COVID-19 Coronavirus. Many asked where God was in the midst of all the suffering and death. Cf. the responses by John Lennox in *Where Is God in a Coronavirus?* (London: The Good Book, 2020).
2. Cf. the remark by Shabbir Akhtar, *The Qur'an and the Secular Mind: A Philosophy of Islam* (Oxford: Routledge, 2008), 82 n.39, and 358.
3. William M. Watt, "Suffering in Sunnite Islam," *Studia Islamica* 50 (1979): 5–6.
4. While completing the final editing of this book, I was unable to properly assess a recently published book on theodicy by Tallal Zeni entitled *Revival of Piety Through and Islamic Theodicy* (Independent Publication, 2020). I am grateful to the author for personal correspondence regarding its contents.
5. Imran Aijaz, *Islam: A Contemporary Philosophical Investigation* (Oxford: Routledge, 2018), 117.

Chapter 1

1. The literature on this topic is vast but for a comprehensive set of chapters, see the contributions in Justin McBrayer and Daniel Howard-Snyder, eds., *The Blackwell Companion to the Problem of Evil* (Oxford: Wiley Blackwell, 2013).
2. Adapted from Nick Trakakis, ed., *The Problem of Evil: Eight Views in Dialogue* (Oxford: Oxford University Press, 2018), 1–4.
3. On this notion, see Yujin Nagasawa, *Maximal God: A New Defense of Perfect Being Theism* (Oxford: Oxford University Press, 2011), 7–39.
4. Trakakis, *The Problem of Evil*, 3.

5. J. L. Mackie, "Evil and Omnipotence," *Mind* 64 (1955): 200–212.

6. H. J. McCloskey, "God and Evil," *Philosophical Quarterly* 10 (1960): 97–114, and his *God and Evil* (The Hague: Martinus Nijhoff, 1974).

7. William Rowe, "The Problem of Evil and Some Varieties of Atheism," *American Philosophical Quarterly* 16 (1979): 335–41.

8. Trakakis, *The Problem of Evil*, 3.

9. On this, see *Skeptical Theism: New Essays*, Trent Dougherty and Justin P. McBrayer, eds. (Oxford: Oxford University Press, 2014). See specifically, Michael Bergmann, "Skeptical Theism and the Problem of Evil" in *The Oxford Handbook of Philosophical Theology*, Thomas Flint and Michael Rea, eds. (Oxford: Oxford University Press, 2009); Timothy Perrine and Stephen J. Wykstra, "Skeptical Theism" in *The Cambridge Companion to the Problem of Evil*, Chad Meister and Paul K. Moser, eds. (New York: Cambridge University Press, 2017), 85–107, and T. M. Rudavsky, "A Brief History of Skeptical Responses to Evil" in *The Blackwell Companion to the Problem of Evil*, 379–95.

10. Trakakis, *The Problem of Evil*, 3.

11. See Trakakis, *The Problem of Evil*, 4–11 and the contributions in that volume.

12. Ibn Sina, *Al-Shifa': The Metaphysics of the Healing*, trans. Michael Marmura (Utah: Brigham Young University Press, 2005), 339–47.

13. Chad Meister, *Evil: A Guide for the Perplexed* (London: Continuum International, 2012), 3–4.

14. Nadja Germann, *"But Draw Not Nigh This Tree*: Evil in Early Islamic Thought" in *Evil: A History*, Andrew P. Chignell, ed. (New York: Oxford University Press, 2019), 198–209.

15. Tubanur Y. Ozkan, *A Muslim Response to Evil: Said Nursi on the Theodicy* (London and New York: Routledge/Ashgate, 2015), 19–35.

16. Ozkan, *A Muslim Response to Evil*, 34–35.

17. On overviews of his life and thought, refer to Soheil M. Afnan, *Avicenna: His Life and Works* (London: George Allen & Unwin, 1958); Lenn E. Goodman, *Avicenna: Arabic Thought and Culture* (Oxford: Routledge, 1992), and Jon McGinnis, *Avicenna* (New York: Oxford University Press, 2010), 3–26.

18. On evil in Ibn Sina's thought, refer to Shams C. Inati, *The Problem of Evil: Ibn Sina's Theodicy* (Albany: State University of New York Press, 2000), 65–102; Yahya Michot, *La destinée de l 'homme selon Avicenne: Le retour a Dieu (ma'ad) et l'imagination* (Louvain: Peeters, 1986), 59–68; McGinnis, *Avicenna*, 220–26; Ozkan, *A Muslim Response to Evil*, 51–56; Ayman Shihadeh, *The Teleological Ethics of Fakhr al-Din al-Razi* (Brill: Leiden and Boston, 2006), 160–69; Carlos Steel, "Avicenna and Thomas Aquinas on Evil"

in *Avicenna and His Heritage: Acts of the International Colloquium Leuven-Louvain-la-Neuve, September 8–September 11, 1999*, Jules Janssens and Daniel De Smet, eds. (Leuven: Leuven University Press, 2002), 171–96; Nada El-Bizri, *The Phenomenological Quest between Avicenna and Heidegger* (Binghamton: State University of New York Press, 2000), 95–128; Peter Adamson, "From the Necessary Existent to God" in *Interpreting Avicenna: Critical Essays*, Peter Adamson, ed. (New York and Cambridge: Cambridge University Press, 2013), 185–88; Maria De Cillis, "Avicenna on Matter, Matter's Disobedience and Evil: Reconciling Metaphysical Stances and Quranic Perspective," *Transcendent Philosophy Journal* 12 (2011):147–68; Sayeh Meisami, "Ibn Sina's Philosophical Interpretation of Sūrat al-Falaq," *Al-Bayan Journal of Qur'an and Hadith Studies* 15 (2017): 1–16, and Olga Lizzini, "Matter and Nature: On the Foundations of Avicenna's Theory of Providence: An Overview," *Intellectual History of the Islamicate World* 7 (2019): 7–34.

19. McGinnis, *Avicenna*, 222.
20. Inati, *The Problem of Evil*, 82–84.
21. Kenneth Seeskin, "Moses Maimonides" in *The History of Evil in the Middle Ages 450–1450*, Andrew Pinsent, ed. (London: Routledge, 2018), 109.
22. McGinnis, *Avicenna*, 222.
23. McGinnis, *Avicenna*, 222–23.
24. Inati, *The Problem of Evil*, 103–25.
25. Inati, *The Problem of Evil*, 127–67 and Mulla Sadra's very similar account analyzed in Ibrahim Kalin, "Why Do Animals Eat Other Animals? Mulla Ṣadra on Theodicy and the Best of All Possible Worlds," *Journal of Islamic Philosophy* 2 (2006): 157–82.
26. Consult the entries in parts 1 and 3 of *The Oxford Handbook of Islamic Theology* and the references therein.
27. The summary account of each school is adapted from Sherman A. Jackson, *Islam and the Problem of Black Suffering* (New York: Oxford University Press, 2009), 48–156 from whom I take the four-fold typology. For general elaborations on some of the four theological schools, see Eric L. Ormsby, *Theodicy in Islamic Thought: The Dispute over Al-Ghazali's Best of All Possible Worlds* (Princeton, NJ: Princeton University Press, 1984), 16–31; Timothy Winter, "Islam and the Problem of Evil" in *The Cambridge Companion to the Problem of Evil*, 230–48, and Ozkan, *A Muslim Response to Evil*, 37–65.
28. Margaretha T. Heemskerk, *Suffering in Mu'tazilite Theology: 'Abd al-Jabbar's Teaching on Pain and Divine Justice* (Leiden: Brill, 2000), 72–189, and Fauzan Saleh, "The Problem of Evil in Islamic Theology: A Study of the Concept of Al-Qabih in Al-Qadi 'Abd al-Jabbar Al-Hamadhani's Thought" (MA diss., McGill University, 1992), 54–117.

29. For Ash'arite accounts of evil, see Peter Antes, "The First Aš'arites' Conception of Evil and the Devil" in *Mélanges offerts à Henry Corbin*, Seyyed H. Nasr, ed. (Tehran: McGill University, Institute of Islamic Studies, Tehran Branch, 1977), 177–89; Mohammed Y. Hussain, "Al-Ash'ari's Discussion of the Problem of Evil," *Islamic Culture* 64 (1990): 25–38; G. Legenhausen, "Notes towards an Ash'arite Theodicy," *Religious Studies* 24 (1988): 257–66; Jackson, *Islam and the Problem of Black Suffering*, 75–98, and cf. Muhammad U. Faruque, "Does God Create Evil? A Study of Fakhr al-Din al-Razi's Exegesis of Surat al-Falaq," *Islam and Christian-Muslim Relations* 28 (2017): 271–91.

30. On evil in Maturidite theology, see James Pessagno, "The Uses of Evil in Maturidian Thought," *Studia Islamica* 60 (1984): 59–82, and Jackson, *Islam and the Problem of Black Suffering*, 99–125.

31. The Traditionalist account here is based mainly on the ideas of Ibn Taymiya; see Jon Hoover, *Ibn Taymiya's Theodicy of Perpetual Optimism* (Leiden: Brill, 2007), 177–208; Hoover, "God's Wise Purposes in Creating Iblis: Ibn Qayyim al-Ǧawziyyah's Theodicy of God's Names and Attributes," in *A Scholar in the Shadow: Essays in the Legal and Theological Thought of Ibn Qayyim al-Ǧawziyyah*, Bori, Caterina and Livnat Holtzman, ed., Oriente Moderno monograph series, 90.1 (2010): 113–34, and Jackson, *Islam and the Problem of Black Suffering*, 127–56.

32. Ormsby, *Theodicy in Islamic Thought*, 253–58, and cf. Justin P. McBrayer, "Counterpart and Appreciation Theodicies" in *The Blackwell Companion to the Problem of Evil*, 192–204.

33. Daniel Speak, "Free Will and Soul-Making Theodicies" in *The Blackwell Companion to the Problem of Evil*, 205–221.

34. Ormsby, *Theodicy in Islamic Thought*, 217–58, and cf. Hud Hudson, "Best Possible World Theodicy" in *The Blackwell Companion to the Problem of Evil*, 236–50.

35. Ormsby, *Theodicy in Islamic Thought*, 182–216.

36. Ormsby, *Theodicy in Islamic Thought*, 254–57.

37. Ormsby, *Theodicy in Islamic Thought*, 253–54.

38. I have found Mark Scott's *Pathways to Theodicy: An Introduction to the Problem of Evil* (Minneapolis, MN: Fortress Press, 2015) extremely helpful and this section is broadly adapted from pages 11–68.

39. See Immanuel Kant, "On the Miscarriage of All Philosophical Trials in Theodicy" in *Religion within the Boundaries of Mere Reason and Other Writings*, Allen Wood and George Di Giovanni, trans. and eds. (Cambridge: Cambridge University Press, 1998), 17.

40. Scott, *Pathways to Theodicy*, 56.

41. Peter van Inwagen, *The Problem of Evil* (New York: Oxford University Press, 2006), 6.

42. Chad Meister and Charles Taliaferro, *Contemporary Philosophical Theology* (London: Routledge, 2016), 16.

43. From Scott, *Pathways to Theodicy*, 64.

44. From Scott, *Pathways to Theodicy*, 65–66. Antecedents to Scott's own criteria are that of John Hick's dual criteria of (1) internal coherence (possibility) and (2) consistency with religious data and the experience of the world (plausibility), in "An Irenaean Theodicy" in *Encountering Evil: Live Options in Theodicy*, Stephen T. Davis, ed. (Louisville, KY: Westminster John Knox, 2001), 38–39, and Sarah K. Pinnock, *Beyond Theodicy: Jewish and Christian Continental Thinkers Respond to the Holocaust* (Albany: State University of New York Press, 2002), 138–44: (1) epistemic humility, (2) moral sensitivity, (3) religious practice, and (4) narrative memory.

45. Nick Trakakis, "Antitheodicy" in *The Blackwell Companion to the Problem of Evil*, 363–76.

46. Scott, *Pathways in Theodicy*, 173–92; Nick Trakakis, *The End of Philosophy of Religion* (London: Continuum, 2008), 11–30; Toby Betenson, "The Problem of Evil as a Moral Objection to Theism" (PhD diss., University of Birmingham, UK, 2014), 84–122; Kenneth Surin, *Theology and the Problem of Evil* (Eugene, OR: Wipf & Stock, 2004); Terrence W. Tilley, *The Evils of Theodicy* (Washington, DC: Georgetown University Press, 1991); D. Z. Phillips, "Theism without Theodicy" in *Encountering Evil: Live Options in Theodicy*, Stephen T. Davis, ed. (Louisville, KY: Westminster John Knox, 2001), 145–61, and Navid Kermani, *The Terror of God: Attar, Job and the Metaphysical Revolt* (Cambridge: Polity Press, 2011), 36–222.

47. On this school, see Amr Osman, *The Ẓahiri Madhhab (3rd/9th–10th/16th Century): A Textualist Theory of Islamic Law* (Leiden: Brill, 2014).

48. Mohammed Ghaly, *Islam and Disability: Perspectives in Theology and Jurisprudence* (London: Routledge, 2010), 25.

49. Ghaly, *Islam and Disability*, 25.

50. Omar Farahat, *The Foundations of Norms in Islamic Jurisprudence and Theology* (Cambridge: Cambridge University Press, 2019), 131–97.

51. Ayman Shihadeh, "Avicenna's Theodicy and al-Razi's Anti-Theodicy," *Intellectual History of the Islamicate World* 7 (2019): 67–76, 82.

52. Ibn al-ʿArabi, *Ahkam al-Qurʾan* (Beirut: Dar al-Kutub al-ʿIlmiya, 2003), 2:336.

Chapter 2

1. For an overview of disability studies, see Brendan Gleeson, *Geographies of Disability* (London: Routledge, 1999), 15–56.

2. See the Oxford bibliography entry "Islam and Disability" by Kristina Richardson at http://www.oxfordbibliographies.com (accessed March 2017).

3. Sa'diyya Shaikh, "Engaging Disability and Religion in the Global South," section: "A Constructive Ethical Reflection on the Quran and Disability" in *The Palgrave Handbook of Disability and Citizenship in the Global South* (Cham, Switzerland: Palgrave Macmillan, 2018), 156.

4. al-Razi, *Mafatih al-ghayb* (Beirut: Dar al-Fikr, 1981), 12:246–47.

5. Shaikh, "Engaging Disability and Religion in the Global South," 154–57.

6. Shaikh, "Engaging Disability and Religion in the Global South," 157.

7. Shaikh, "Engaging Disability and Religion in the Global South," 157.

8. For which see http://www.who.int/topics/disabilities/en/ (accessed November 2017).

9. As argued by Maysaa S. Bazna, and Tarek A. Hatab in "Disability in the Qur'an: The Islamic Alternative to Defining, Viewing and Relating to Disability," *Journal of Religion, Disability and Health* 9 (2005): 5–27.

10. See Mohammed Ghaly, *Islam and Disability: Perspectives in Theology and Jurisprudence* (Oxon: Routledge, 2010), 11–14 for a discussion on Arabic usage.

11. See, for example, Matthew L. Long, "Leprosy in Early Islam" in *Disability in Judaism, Christianity and Islam: Sacred Texts, Historical Traditions and Social Analysis*, Darla Schumm and Michael Stoltzfus, eds. (New York: Palgrave Macmillan, 2011), 43–62.

12. See Isra Bhatty, Asad A. Moten, Mobin Tawakkul, and Mona Amer, "Disability in Islam: Insights into Theology, Law, History and Practice" in *Disabilities: Insights from across Fields and around the World*, Catherine A. Marshall, Elizabeth Kendall, Martha E. Banks, and Reva M. S. Gover, eds. (Westport, CT: Praeger, 2009), 1:160.

13. See Bhatty et al., "Disability in Islam," 1:164.

14. For discussions around this, refer to the essays in *Cognitive Disability and Its Challenge to Moral Philosophy*, Eva Feder Kittay and Licia Carlson, eds. (Sussex: Wiley-Blackwell, 2010).

15. For a survey on disability and legal capacity in the Islamic tradition, see Mohammed Ghaly, "The Convention on the Rights of Persons with Disabilities and the Islamic Tradition: The Question of Legal Capacity in Focus," *Journal of Disability and Religion* 23 (2019): 257–78.

16. Ibn Taymiya, *Minhaj al-sunna al-nabawiya*, Muhammad Salim, ed. (Riyadh: Muhammad Ibn Saud University, 1987), 3:32.

17. Abdulaziz Sachedina, *Islamic Bio-Medical Ethics: Principles and Applications* (New York: Oxford University Press, 2009), 83.

18. Michael J. Murray, "Theodicy" in *The Oxford Handbook of Philosophical Theology*, 360–62. I take up the issue of hell and divine punishment in Chapter 5.

19. Sachedina, *Islamic Bio-Medical Ethics*, 77–78.

20. Sachedina, *Islamic Bio-Medical Ethics*, 78.

21. Vardit Rispler-Chaim, *Disability in Islamic Law* (Dordrecht: Springer, 2007), 8.

22. Sara Scalenghe, *Disability in the Ottoman Arab World, 1500–1800* (New York: Cambridge University Press, 2014), 67–68.

23. Ibn al-Jawzi, *Zad al-masir fi 'ilm al-tafsir* (Beirut: Dar Ibn Hazm, 2002), 303, and al-Qurtubi, *al-Jami' li-ahkam al-qur'an* (Beirut: Mu'assasat al-Risala, 2006), 6:468–69.

24. Sachedina et al., "Religious Perspectives on Human Suffering: Implications for Medicine and Bioethics," *Journal of Religion and Health* 55 (2016): 169.

25. al-Mawardi, *al-Nukat wa-l-'uyun* (Beirut: Dar al-Kutub al-'Ilmiya and Mu'assasat al-Kutub al-Thaqafiya, n.d.), 1:509.

26. Ibn al-Jawzi, *Zad al-masir*, 1069.

27. al-Razi, *Mafatih al-ghayb* (Beirut: Dar al-Fikr, 1981), 27:173.

28. al-Baydawi, *Anwar al-tanzil wa-asrar al-ta'wil* (Beirut: Dar al-Ma'rifa, 2017), 796.

29. See al-Fatir, verse 45.

30. al-Suyuti, *al-Durr al-manthur fi tafsir al-ma'thur* (Beirut: Dar al-Fikr, 2011), 7:355.

31. Ibn 'Atiya al-Andalusi, *al-Muharrar al-wajiz fi tafsir al-kitab al-'aziz* (Beirut: Dar al-Kutub al-'Ilmiya, 2001), 5:37.

32. al-Bukhari, *al-Sahih* (no. 6720).

33. al-Ghazali, *Ihya' 'ulum al-din* (Beirut: Dar al-Kutub al-'Ilmiya, 2016), 2:478.

34. Abu Dawud, *al-Sunan* (no. 705).

35. Ibn Abi Hatim, *al-Sunan* (Mecca: Maktabat al-Nazar al-Baz, 1997), 10:3279.

36. See al-Qurtubi, *al-Jami' li-ahkam al-qur'an* (Beirut: Mu'assasat al-Risala, 2006), 9:145–48, 17:367–69, and 20:53–54. Cf. Amos Yong, "Disability and the Love of Wisdom," *Ars Disputandi* 9 (2009): 57.

37. See al-Baqara, verse 286.

38. Ghaly, *Islam and Disability*, 44 (italics are author's emphasis).

39. Rispler-Chaim, *Disability in Islamic Law*, 8.

40. Ghaly, *Islam and Disability*, 44.

41. Abu Dawud, *al-Sunan* (no. 3090).

42. al-Bukhari, *al-Sahih* (no. 5641–2).

43. Cited by Mulla 'Ali al-Qari in *Tasliyat al-a'ma 'ala baliyat al-'ama* (Tanta: Dar Sahaba, 1993), 31. See the editor's comments on the nonauthenticity of this narration.

44. Ibn Qayyim, *al-Tibb al-nabawi* (Beirut: Dar al-Fikr, n.d.), 152.

45. See *Theodicy in the World of the Bible: The Goodness of God and the Problem*

of Evil, Laato, Anitti and Johannes de Moor, eds. (Leiden: Brill, 2003), xlviii–liii.

46. Ahmad, *al-Musnad* (no. 649) and Abu Ya'la, *al-Musnad*, 1:351–53 (no. 435) cited and translated in Ghaly, *Islam and Disability*, 44.

47. Ghaly, *Islam and Disability*, 44–45.

48. al-Suyuti, *Jami' al-hadith al-jami' al-saghir wa-zawa'iduhu wa-l-jami' al-kabir* (Beirut: Dar al-Fikr, 1994), 5:364–65 (no. 19322) and al-Hakim, *al-Mustadrak 'ala al-sahihayn*, 1:449 (no. 1287) and others cited and translated in Ghaly, *Islam and Disability*, 45. For a discussion, see Ibn Hajar al-'Asqalani, *Fath al-Bari* (Riyadh: Maktabat al-Malik Fahad al-Wataniya, 2001), 10:107–115 (no. 5442–44).

49. Ghaly, *Islam and Disability*, 45.

50. Taken from Ana-Maria Rizzuto's distinction in her seminal work *The Birth of the Living God: A Psychoanalytic Study* (Chicago: University of Chicago Press, 1979).

51. On this genre, see Scott C. Lucas, "Forty Traditions," *Encyclopaedia of Islam* 3 (Leiden and Boston: Brill, 2017), 107–11.

52. 'Ali al-Qari, *Tasliyat al-a'ma*, 47. On blindness and its privileged status in the cultural hierarchy of impairments, see Scalenghe, *Disability in the Ottoman World*, 52–87.

53. 'Ali al-Qari, *Tasliyat al-a'ma*, 32–36.

54. 'Ali al-Qari, *Tasliyat al-a'ma*, 31.

55. 'Ali al-Qari, *Tasliyat al-a'ma*, 44. One of the meanings of the phrase "brightened face" *(tabayyud al-wajh)* is a figurative reference to the registered expression of happiness, delight, and joy on Judgment Day. Al-Razi, *Mafatih al-ghayb* (Beirut: Dar al-Fikr, 1981), 8:185–6.

56. 'Ali al-Qari, *Tasliyat al-a'ma*, 30, 46.

57. 'Ali al-Qari, *Tasliyat al-a'ma*, 41–42.

58. 'Ali al-Qari, *Tasliyat al-a'ma*, 41–42.

59. For critiques of G-G type theodicies, see Bruce A. Little, *A Creation-Order Theodicy: God and Gratuitous Evil* (Lanham, MD: University Press of America, 2004), 99–128, and his *God, Why This Evil?* (Plymouth: Hamilton Books, 2010), 58–79.

60. Sachedina, *Islamic Bio-Medical Ethics*, 90.

61. Sachedina, *Islamic Bio-Medical Ethics*, 91.

62. al-Bukhari, *Sahih* (no. 2265).

63. Kristina L. Richardson, *Difference and Disability in the Medieval Islamic World: Blighted Bodies* (Edinburgh: Edinburgh University Press, 2010), 41–42.

64. Ibn Hajar al-'Asqalani, *Fath al-bari sharh sahih al-bukhari* (Riyadh: Maktabat Malik Fahad, 2001), 10:120.

65. Anthony H. Johns, "A Comparative Glance at Ayyub in the Qur'an" in *Deconstructing Theodicy: Why Job Has Nothing to Say to the Puzzled Suffering*, David B. Burrell, ed. (Grand Rapids, MI: Brazos Press, 2008), 51–82.

66. On the notion of purification of the soul in Islamic theology, see the extensive treatment by Gavin Picken in *Spiritual Purification in Islam: The Life and Works of al-Muhasibi* (Oxon: Routledge, 2011), 123–67.

67. A. Aslan, "The Fall, Evil and Suffering in Islam" in *The Origin and the Overcoming of Evil and Suffering in the World Religions*, Peter Koslowski, ed. (Dordrecht: Springer, 2001), 42–47, and Ghaly, *Islam and Disability*, 54–62.

68. Nasrin Rouzati, *Trial and Tribulation in the Qur'an* (Berlin: Gerlach Press, 2015), 8–60.

69. Rouzati, *Trial and Tribulation in the Qur'an*, 126.

70. Rouzati, *Trial and Tribulation in the Qur'an*, 126–27.

71. Jalal al-Din Rumi, *Diwan Shams Tabrizi*, 120, 74–79, trans. William C. Chittick in *The Sufi Path of Love: The Spiritual Teachings of Rumi* (Albany: State University of New York Press, 1983), 239.

72. Mohammad Ali Mobini, "Earth's Epistemic Fruits for Harmony with God: An Islamic Theodicy" in *The Blackwell Companion to the Problem of Evil*, 304.

73. Aslan, "The Fall, Evil and Suffering in Islam," 42.

74. Aslan, "The Fall, Evil and Suffering in Islam," 43–44.

75. Aslan, "The Fall, Evil and Suffering in Islam," 44.

76. Rouzati, *Trial and Tribulation in the Qur'an*, 104.

77. I discuss this notion of the primordial covenant in Chapter 5 under the problem of hell.

78. Rouzati, *Trial and Tribulation in the Qur'an*, 127.

79. Jalal al-Din Rumi, *Diwan Shams Tabrizi* 35486–87; 3952, trans. William C. Chittick in *The Sufi Path of Love*, 238.

80. Jalal al-Din Rumi, *Fihi ma fihi*, cited and trans. in Rouzati, *Trial and Tribulation*, 128.

81. 'Ali al-Qari, *Tasliyat al-a'ma*, 29.

82. Ibn 'Ashur, *al-Tahrir wa-l-tanwir* (Tunis: Dar al-Tunisiya, 1984), 17:288–89. See as well the discussion in *Ruh al-ma'ani fi tafsir al-qur'an al-'azim wa-l-Sab' al-mathani* (Beirut: Dar Ihya' al-Turath al-'Arabi, 1985), 17:166–9. See as well Rispler-Chaim, *Disability in Islamic Law*, 8–9; Ghaly, *Islam and Disability*, 13–14, 173, fn.128; "Seeing and Hearing," 4:573–76 (Andrew Rippin), "Vision and Blindness," 5:445–48 (Scott Kugle) in *EQ*, and Scalenghe, *Disability in the Ottoman Arab World*, 68–70.

83. For which see Ze'ev Maghen's study, *Virtues of the Flesh: Passion and Purity in Early Islamic Jurisprudence* (Leiden: Brill, 2005), 3–40.

84. Taken from Bryan S. Turner, *Regulating Bodies: Essays in Medical Sociology* (London: Routledge, 2002).

85. Muslim, *Sahih* (no. 2564).

86. al-Nawawi, *Sharh Sahih Muslim* (Cairo: al-Matba'at al-Misriya, 1930), 16:121.

87. Based primarily on Mona Siddiqui's *Hospitality and Islam: Welcoming in God's Name* (New Haven, CT: Yale University Press, 2015).

88. Alasdair MacIntyre, *Dependent Rational Animals: Why Human Beings Need the Virtues* (Chicago, IL: Carus, 1999).

89. Kevin Timpe and Aaron D. Cobb, "Disability and Theodicy of Defeat," *Journal of Analytic Theology* 5 (2017): 100–120.

90. Marilyn McCord Adams, *Horrendous Evil and the Goodness of God* (Ithaca, NY: Cornell University Press, 1999).

91. See Scott M. Williams, "Horrendous-Difference Disabilities, Resurrected Saints, and the Beatific Vision: A Theodicy," *Religions* 9 (2018): 1–13.

92. Adams, *Horrendous Evil and the Goodness of God*, 26.

93. Adams, *Horrendous Evil and the Goodness of God*, 26.

94. Adams, *Horrendous Evil and the Goodness of God*, 146.

95. Adams, *Horrendous Evil and the Goodness of God*, 148.

96. Adams, *Horrendous Evil and the Goodness of God*, 177–80.

97. Chisholm, "The Defeat of Good and Evil," *Proceedings of the American Philosophical Association* 42 (1968): 61.

98. Adams, *Horrendous Evil and the Goodness of God*, 31.

99. Adams, *Horrendous Evil and the Goodness of God*, 28–29.

100. William Bell, "Horrendous Evil and the Problem of Representation" (MA diss., University of Missouri, St. Louis, 2016), 13.

101. Adams, *Horrendous Evil and the Goodness of God*, 80.

102. Adams, *Horrendous Evil and the Goodness of God*, 167, and Marilyn McCord Adams, "Ignorance, Instrumentality, Compensation, and the Problem of Evil," *Sophia* 52 (2013): 20.

103. Adams, *Horrendous Evil and the Goodness of God*, 28.

104. Adams, *Horrendous Evil and the Goodness of God*, 80–85.

105. Andrew Chignell, "The Problem of Infant Suffering," *Religious Studies* 34 (1998): 205–17.

106. Richard Cross, "Impairment, Normalcy, and a Social Theory of Disability," *Res Philosophica* 93 (2016): 693–714.

107. Williams, "Horrendous-Difference Disabilities," 2.

108. Williams, "Horrendous-Difference Disabilities," 2.

109. Williams, "Horrendous-Difference Disabilities," 2–3.

110. Williams, "Horrendous-Difference Disabilities," 5–6.

111. See book 33 of al-Ghazali's *Ihya'*, trans. William MacKane as *Book of Fear and Hope* (Leiden: Brill, 1965).

112. See book 36 of al-Ghazali's *Ihya'*, trans. Eric Ormsby as *Al-Ghazali on*

Love, Longing, Intimacy, and Contentment (Cambridge: Islamic Texts Society, 2016).

113. See book 25 of al-Ghazali's *Ihya'*, trans. David B. Burrell as *Faith in Divine Unity and Trust in Divine Providence* (Louisville, KY: Fons Vitae, 2002).

114. See book 15 of al-Ghazali's *Ihya'*, partial trans. Muhtar Holland as *Duties of Brotherhood in Islam* (Leicester: Islamic Foundation, 1980).

115. El-Sayed El-Aswad, "Hospitality" in *Encyclopaedia of Islam and the Muslim World*, Richard C. Martin, ed. (New York: Macmillan, 2003), 462.

116. El-Aswad, "Hospitality," 462.

117. El-Aswad, "Hospitality," 462.

118. Siddiqui, *Hospitality and Islam*, 10–11.

119. Siddiqui, *Hospitality and Islam*, 29.

120. Siddiqui, *Hospitality and Islam*, 29.

121. Siddiqui, *Hospitality and Islam*, 18.

122. Siddiqui, *Hospitality and Islam*, 18–19.

123. Siddiqui, *Hospitality and Islam*, 29.

124. Siddiqui, *Hospitality and Islam*, 32–33.

125. Siddiqui, *Hospitality and Islam*, 35.

126. Siddiqui, *Hospitality and Islam*, 55–56.

127. Siddiqui, *Hospitality and Islam*, 82.

128. What is between the square brackets is taken from al-Suyuti's *al-Durr al-manthur fi-l-tafsir al-ma'thur* (Cairo: Markaz al-Hajar, 2003), 6:658–59, and 662–63.

129. al-Bayhaqi, *Shu'ab al-iman*, Sa'id Zaghlul, ed. (Beirut: Dar al-Kutub al-'Ilmiya, 2000), 4:107 (no. 4441).

130. What is between the square brackets is taken from al-Suyuti's *al-Durr al-Manthur*, 6:663.

131. Ormsby, *Theodicy in Islamic Thought*, 197–202.

132. Muslim, *Sahih (no. 2569)* cited and trans. in Siddiqui, *Hospitality and Islam*, 125. I have replaced the Arabic word *rabb* with "Lord."

133. MacIntyre, *Dependent Rational Animals*, 1.

134. MacIntyre, *Dependent Rational Animals*, 82.

135. MacIntyre, *Dependent Rational Animals*, 120.

136. Timpe and Cobb, "Disability and the Theodicy of Defeat," 112.

137. Timpe and Cobb, "Disability and the Theodicy of Defeat," 111. See as well a very similar account of vulnerability and host–guest reciprocity in Reynolds, *Vulnerable Communion*, 104–132, 137–38 and 164–65.

138. A. Cobb, "Acknowledged Dependence and the Virtues of Perinatal Hospice," *Journal of Medicine and Philosophy* 42 (2016): 31.

139. Cobb, "Acknowledged Dependence and the Virtues of Perinatal Hospice," 31.

140. Timpe and Cobb, "Disability and the Theodicy of Defeat," 110–11.

141. Reynolds, *Vulnerable Communion*, 41. See as well Kathy Black, *A Healing Homiletic: Preaching and Disability* (Nashville, TN: Abingdon Press, 1996), 27–28.

142. Reynolds, *Vulnerable Communion*, 41.

143. Reynolds, *Vulnerable Communion*, 41.

144. Reynolds, *Vulnerable Communion*, 42.

145. Nancy L. Eiesland, *The Disabled God: Toward a Liberatory Theology of Disability* (Nashville, TN: Abingdon Press, 1994), 48.

146. Reynolds, *Vulnerable Communion*, 42 and cf. Sachedina, *Islamic Bio-Medical Ethics*, 79.

147. Deborah R. Barnbaum, *The Ethics of Autism: Among Them but Not of Them* (Bloomington: Indiana University Press, 2008), 104.

148. Barnbaum, *The Ethics of Autism*, 104.

149. Reynolds, *Vulnerable Communion*, 38.

150. Reynolds, *Vulnerable Communion*, 39.

151. Shaikh, "Engaging Disability and Religion," 160.

152. Shaikh, "Engaging Disability and Religion," 160.

153. al-Tirmidhi, *al-Sunan* (no. 3292).

Chapter 3

1. See the brief treatments in al-'Amiri, *Mushkilat al-sharr*, 166–86; Didier Gazagnadou, "Note on the Question of Animal Suffering in Medieval Islam: Muslim Mu'tazilite Theology Confronted by Manichean Iranian Thought," *Anthropology of the Middle East* 11 (2016): 30–35, and Cüneyt M. Şimsek, "The Problem of Animal Pain: An Introduction to Nursi's Approach" in *Theodicy and Justice in Modern Islamic Thought: The Case of Said Nursi*, Ibrahim M. Abu Rabi', ed. (Farnham: Ashgate, 2010), 111–34. On Heemskerk's treatment, see my discussion below.

2. On animals within the Islamic sources, see Richard Foltz, *Animals in Islamic Traditions and Muslim Cultures* (London: Oneworld, 2006), 11–27 with broad summaries in his chapter "'This She-Camel Is a Sign to You'": Dimensions of Animals in Islamic Tradition and Muslim Culture" in *A Communion of Subjects: Animals in Religion, Science and Ethics*, Paul Waldau and Kimberley Patton, eds. (New York: Columbia University Press, 2006), 149–59; *L'Animal en Islam*, Mohammed H. Benkheira, C. Mayeur-Jaouen, and J. Sublet, eds. (Paris: Les Indes Savantes, 2005); Katherine Perlo, *Kinship and Killing: The Animals in World Religions* (New York: Colombia University Press, 2009), 95–113; Neil Robinson, *The Sayings of Muhammad* (London: Duckworth, 1991), 48–49; Sara Tlili, *Animals in the Qur'an* (New York: Cambridge University Press, 2012), part 2; Basheer Masri, *Animal*

Welfare in Islam (Leicester: Islamic Foundation, 2007), 2–55; Daniel Capper, *Learning Love from a Tiger: Religious Experiences with Nature* (Oakland: University of California Press, 2016), 68–97; Barbara Allen, *Animals in Religion: Devotion, Symbol and Ritual* (London: Reaktion Books, 2016), 242–88; Lisa Kemmerer, *Animals and World Religions* (New York: Oxford University Press, 2012), 241–76; A. Gazonneau, "L'Animal et L'Islam à Travers le Temps" (PhD diss., National Veterinary School of Alfort, 2019), 19–89, and G. H. Bousquet, "Des Animaux et de leur traitement selon le Judaïsme, le Christianisme et l'Islam," *Studia Islamica* 9 (1958): 31–48. Tlili reviews the current state of scholarship on animal ethics in Islam in her article "Animal Ethics in Islam: A Review Article," *Religions* 9 (2018): 1–18. By the term 'animal' I am referring in general to any nonhuman creature.

3.   On speciesism, see Richard Ryder, *Speciesism, Painism and Happiness: A Morality for the Twentieth Century* (Exeter: Imprint Academic, 2015), 38–61 as well as the essays in Rob Boddice, ed., *Anthropocentricism: Humans, Animals and Environments* (Leiden: Brill, 2011).

4.   On the material and spiritual benefits animals offer for human flourishing, see Tlili, *Animals in the Qur'an*, 79–91.

5.   See Foltz, *Animals in Islamic Tradition*, 19–36 for the examples and their references. On animal rights in Islam, see M. Azzam, "Islamic Philosophy on Human Rights" in *Animal Ethics and Trade: The Challenge of Animal Sentience*, Joyce D'Silva and Jacky Turner, eds. (London: Earthscan, 2006), 129–33; Bagher Larijani, Nazafarin Ghasemzadeh, and Mansoureh Madani, "Animal Rights in Islam: The Use of Animals for Medical Research" in *Islamic Bioethics: Current Issues and Challenges*, Alireza Bagheri and Khalid Alali, eds. (London: World Scientific Publishing, 2017), 183–96, and Mawil Izzi Dien, *The Environmental Dimensions of Islam* (Cambridge: Lutterworth, 2000), 45–46 who translates a list of obligations drafted in *Qawa'id al-ahkam fi masalih al-anam* by the Shafi'ite jurist al-'Izz b. 'Abd al-Salam al-Sulami (d. 660/1262). Cf. as well Musa Furber, "Rights and Duties Pertaining to Kept Animals: A Case Study in Islamic Law and Ethics," *Tabah Paper Series* no. 9 (2015): 30–34.

6.   al-Bukhari, *al-Sahih* (no. 3318).

7.   See *The Case of the Animals versus Man before the King of the Jinn: An Arabic Critical Edition and English Translation of Epistle 22*, Lenn Goodman and Richard McGregor, eds. (Oxford: Oxford University Press in Association with The Institute of Ismaili Studies, 2010). On this epistle, see Godefroid de Callataÿ, "'For Those With Eyes to See': On the Hidden Meaning of the Animal Fable in the Rasa'il Ikhwan al-Safa," *Journal of Islamic Studies* 29 (2018): 1–36; Zayn Kassam, "The Case of the Animals Versus Man: Toward an Ecology of Being" in *A Communion of Subjects*, 160–69, and Sara Tlili,

"All Animals Are Equal, or Are They? The Ikhwan al-Safa's Animal Epistle and Its Unhappy End," *Journal of Qur'anic Studies* 16 (2014): 42–88.

8. For overviews on the Ikhwwn al-Safa, see Ian R. Netton, *Muslim Neoplatonists: An Introduction to the Thought of the Brethren of Purity* (London: RoutledgeCurzon, 2013), and Godefroid de Callataÿ, *Ikhwan al-Safa': A Brotherhood of Idealists on the Fringe of Orthodox Islam* (Oxford: Oneworld, 2005).

9. See al-Razi, *Mafatih al-ghayb*, 1st ed. (Beirut: Dar al-Fikr, 1987), 12:223–25.

10. See al-Alusi, *Ruh al-ma'ani fi tafsir al-qur'an al-'azim wa-l-sab' al-mathani* (Beirut: Dar Ihya' al-Turath al-'Arabi, n.d.), 7:146–47.

11. al-Alusi, *Ruh al-ma'ani*, 7:146.

12. al-Alusi, *Ruh al-ma'ani*, 7:146.

13. al-Alusi, *Ruh al-ma'ani*, 7:146.

14. al-Alusi, *Ruh al-ma'ani*, 7:147. On this discussion, see as well al-Razi, *Mafatih al-ghayb*, 12:224.

15. On al-Daylami, see the introduction in *A Treatise on Mystical Love*, xii–lxix (fully cited below).

16. al-Daylami, *Kitab 'atf al-alif al-ma'luf 'ala al-lam al-ma'tuf* ('A Treatise on Mystical Love'), trans. Joseph Norman Bell and Hassan Al Shafie (Edinburgh: Edinburgh University Press, 2005), 160–61.

17. On this idea, see Robert Mitchell, Thompson Nicholas, and H. Lyn Miles, eds., *Anthropomorphism, Anecdotes and Animals* (Albany: State University of New York Press, 1997), especially part 4.

18. Tlili, *Animals in the Qur'an*, 166–220. I have also added examples from the Hadith. Cf. as well "Animal Life," *EQ*, 1:93–102 (Eisenstein), and John Kaltner, *Introducing the Qur'an: For Today's Reader* (Minneapolis, MN: Fortress Press, 2011), 61–66 for a survey of animal themes in the Qur'an.

19. See al-Munawi, *Fayd al-qadir sharh al-jami' al-saghir*, 2nd ed. (Beirut: Dar al-Ma'rifa, 1972), 4:268 (no. 5266) and 5:525 (no. 8190).

20. al-Bukhari, *al-Sahih* (no. 3663).

21. Tlili, *Animals in the Qur'an*, 184–91.

22. See Ibn al-'Arabi, *Ahkm al-Qur'an* (Beirut: Dar al-Kutub al-'Ilmiya, 2002), 3:472–73 citing al-Isfarayini.

23. Heemskerk, *Suffering in Mu'tazilite Theology*, 165.

24. On this term, see "Revelation and Inspiration," *EQ*, 4:437–48 (Madigan).

25. See Abu Hayyan al-Andalusi, *al-Bahr al-muhit* (Beirut: Dar al-Kutub al-'Ilmiya, 1993), 5:496.

26. This is mentioned by al-Qurtubi, *al-Jam' li-ahkam al-qur'an* (Beirut: Dar al-Fikr, 1987), 10:122 taken from Ibn al-'Arabi's *Ahkam al-qur'an*.

27. On resurrection, see al-Qurtubi, *Kitab al-tadhkira fi ahwal al-mawta wa*

umur al-akhira (Riyadh: Maktabat Dar al-Minhaj, 1425 H), 1:515–21. See as well, "Resurrection," *EQ*, 4:434–35 (Borrmans).

28. al-Qurtubi, *Kitab al-tadhkira*, 1:651–59.

29. al-Mawardi, *al-Nukat wa-l-'uyun* (Beirut: Dar al-Kutub al-'Ilmiya, 1992), 2:112–13.

30. On these narrations, see Foltz, *Animals in Islamic Traditions and Muslim Cultures*, 11–27, and Robinson, *The Sayings of Muhammad*, 48–49. On other postresurrection modalities of being in animals, see al-Ash'ari's segment from *al-Maqalat al-islamiyin* below.

31. The doctrine of *'iwad* is discussed below.

32. Tlili, *Animals in the Qur'an*, 184–91.

33. Tlili, *Animals in the Qur'an*, 182–84. See as well "Sheba," *EQ*, 4:585–87 (Veronica Gonzalez).

34. On Descartes' views regarding animals as automata as well as reinterpretations of this view by modern commentators, see the discussion by Gary Steiner in *Anthropocentricism and Its Discontents: The Moral Status of Animals in the History of Western Philosophy* (Pennsylvania: Pittsburgh University Press, 2005), 132–52. On criticisms regarding the neo-Cartesian idea that animals do not suffer in a morally significant way, see Trent Dougherty's excellent discussion in *The Problem of Animal Suffering: A Theodicy for all Creatures Great and Small* (New York: Palgrave Macmillan, 2014), 56–95.

35. Followers of a man called Bakr b. Ukht 'Abd al-Wahid b. Zayd (d. 182/798). See al-Ash'ari, *al-Maqalat al-islamiyin*, 286–87, and Van Ess, *Theologie und Gesellschaft*, 2:108–118.

36. al-Juwayni, *A Guide to Conclusive Proofs for the Principles of Belief: Kitab al-Irshad ila Qawati' al-Adilla fi Usul al-I'tiqad* (Reading: Garnet, 2001), 152.

37. Named after MuHammad b. Karram al-Sijistani (d. 255/869) for which see Clifford Edmund Bosworth, "The Rise of the Karramiyya in Khurasan," *Muslim World* (1960): 6–14; Richard Bulliet, *The Patricians of Nishapur: A Study in Medieval Islamic Social History* (Cambridge, MA: Harvard University Press, 1972), 62–64; Wilfred Madelung, *Religious Trends in Early Islamic Iran* (Albany, NY: Persian Heritage Foundation, 1988), 39–46; Margret Malamud, "The Politics of Heresy in Medieval Khurasan: The Karramiyya in Nishapur," *Iranian* Studies 27 (1994): 37–51, and Aron Zysow, "Two Unrecognized Karrami Texts," *Journal of the American Oriental Society* 108 (1988): 577–87 and his "Karramiyya" in *The Oxford Handbook of Islamic Theology*, 252–62.

38. al-Razi, *Mafatih al-ghayb*, 11:99.

39. On animal cognition and consciousness see Robert Lurz, ed., *The Philosophy of Animal Minds* (New York: Cambridge University Press, 2009); Kristin

Andrews, ed., *The Animal Mind: An Introduction to the Philosophy of Animal Cognition* (London: Routledge, 2014); Kristin Andrews and Jacob Beck, eds., *The Routledge Handbook of Philosophy of Animal Minds* (Oxford: Routledge, 2017), and Clive Wynne and Monique Udell, eds., *Animal Cognition: Evolution, Behaviour and Cognition* (London: Palgrave Macmillan, 2013). For accounts of animal psychology in Islamic philosophy, see Peter Adamson, "Human and Animal Nature in the Philosophy of the Islamic World" in *Animals: A History* (New York: Oxford University Press, 2018), 91–114.

40. See Andrews, *The Animal Mind*, 80–109 for an extensive survey that addresses each point.

41. Andrews, *The Animal Mind*, 51–79.

42. This argument is based on William Rowe's evidential argument from evil in his celebrated paper "The Problem of Evil and Some Varieties of Atheism," *American Philosophical Quarterly* 16 (1979): 335–41. See as well William Rowe on *Philosophy of Religion: Selected Writings*, ed. Nicholas Trakakis (Aldershot: Ashgate, 2007), parts 2–4. On gratuitous evil, see Bryan Frances, *Gratuitous Suffering and the Problem of Evil: A Comprehensive Introduction* (New York: Routledge, 2013), 13–39.

43. Peter Harrison, "God and Animal Minds: A Response to Lynch," *Sophia* 35 (1996), 71.

44. On this doctrine in relation to animal pain, see 'Abd al-Jabbar, *Sharh usul al-khamsa*, 483–505; Heemskerk, *Suffering in Mu'tazilite Theology*, 142–89; Peter Adamson, "Abu Bakr al-Razi on Animals," *Archiv für Geschichte der Philosophie* 94 (2012): 250–53; Tlili, *Animals in the Qur'an*, 199–202; Daniel Lasker, "The Theory of Compensation ('Iwad) in Rabbanite and Karaite Thought: Animal Sacrifices, Ritual Slaughter and Circumcision," *Jewish Studies Quarterly* 11 (2004): 59–72 reproduced in Daniel Lasker, *From Judah Hadassi to Elijah Bashyatchi: Studies in Late Karaite Philosophy* (Leiden: Brill, 2008), 203–16.

45. 'Abd al-Jabbar, *al-Mughni*, 13:481.

46. 'Abd al-Jabbar, *al-Mughni*, 13:468.

47. 'Abd al-Jabbar, *al-Mughni*, 13:468.

48. 'Abd al-Jabbar, *al-Mughni*, 13:475–76.

49. 'Abd al-Jabbar, *al-Mughni*, 13:476.

50. 'Abd al-Jabbar, *al-Mughni*, 13:468.

51. 'Abd al-Jabbar, *al-Mughni*, 13:468, and Heemskerk, *Suffering in Mu'tazilite Theology*, 163–66.

52. 'Abd al-Jabbar, *al-Mughni*, 13:452.

53. 'Abd al-Jabbar, *al-Mughni*, 13:457–59.

54. 'Abd al-Jabbar, *al-Mughni*, 13:459: *kana anfa'u laha wa sara dhalik fi babihi*

manzila an yakhtara ta'ala li-l-'abd al-taklif alladhi yusaluhu ila darajat al-thawab.

55. 'Abd al-Jabbar, *al-Mughni*, 13:458.

56. Cf. Heemskerk's explanation in *Suffering in Mu'tazilite Theology*, 167. On the notion of *i'tibar*, see the discussion by Diana Lobel, *A Sufi-Jewish Dialogue: Philosophy and Mysticism in Bahya Ibn Paquda's Duties of the Heart* (Philadelphia: University of Pennsylvania Press, 2007), 124–45.

57. Ormsby, *Theodicy in Islamic Thought*, 246–47.

58. Winter, "Islam and the Problem of Evil," 245.

59. Ormsby, *Theodicy in Islamic Thought*, 247.

60. On Iblis, see "Devil," *EQ*, 1:524–27 (Andrew Rippin). For the wisdom behind why God created Iblis, al-Maturidi writes in *Ta'wilat ahl al-sunna*, 6:440:

A matter they discussed was what the wisdom behind God (Most High) creating Iblis was despite knowing what he would do like causing corruption in His creation, calling them to disobedience and warning them against the Last Day. [God] knew that [Iblis] would warn against this Day and corrupt His devotees and despite knowing this, what is the wisdom behind creating Him? Some have replied saying that Iblis and the iniquitous were created despite [God] knowing [what they will do] in order to teach them that He created them not for His benefit or because He is need of them or that He will be harmed by that they will do or that His dominion will diminish in any way as a result; rather He created them to teach them it is for their benefit, their need. Others have said [God] created enemies and friends with a view towards knowing the friends in order to teach their distinguished qualities they have been given. If everyone is His friends, then God's bounty would not be known and neither would that which He distinguished [His] friends with. This is how God's favours and excellence are known; not through favour and excellence themselves but through trials and hardship that occur. God's friends are known in a similar way. If there were no enemies, then God distinguishing them and the bounties He has honoured them with could not be known. Yet others have said something along the lines of what we have mentioned but from another angle.

61. See Gregory Boyd, *Satan and the Problem of Evil: Constructing a Trinitarian Warfare Theodicy* (Downers Grove, IL: InterVarsity Press, 2001), 302, and Gregory Boyd, "Evolution as Cosmic Warfare: A Biblical Perspective on Satan and 'Natural Evil'" in *Creation Made Free*, T. Oord, ed. (Eugene, OR:

Wipf & Stock, 2009), 125–45, and Ronald Osborn, *Death Before the Fall: Biblical Literalism and the Problem of Animal Suffering* (Downers Grove, IL: InterVarsity Press, 2014), 140–49. For Boyd, although demonic activity supervised by Satan does not explain all animal pain and suffering, it cannot be ignored as a factor. Cf. C. S. Lewis, *Problem of Pain* (London: Harper-Collins, 2009, repr.), 132–47, and Gijsbert Van den Brink, "God and the Suffering of Animals" in *Playing with Leviathan: Interpretation and Reception of Monsters from the Biblical World*, Koert Van Bekkum, Jaap Dekker, Henk Van de Kamp and Eric Peels, eds. (Leiden: Brill, 2017), 179–99.

62. al-'Azim Abadi, *'Awn al-ma'bud 'ala sunan Abi Dawud* (Amman: Bayt al-Afkar al-Dawliya, n.d.), 2228 (no. 5247).

63. al-Maturidi, *Ta'wilat ahl al-sunna*, 11 vols. ed. Majdi Basallum (Beirut: Dar al-Kutub al-'Ilmiya, 2005), 8:108.

64. See Michael Murray, *Nature Red in Tooth and Claw* (Oxford: Oxford University Press, 2008), 41–72. See as well Dougherty's extremely helpful survey in *The Problem of Animal Pain*, 16–35.

65. Rose, James, et al, "Can Fish Feel Pain?" *Fish and Fisheries* 15 (2013): 99.

66. Rose, "Can Fish Feel Pain?," 99.

67. Rose, "Can Fish Feel Pain?," 99.

68. Rose, "Can Fish Feel Pain?," 99

69. Rose, "Can Fish Feel Pain?," 100.

70. Rose, "Can Fish Feel Pain?," 100.

71. James Rose, "The Neurobehavioral Nature of Fishes and the Question of Awareness and Pain," *Reviews in Fisheries Science* 10 (2002): 2–10.

72. Roger Scruton, *Animal Rights and Wrongs* (London: Continuum, 1999), 42.

73. Scruton, *Animal Rights and Wrongs*, 36.

74. Pessagno, "The Uses of Evil in Maturidian Thought," 59–82, and Jackson, *Islam and the Problem of Black Suffering*, 103–117.

75. Jackson, *Islam and the Problem of Black Suffering*, 113.

76. Feisal Abdul Rauf, "What Is Sunni Islam?" in *Voices of Islam*, Vincent Cornell, ed., volumes 1–5 (London and Connecticut: Praeger, 2007), 1:198.

77. al-Maturidi, *Ta'wilat ahl al-sunna*, 7:367.

78. al-Maturidi, *Ta'wilat ahl al-sunna*, 6:181.

79. al-Maturidi, *Ta'wilat ahl al-sunna*, 2:454.

80. al-Maturidi, *Ta'wilat ahl al-sunna*, 9:55:

This verse contains a critique of the Mu'tazilite position because they hold that God cannot cause pain to children or animals unless He compensates them for it. No doubt, God has subjected animals and beasts for human beings and given them control over them to use and benefit from in various ways and this leads to their being hurt and harmed. There view necessitates that God cannot cause them harm unless he compensates them for it subject to their approval of it. This is the case for everything that is a recipient of compensation, namely that approval of the recipient is a condition for receiving the compensation. But if these [animals] are not those who have approved in that they cannot receive compensation, then this proves that it is based on what we said which is that doing the optimal is not obligatory on God.

81. al-Maturidi, *Ta'wilat ahl al-sunna*, 1:421.
82. al-Maturidi, *Ta'wilat ahl al-sunna*, 3:421. He surveys different meanings of the term "Hikma" under al-Baqara, verse 269. See as well al-Maturidi, *Kitab al-tawhid*, ed. Fathalla Kholeif (Beirut: Dar al-Mashriq, 1986), 217, and Abu al-Mu'in al-Nasafi, *Tabsirat al-adilla fi usul al-din*, 2 vols. Hüseyin Atay and Şaban Ali Düzügün, eds. (Ankara: Nashriyat Ri'asat al-Shu'un al-Diyana li-l-Jumhuriya al-Turkiya, 2003), 2:252.
83. Pessagno, "Uses of Evil in Maturidian Thought," 68–69. See al-Maturidi, *Ta'wilat ahl al-sunna*, 4:401.
84. See Shaykh Zadah, *Nazm al-fara'id wa-jam' al-fawa'id*, 1st ed. (Cairo: al-Matba'a al-Adabiya, 1317 H), 27–28.
85. Ibn al-Humam, *al-Musayara fi al-'aqa'id al-munjiya fi al-akhira* (Cairo: al-Maktaba al-Mahmudiya al-Tijariya, 1929), 117–18.
86. *Kitab al-musamara fi sharh al-musayara* by al-Kamal Ibn Abi Sharif and the sublinear notes by Qasim b. Qutlubugha (Cairo: al-Maktaba al-Azhariya, 2006), 2:71. Cf. al-Maturidi, *Kitab al-tawhid*, 97, 100, 108; al-Nasafi, *Tabsirat al-adilla fi usul al-din*, 2:249, and al-Lamishi, *Kitab al-tamhid li-qawa'id al-tawhid*, ed. 'A. al-Turki (Beirut: al-Gharb al-Islami, 1995), 102.
87. al-Maturidi *Ta'wilat ahl al-sunna*, 6:440.
88. al-Maturidi, *Ta'wilat ahl al-sunna*, 2:70.
89. Ibn al-Humam, *al-Musayara*, 117.
90. Ibn Qayyim, *Shifa' al-'alil*, 362–65.
91. Ibn Qayyim, *Shifa' al-'alil*, 368–70.
92. Cf. Richard Swinburne's animal virtue theodicy in *Providence and the Problem of Evil* (Oxford: Clarendon Press, 1998), 189–90 and passim and Atle Søvik's telling criticisms in *The Problem of Evil and the Power of God* (Leiden: Brill, 2011), 23–32, 161–94 echoed by Beth Seacord in "Unto the Least of These: Animal Suffering and the Problem of Evil" (PhD diss., University of Colorado, 2013), 163–78.
93. Ibn Qayyim, *On Divine Wisdom and the Problem of Evil*, trans. Tallal Zeni (Cambridge: Islamic Texts Society, 2017), 160–61.
94. Ibn Qayyim like many of his predecessors does not elaborate on animal cognition and so we cannot really construct much from sparse references

here and there. A cursory survey on the section on the wisdom in God's creative design of animals in *Miftah dar al-sa'ada* suggests the following notions regarding animals, 669, 671, 667–78, 67–80, 692 and 723–25, respectively:

1. Animal traits can be transferred through their meat consumption (*al-mughtadhi shabih bi-l-ghadhi*).
2. Animals lack advanced levels of mutual care, empathy (*mulatafa*), or compassion (*rifq*).
3. Animals lack aesthetic appreciation or sensuality (*taladhdhudh*).
4. Animals have the capacity for instructing others (based on al-Ma'ida, verse 31).
5. Animals engage in species-specific mating patterns (*idh laysa fi al-haywan sinfun yalhaqu sinfan akhar*), meaning that animals of one species cannot be a hybrid of different species.
6. Animals praise God.
7. The possibility of human–animal metamorphosis (*maskh*).

95. *Miftah dar al-sa'ada*, 665–66 and trans. in Al-Qoz, *Men and the Universe: Reflections of Ibn Al-Qayyem* (Riyadh: Darussalam, 2004), 194–95.
96. Ibn Qayyim, *Miftah dar al-sa'ada*, 665–719 and trans. in Al-Qoz, *Men and the Universe*, 193–252.
97. Ibn Qayyim, *Miftah dar al-sa'ada*, 586.
98. Ibn Qayyim, *Miftah dar al-sa'ada*, 594.
99. Ibn Qayyim, *Miftah dar al-sa'ada*, 587–88. On formulations of the teleological argument in medieval Islamic philosophy and theology, see Herbert Davidson, *Proofs for Eternity, Creation and the Existence of God in Medieval Islamic and Jewish Philosophy* (New York: Oxford University Press, 1987), 213–36. See as well the comparative account of teleological arguments in Cafer Yaran, *Islamic Thought on the Existence of God: With Contributions from Contemporary Western Philosophy of Religion* (Washington: Council for Research in Value and Philosophy, 2003), 33–161.
100. Ibn Qayyim, *Miftah dar al-sa'ada*, 669–70 and an extensive survey in Benjamin Jantzen, *An Introduction to Design Arguments* (Cambridge: Cambridge University Press, 2014), especially 29–57. Thomas Aquinas a century earlier than Ibn al-Qayyim stated in a similar fashion that God's decision to create originates from an outpouring or overflowing of God's being. Creation is an emanative expression of divine goodness. In order to manifest this goodness, the panoply of plants and animals—sentient and non-sentient—is created. He states:

For he brought things into being in order that His goodness might be communicated to creatures, and be represented by them; and because

His goodness could not be adequately represented by one creature alone, He produced many and diverse creatures, that what was wanting to one in the representation of the divine goodness might be supplied by another. For goodness, which in God is simple and uniform, in creatures is manifold and divided and hence the whole universe together participates in the divine goodness more perfectly, and represents it better than any single creature whatever (Aquinas, *Summa Theologiae* 47, a1, Fathers of the English Dominican province, trans. [Wheaton: Christian Classics, 1981]), quoted in Murray, *Nature Red in Tooth and Claw*, 115.

101. Ibn Qayyim, *Bada'i' al-fawa'id*, ed. 'A. al-'Imran (Jeddah: Dar 'Alam al-Fawa'id, 2003), 4:1593–94.

Chapter 4
1. From Yaqut, *Irshad al-arib*, 1:199 cited and trans. in Ormsby, *Theodicy in Islamic Thought*, 26.
2. Karen Armstrong, *A History of God* (London: Heinemann, 1992), 362 and 335–36, and Stanley Grenz and Roger Olson, eds., *Twentieth-Century Theology: God and the World in a Transitional Age* (Downers Grove, IL: InterVarsity Press, 1992), 18–23.
3. Darwin 1985, 8, 224 cited in Michael Ruse, *Darwinism as Religion: What Literature Tells Us about Evolution* (Oxford: Oxford University Press, 2017), 89.
4. Neil Gillespie, *Charles Darwin and the Problem of Creation* (Chicago, IL: University of Chicago Press, 1979), 72, 77–79, 126–27.
5. Cornelius Hunter, *Darwin's God. Evolution and the Problem of Evil* (Grand Rapids, MI: Baker, 2001), 11–18.
6. I am extremely grateful for Christopher Southgate's feedback on this chapter and pointing out some errors in it.
7. Southgate, *The Groaning of Creation*, 1–17.
8. Southgate, *The Groaning of Creation*, 45.
9. Southgate, *The Groaning of Creation*, 40.
10. Southgate, *The Groaning of Creation*, 28–31.
11. Southgate, *The Groaning of Creation*, 34.
12. Southgate, *The Groaning of Creation*, 16. See also Southgate, "Cosmic Evolution and Evil" in *The Cambridge Companion to the Problem of Evil*, 156–58.
13. Stephen Webb, Review of *The Groaning of Creation* in *Reviews in Religion and Theology* 16 (2009): 471.
14. Southgate, *The Groaning of Creation*, 18–39.
15. Southgate, *The Groaning of Creation*, 65.
16. Southgate, *The Groaning of Creation*, 15–17.

17.	Southgate, *The Groaning of Creation*, 15–16. Points (1)–(4) have been taken from Sollereder, "Animal Suffering in an Unfallen World," 93–94 with minor changes and helped by the discussion in Paul Blowers, "Unfinished Creative Business: Maximus the Confessor, Evolutionary Theodicy and Human Stewardship in Creation" in *On Earth as It Is in Heaven: Cultivating a Contemporary Theology of Creation*, David Meconi S. J., ed. (Grand Rapids, MI: Eerdmans, 2016), 174–77, and White, "God, Evolution and the Problem of Evil," 48–54. An entire honorary volume of *Zygote* was devoted to Southgate and his theodicy (September 2018).

18.	Norman Wirzba, Review of *The Groaning of Creation* in *Theology Today* 66 (2010): 507.

19.	Southgate, *The Groaning of Creation*, 18–39.

20.	Southgate, *The Groaning of Creation*, 55–77.

21.	See, for example, the two-part post by Stuart, 2010. "Southgate's 'only way' the Wrong Way: God's Omnipotence and Benevolence in the Problem of Natural Evil," *thinkingmatters.org.nz*, http://thinkingmatters.org.nz/2010/12/southgates-only-way-the-wrong-way.

22.	Southgate, *The Groaning of Creation*, 55–77.

23.	For this distinction, see the articles in Charles Pigden, ed., *Hume on Is and Ought* (New York: Palgrave Macmillan, 2010).

24.	Robin Attfield, *Wonder, Value and God* (Oxford: Routledge, 2017), 87–88.

25.	See Janel Bakker, "Debunking 'Bambi Theology'," interview with Christopher Southgate. *Bearingsonline*, June 7, 2013. http://collegevilleinstitute.org/bearings/debunking-bambi-theology-interview-christopher-southgate/.

26.	Murray, *Nature Red in Tooth and Claw*, 1–2.

27.	Murray, *Nature Red in Tooth and Claw*, 16.

28.	Murray, *Nature Red in Tooth and Claw*, 21.

29.	Murray, *Nature Red in Tooth and Claw*, 37.

30.	Murray, *Nature Red in Tooth and Claw*, 40.

31.	Murray, *Nature Red in Tooth and Claw*, 130–65.

32.	Murray, *Nature Red in Tooth and Claw*, 14–16, and Murray, "Theodicy," 356. Cf. Swinburne, *Providence and the Problem of Evil*, parts 2–4.

33.	Murray, *Nature Red in Tooth and Claw*, 39.

34.	Murray, *Nature Red in Tooth and Claw*, 41–72.

35.	Murray, *Nature Red in Tooth and Claw*, 73–106.

36.	Murray, *Nature Red in Tooth and Claw*, 107–129.

37.	Murray, *Nature Red in Tooth and Claw*, 130–65.

38.	Murray, *Nature Red in Tooth and Claw*, 139–40.

39.	On Malebranche's theodicy of justice, see Donald Rutherford, "Malebranche's Theodicy" in *The Cambridge Companion to Malebranche*, Steven Nadler, ed. (Cambridge: Cambridge University Press, 2000), 165–89, and

Denis Moreau, "Malebranche on Disorder and Physical Evil: Manichaeism or Philosophical Courage?" in *The Problem of Evil in Early Modern Philosophy*, Elmer Kremer and Michael Latzer, eds. (Toronto: University of Toronto Press, 2001), 81–100.

40. Murray, "Theodicy," 370.

41. Murray, *Nature Red in Tooth and Claw*, 8.

42. Murray, *Nature Red in Tooth and Claw*, 130–65.

43. For a more detailed response to Murray's version, see Robert Francescotti, "The Problem of Animal Pain and Suffering," 121–25 in *The Blackwell Companion to the Problem of Evil*. See as well brief critiques by Mylan Engel, review of *Nature Red in Tooth and Claw* by Murray in *Notre Dame Philosophical Reviews*, 2009, http://ndpr.nd.edu/news/nature-red-in-tooth-and-claw-theism-and-the-problem-of-animal-suffering/; Creegan, *Animal Suffering and the Problem of Evil*, 51–53, and Seacord, "Unto the Least of These," 135–62.

44. Engel, Review of *Nature Red in Tooth and Claw*.

45. Murray, *Nature Red in Tooth and Claw*, 184.

46. Sollereder, "Animal Suffering in an Unfallen World," 37, fn. 41.

47. Engel, Review of *Nature Red in Tooth and Claw*.

48. Creegan, *Animal Suffering and the Problem of Evil*, 1–5.

49. Creegan, *Animal Suffering and the Problem of Evil*, 1–5.

50. Creegan, *Animal Suffering and the Problem of Evil*, 97, ". . . random mutation plus selection and intense competition for survival."

51. Creegan, *Animal Suffering and the Problem of Evil*, 7–13 and 27–43.

52. Creegan, *Animal Suffering and the Problem of Evil*, 13.

53. Creegan, *Animal Suffering and the Problem of Evil*, 14–26 and cf. her own reformulation of the fall account in 138–53.

54. Creegan, *Animal Suffering and the Problem of Evil*, 44–55 and 56–70.

55. Creegan, *Animal Suffering and the Problem of Evil*, 7–13 and 27–43.

56. See Jacques Maritain, *On the Philosophy of History*, ed. Joseph Evans (London: Geoffrey Bles, 1959), 36–42.

57. See Reinhold Niebuhr, "The Wheat and the Tares" in *Justice and Mercy*, Ursula Niebuhr, ed. (New York: Harper & Row, 1974), 51–58.

58. Creegan, *Animal Suffering and the Problem of Evil*, 82–96.

59. Creegan, *Animal Suffering and the Problem of Evil*, 111.

60. See Jan Sapp, *Genesis: The Evolution of Biology* (New York: Oxford University Press, 2003).

61. Creegan, *Animal Suffering and the Problem of Evil*, 117.

62. Creegan, *Animal Suffering and the Problem of Evil*, 125.

63. Creegan, *Animal Suffering and the Problem of Evil*, 102–104.

64. Creegan, *Animal Suffering and the Problem of Evil*, 93.

65. Also known and preferred by many as "evolutionary creationism." On a survey of some prominent theistic evolutionists, see Allenne Phy-Olsen, *Evolution, Creationism and Intelligent Design* (California: Greenwood, 2010), 45–58. For perhaps the most formidable critique of theistic evolution to date, see *Theistic Evolution: A Scientific, Philosophical and Theological Critique*, ed. James Porter Moreland et al. (Wheaton, IL: Crossway Books, 2017).

66. From Farid Younos, *Principles of Islamic Sociology* (Bloomington, IN: Author House, 2011), 134.

67. Which amounts to deism.

68. Taken from Gerald Rau's *Mapping the Origins Debate: Six Models on the Beginning of Everything* (Downers Grove, IL: InterVarsity Press, 2012), 38–51.

69. Some general justifications for why an ITE may be more favorable than premodern Islamic scholastic theological accounts include: (1) it allows for reconciliation between the Qur'anic claims and current established biological and physical sciences; (2) creation and its nature are truly separate from God and thus transcendence is affirmed in a clearer way; (3) God is not enlisted as cooperating in evil as it is attributed to the unfolding evolutionary process; and (4) the bad design we observe is not attributed to the direct handiwork of God but random mutation.

70. For an account of Islam and evolution, see Nidhal Guessoum's *Islam's Quantum Question: Reconciling Muslim Tradition and Modern Science* (London: I.B. Tauris, 2011), 271–324 and for a survey of views of Muslim academics toward evolution with further references, see his "Islamic Theological Views on Darwinian Evolution," *Oxford Research Encyclopaedia of Religion*, available online at http://religion.oxfordre.com (accessed November 2016).

71. See "Fall of Man," *EQ*, 2:172–73 (Anthony Johns).

72. A notion used by Hick to predicate his response that in order for human beings to freely develop love for God, they require autonomy; an absence of pressure to love Him so it does not seem coercive. See *Evil and the God of Love*, 281 and elsewhere. See Trakakis' critique in "An Epistemically Distant God? A Critique of John Hick's Response to the Problem of Divine Hiddenness," *Heythrop Journal* 48 (2007): 214–26.

73. See al-Hadid, verse 3.

74. This narration is unanimously classed as a forgery by hadith specialists even though the general purport is affirmed by al-Dhariyat, verse 56: *I have not created humans and jinn except to worship Me*. See 'Ali al-Qari, *al-Asrar al-marfu'a fi al-akhbar al-mawdu'a* (Beirut: Dar al-Kutub al-'Ilmiya, 2018), 172 (no. 353).

75. *Ruh al-ma'ani*, 19:418.

76. There are a cluster of arguments that attempt to undermine confidence in belief in God as a benevolent, powerful, and just Creator with the reality of

evolution. Specific disvalues that arise from evolution through natural selection such as mass extinction, predation, death, suffering, parasitism, and unnecessary waste (I will call it "E-disvalues") seem incompatible with such a characterization of a Deity worthy of total worship. There are a number of argument formulations for this type of challenge, three of which are the following:

1.
   (1) Any world in which there are E-disvalues ought not to be created by God.
   (2) This world contains immense E-disvalue.
   (3) Therefore, this world ought not to have been created by God.
2.
   (1) If God is a benevolent and value-loving Creator, He would not create a world containing E-disvalues.
   (2) This world contains immense E-disvalue.
   (3) Therefore, God is not a benevolent and value-loving Creator.
3.
   (1) If God is a benevolent and value-loving Creator, He would desire to create a world outweighed by value.
   (2) This world contains immense E-disvalue that outweighs any value.
   (3) Therefore, God is not a benevolent and value-loving Creator.

I take up these arguments and others with responses in a paper entitled "Evil in the Biosphere: Towards an Islamic Evolutionary Theodicy," British Academy of Islamic Studies, Exeter University, April 11, 2018, Exeter 2018. See as well Attfield, *Wonder, Value and God*, 71–90.

77. On this term, see Wadad Al-Qadi, "The Term 'Khalifa' in Early Exegetical Literature," *Die Welt des Islams* 28 (1988): 392–411, and "Caliph," *EQ*, 1:276–78 (Wadad Al-Qadi); Watt, "God's Caliph, Qur'anic Interpretations and Umayyad Claims" in *Iran and Islam in Memory of the Late Vladimir Minorsky*, Clifford Bosworth, ed. (Edinburgh: Edinburgh University Press, 1971), 565–74; Fritz Steppat, "God's Deputy: Materials on Islam's Image of Man," *Arabica* 36 (1989):163–72; Bernard Lewis, *The Political Language of Islam* (Chicago, IL: University of Chicago Press, 1988), 43–70, and Tlili's *Animals in the Qur'an*, 114–23. See as well "Adam and Eve," *EQ*, 1:22 (Cornelia Schöck) and David Johnston, *Earth, Empire and Sacred Text: Muslims and Christians as Trustees of Creation* (London: Equinox, 2013), 239-403. On al-Tabari's exegesis of al-Baqara verses 35–36 in relation to Adam and Eve, see *The Commentary on the Qur'an*, trans. John Cooper and ed. Wilfred Madelung and Alan Jones (Oxford: Oxford University Press, 1987),

1:244–46, 251–55, 257–58 reproduced in *Eve and Adam: Jewish, Christian and Muslim Readings of Genesis and Gender*, Kristen Kvam, Linda Shearing and Valarie Ziegler, ed. (Bloomington: Indiana University Press, 1999), 185–99.

78. "Adam and Eve," *EQ*, 1:22–23. Cf. "Biology as the Creation and Stages of Life," *EQ*, 1:229–32 (Abul Fadl Mohsin Ebrahim).

79. Cf. Q.55:8–9.

80. Cf. here Ibn al-Qayyim's near two dozen possible reasons why God created Adam and subsequently placed him on earth in *On Divine Wisdom*, 1–18 and the mystical account of Adam's fall and its significance in Ahmad Sam'ani's *Rawh al-arwah fi sharh asma' al-malik al-fattah* discussed in Chittick, *Sufism*, 112–36. On Adamic themes in Sufi thought, see as well Chittick, *The Sufi Path of Knowledge*, 275–77; Schimmel, *Mystical Dimension of Islam*, 187–91; Johnston, *Earth, Empire and Sacred Text*, 304–13 and Sa'diyya Shaikh, *Sufi Narratives of Intimacy: Ibn 'Arabi, Gender and Sexuality* (Chapel Hill: University of North Carolina Press, 2012), 141–72.

81. See "Eschatology," *EQ*, 2:44–54 (Smith) for a summary of the Qur'anic depiction of the universe's destruction.

Chapter 5

1. See, for example, John McTaggart's *Some Dogmas of Religion* (London: E. Arnold, 1906), section 177 and its discussion in Jonathan Kvanvig, *Destiny and Deliberation: Essays in Philosophical Theology* (Oxford: Oxford University Press, 2011), 41–42.

2. David Lewis and Philip Kitcher, "And Lead Us Not," *Harper's Magazine*, December 2007, 28. For a Thomist response to this argument, see John Lamont, "The Justice and Goodness of Hell," *Faith and Philosophy* 28 (2011): 152–73.

3. See "Hell and Hellfire," 2:414–20 (Rosalind Gwynne), "Chastisement and Punishment," 1:294–98 (Mohammed Fadel) and "Eschatology," 2:44–54 (Jane Smith) all in *EQ*. Cf. as well "Hell," *Qur'an: An Encyclopaedia*, 259–62 (Stefan Wild) and "Hell," *Encyclopedia Iranica*, 12:154–6, updated version available online at http://www.iranicaonline.org/articles/hell-ii-islamic-period (accessed online December 5, 2017) (Mahmoud Omidsalar).

4. For which see 'Umar S. al-Ashqar, *al-Janna wa-l-nar* (Amman: Dar al-Nafa'is, 1998), 13–111, and Marco Demichelis, *Salvation and Hell in Classical Islamic Thought: Can Allah Save Us All?* (London: Bloomsbury, 2018), 18–25. Stefan Wild in his encyclopedia entry summarizes succinctly the description of hell within the Qur'an that offers for us a glimpse into the kind of destination it is and why it is judged as so disturbing, see "Hell," *Qur'an: An Encyclopaedia*, 259–62.

5. See, for example, Christian Lange, *Justice, Punishment and Medieval Muslim Imagination* (Cambridge: Cambridge University Press, 2008), 101–75; Christian Lange, *Paradise and Hell in Islamic Traditions* (New York: Cambridge University Press, 2016), and "Introducing Hell in Islamic Studies," *Locating Hell in Islamic Traditions* (Boston: Brill, 2016), 1–28, and Nerina Rustomji, *The Garden and the Fire: Heaven and Hell in Islamic Culture* (New York: Colombia University Press, 2009), 1–20 and 98–122.

6. I take these terms and the theses with slight variation from Jonathan Kvanvig, *The Problem of Hell* (New York: Oxford University Press, 1993), 19, and Jonathan Kvanvig, "Hell" in *The Oxford Handbook of Eschatology*, Jerry Walls, ed. (New York: Oxford University Press, 2016), 413–27. See also Robert Arp and Benjamin McCraw, eds., *The Concept of Hell* (New York: Palgrave Macmillan, 2015), introduction, 1–15 for an overview of (H1)–(H4).

7. I take (H5) following Andrew Rogers and Nathan Conroy, "The New Defense of the Strong View of Hell" in *The Concept of Hell*, 50.

8. I have omitted discussions of those views of hell that form part of an imaginary eschatology that deny any literal reality to afterlife events such as bodily resurrection or hell and paradise as actual locations. This can be found in, for example, Ibn Sina and others such as Isma'ili thinkers.

9. Kvanvig, *The Problem of Hell*, 3–4. See James S. Spiegel, *Hell and Divine Goodness: A Philosophical-Theological Inquiry* (Eugene, OR: Cascade Books, 2019), 57–79.

10. Other responses would be to abandon the Mainstream View altogether through reconceptualizing hell in an allegorical way or rejecting it outright as morally untenable.

11. See, for example, the various exegetical discussions by Muslim commentators on Al 'Imran, verse 26, al-Ghafir, verse 16 and many other verses regarding God's eternal sovereignty and control over the entire temporal order. See as well particular glosses by al-Baydawi and others mentioned in Helmut Gätje, *The Qur'an and Its Exegesis: Selected Texts with Classical and Modern Muslim Interpretations* (Oxford: Oneworld, 2004), 146–63; "Kings and Rulers," 3:91–94 (Louise Marlowe), "God and His Attributes, 2:329–31 (Gerhard Böwering); "Possession and Possessions," 4:184–87 (Alexander Knysh) and "Power and Impotence," 4:210–13 (Alexander Knysh) all in *EQ*. On the divine name *malik* and *malik* see al-Qurtubi, *al-Jami' li-Ahkam al-Qur'an*, trans. Aisha Bewley (London: Dar al-Taqwa, 2003), 1:120–22, and *Bada'i' al-fawa'id*, *Shifa' al-'alil* and *al-Tibyan* of Ibn al-Qayyim cited in Ashqar, *Sharh Ibn al-Qayyim li-asma' Allah*, 46–51.

12. al-Ghazali, *Maqsad al-asna sharh asma' Allah al-husna*, MS Sarajevo, Gazi Hüsrev Beg, fols 29b–30a, and *The Ninety-Nine Beautiful Names of God*,

trans. David Burrell and Nazih Daher (Cambridge: Islamic Texts Society, 2007), 57.

13. al-Ghazalii *Maqsad al-asna*, fol. 23a/b, and *The Ninety-Nine Beautiful Names of God*, 139–40.

14. See "Good and Evil," *EQ*, 2:335–39 (Brannon Wheeler).

15. Referring to the names "al-Khafid" ('The Abaser') and "al-Rafi'" ('The Exalter').

16. See al-Qurtubi, *al-Asna fi sharh asma' Allah al-husna* (Tanta: Dar al-Sahaba li-l-Turath, 1995), 1:367.

17. al-Ghazali, *Maqsad al-asna*, fol. 43a, and *The Ninety-Nine Beautiful Names of God*, 82 (trans. Burrell and Daher).

18. On this and related notions, see Majid Khadduri, *The Islamic Conception of Justice* (Baltimore: Johns Hopkins University Press, 1984), 39–134; "Justice and Injustice" *EQ*, 3:69–74 (Jonathan E. Brockopp); Sheryl L. Burkhalter, "Completion in Continuity: Cosmogony and Ethics in Islam" in *Cosmogony and Ethical Order: New Studies in Comparative Ethics*, Robin Lovin and Frank E. Reynolds, eds. (Chicago: University of Chicago Press, 1985), 225–50; Lutpi Ibrahim, "The Concept of Divine Justice According to al-Zamakhshari and al-Baydawi," *Hamdard Islamicus* 3 (1980): 3–17; Safraz Bacchus, *The Concept of Justice in Islam* (Victoria: Friesen Press, 2014), M. A. Draz, *The Moral World of the Qur'an* (London: I.B. Tauris, 2008), 13–292, and Ramon Harvey, *The Qur'an and the Just Society* (Edinburgh: Edinburgh University Press, 2018), 119–68 and 169–90.

19. On these epithets, see al-Qurtubi, *al-Asna fi sharh asma' Allah al-husna*, 1:482–84.

20. al-Qurtubi, *al-Asna fi sharh asma' Allah al-husna*, 1:486–90.

21. 'Ali al-Qari, *Mirqat al-mafatih sharh Mishkat al-Masabih* (Beirut: Dar al-Kutub al-'Ilmiya, 2015), 5:198 (no. 2288).

22. al-Ghazali, *The Ninety-Nine Beautiful Names of God*, 138.

23. Hakan Gok, "Said Nursi's Arguments for the Existence of God in Risale-i Nur" (PhD diss., Durham University, 2014), 256–62, and Ian S. Markham, *Engaging with Bediuzzaman Nursi: A Model of Interfaith Dialogue* (New York: Routledge, 2016), 35–41.

24. See "Sin, Major and Minor," *EQ*, 5:19 (Qasim Zaman).

25. Toshiko Izutsu, *Ethico-Religious Concepts in the Qur'an* (McGill-Queens University Press, 2002), 241–49, and Zaman, "Sin, Major and Minor," *EQ*, 5:19–28.

26. For a survey of scholarly discussions of sin and a catalogue of them, refer to al-Dhahabi, *Kitab al-kaba'ir* (Beirut: al-Maktaba al-Umawiya, 1970); Ibn Nujaym's *al-Sagha'ir wa-l-kaba'ir* with its commentary by his grandson

Zayn al-Din, Khalil al-Mays (Beirut: Dar al-Kutub al-'Ilmiya, 1981) and al-Haythami, *al-Zawajir 'an iqtiraf al-kaba'ir* (Beirut: Dar al-Kutub al-'Ilmiya, 1987). See as well Toshiko Izutsu, *The Concept of Belief in Islamic Theology: A Semantic Analysis of Iman and Islam* (New York: The Other Press, 2006), 43–70, and Lange, *Justice, Punishment and the Medieval Muslim Imagination*, 101–111.

27. In al-Tabari, *Tafsir*, 4:44 on Qur'an 4:31 [no. 9213] cited in "Sin, Major and Minor," *EQ*, 5:19.

28. al-Qurtubi, *al-Mufhim li-ma ashkala min talkhis Kitab Muslim* (Damascus and Beirut: Dar Ibn Kathir and Dar Kalim al-Tayyib, 1996), 1:284.

29. al-Qurtubi, *al-Mufhim*, 1:284.

30. al-Haythami, *al-Zawajir 'an iqtiraf al-kaba'ir*, 1:8.

31. See Ayman Shabana, "The Concept of Sin in the Qur'an in Light of the Story of Adam," in *Sin, Forgiveness and Reconciliation: Christian and Muslim Perspectives*, Lucinder Mosher and David Marshall, eds. (Virginia: George-town University Press, 2016), 40–65.

32. "Sins," *Qur'an: An Encyclopaedia*, 594 (Oliver Leaman).

33. Leaman, "Sins," 594.

34. See *Arabic–English Dictionary of Qur'anic Usage*, Elsaid Badawi and Muhammad Abdel Haleem, eds. (Leiden and Boston: Brill, 2008), 742–43.

35. Ibn Qayyim al-Jawziya, *Shifa' al-'alil*, 2:510–511 cited in *Sharh Ibn Qayyim asma' Allah al-husna*, Sulayman al-Ahsqar, ed. (Amman: Dar al-Nafa'is, 2008), 52–53.

36. al-Ghazali, *Maqsad al-asna*, fol. 30a and *The Ninety-Nine Beautiful Names of God*, 59–60.

37. al-Alusi, *Ruh al-ma'ani*, 28:62.

38. al-Maturidi, *Ta'wilat ahl al-sunna*, 9:59–60. This was the view of al-Qatada as mentioned by al-Tabari in *al-Jami' al-bayan*, 23:302.

39. See "Covenant (religious) pre-eternal," *Encyclopaedia of Islam* (Third Edition), 1:74–78 (Michael Ebstein); "Covenant," *EQ*, 1:464–67 (Gerhard Böwering); "Mithaq," 408–409 (Rafik Berjak) and "'Ahd/'Ahada," 14–16 (Ibrahim Sumer) both in *The Qur'an: An Encyclopaedia*; Clifford E. Bosworth, "Mithak," *Encyclopaedia of Islam* (Second Edition), 7:187; Robert Darnell, "The Idea of Divine Covenant in the Qur'an" (PhD diss., University of Michigan, 1970); Louis Massignon, Le "jour du covenant" (*yawm al-mithaq*), *Oriens* (1962): 86–92; Richard Gramlich, "Der Urvertrag in der Koranauslegung," *Der Islam* 60 (1983): 205–230; Joseph Lumbard, "Covenant and Covenants in the Qur'an," *Journal of Qur'anic Studies* 17 (2015): 1–23; Torsten Hylén, "*The Hand of God is over their Hands* (Q. 48:10): On the Notion of Covenant in al-Tabari's Account of Karbala'," *Journal of*

Qur'anic Studies (2016): 58–68; Tariq Jaffer, "Is There Covenant Theology in Islam?" in *Islamic Studies Today: Essays in Honour of Andrew Rippin*, Majid Daneshgar and Walid Saleh, eds. (Leiden: Brill, 2016), 98–121; Rosalind Gwynne, *Logic, Rhetoric and Legal Reasoning in the Qur'an* (London: Routledge, 2004), 1–24, and finally, Abdel-Kader, *The Life, Personality and Writings of Al-Junayd*, 76–80, 160–64 (English trans.), and 40–43 (Arabic text) and Harvey, *The Qur'an and the Just Society*, 10–13.

40. Wadad Kadi, "The Primordial Covenant and Human History in the Qur'an," *Proceedings of the American Philosophical Society* 174 (2003): 333.

41. For a discussion of this concept, see al-Qurtubi, *al-Jami' li-ahkam al-Qur'an* (Beirut: Mu'assasat al-Risala, 2006), 19:158–62.

42. al-Ghazali, *al-Arba'in fi Usul al-Din*, trans. N. Abdassalam (London: Turath Publishing, 2016), 280–86.

43. See Jane Idleman Smith and Yvonne Yazbeck Haddad, *The Islamic Understanding of Death and Resurrection* (New York: Oxford University Press, 2002), 31–98.

44. Ibn Rajab, *al-Takhwif min al-nar wa-l-ta'rif bi-hal dar al-bawar* (Damascus-Beirut: Maktabat al-Mu'ayyad, 1988), 195–96.

45. Ibn Hazm, *Maratib al-ijma' fi al-'ibadat wa-l-mu'amalat wa-l-i'tiqadat* (Beirut: Dar Ibn Hazm, 1998), 268. See as well the relevant articles from various creeds translated in William Montgomery Watt's *Islamic Creeds: A Selection* (Edinburgh: Edinburgh University Press, 1994).

46. Ibn Hazm, *al-Faal fi al-milal wa-l-nihal* (Saudi Arabia: Sharikat Maktabat 'Ukkaz), 4:145. Cf. Al-Ash'ari, *Maqalat al-Islamiyin*, 148–49 (Ritter's edn.).

47. See Hamza, "To Hell and Back," 156–59; Lange, *Justice, Punishment and the Medieval Muslim Imagination*, 101–103 and his *Paradise and Hell*, 176–78. For some of the arguments against the Mu'tazilite position, see al-Maturidi, *Ta'wilat ahl al-sunna*, 1:402–403, 2:477–78, 3:331 and 4:375. Cf. as well the discussion in Sophia Vasalou, *Moral Agents and their Deserts: The Character of Mu'tazilite Ethics* (Princeton, NJ: Princeton University Press, 2008), 121–32.

48. Al-Ash'ari, *Maqalat al-Islamiyin*, 474 (Ritter's ed.).

49. Although on Muslim doubts regarding assurances of salvation (*Heilsgewissheit*), see Lange, *Justice, Punishment and the Medieval Muslim Imagination*, 111–15.

50. al-Taftazani, *Sharh al-maqasid* (Beirut: 'Alam al-Kutub, 1998), 5:137. Cf. al-Maturidi's argument in *Ta'wilat ahl al-sunna*, 2:477–78.

51. See the statements of Ibn Hajar al-'Asqalani quoting al-Qurtubi regarding the varying degrees of punishment according to the type of sinful action in *'Awn al-murid li-sharh jawharat al-tawhid fi 'aqidat ahl al-sunna wa-l-jamaia*, Tattan, 'Abd al-Karim and Mahmud al-Kiylani, eds. (Beirut:

Dar al-Basha'ir, 1999), 1117. See as well Lange, *Justice, Punishment and the Medieval Muslim Imagination*, 139–75.

52. Cf. Parry, *The Evangelical Universalist*, 13, fn.9.

53. al-Nisa', verse 56. Al-Taftazani, *Sharh al-maqasid*, 5:134 and al-Jurjani, *Sharh al-mawaqif* of al-Iji (Beirut: Dar al-Kutub al-'Ilmiya, 1998), 8:335–37.

54. "Devil," *The Qur'an: An Encyclopaedia*, 179 (Stefan Wild).

55. Oliver Crisp, "Divine Retribution: A Defense," *Sophia* 42 (2003): 40. On the status principle, see Paul Kabay, "Is the Status Principle beyond Salvation? Toward Redeeming an Unpopular Theory of Hell," *Sophia* 44 (2005): 91–103; Kvanvig, *The Problem of Hell*, 29; Seymour, *A Theodicy of Hell*, 48–81, and Shawn Bawulski, "The Fire that Reconciles: Theological Reflections on the Doctrine of Eternal Punishment, with Special Consideration of Annihilationism and Traditionalism" (PhD. diss., University of St Andrews, 2012), 154–61.

56. Cf. as well al-Fatir, verse 37.

57. al-Razi, *Mafatih al-ghayb* (Beirut: Dar al-Fikr, 1981), 12:204.

58. al-Razi, *Mafatih al-ghayb*, 12:205.

59. Ibn Hajar al-'Asqlani, *Fath al-bari*, 15:204–206.

60. *Mirqat al-mafatih sharh Mishkat al-Masabih* (Beirut: Dar al-Kutub al-'Ilmiya, 2001), 1:273.

61. *Kitab al-tawhid*, 167.

62. al-Babarti, *Sharh wasiyat al-Imam Abi Hanifa* (Amman: Dar al-Fath, 2009), 140. See as well A. J. Wensinck, *The Muslim Creed: Its Genesis and Historical Development* (New Delhi: Oriental Books Reprint Corporation, 1979, repr.), 165–67, 184–85, and al-Maghnisawi, *Imam Abu Hanifa: al-Fiqh al-Akbar Explained*, trans. Abdur-Rahman Mangera (Santa Barbara, CA: Whitethread Press, 2007), 190–91.

63. al-Razi, *Mafatih al-ghayb* as cited in al-Munawi, *Fayd al-qadir sharh Jami' al-Saghir* (Beirut: Dar al-Ma'rifa, 1972), 1:39–40 (no. 3). See as well Ibn 'Adil al-Dimashqi, *al-Lubab fi 'ulum al-kitab* (Beirut: Dar al-Kutub al-'Ilmiya, 1998), 10:568–73 for a discussion.

64. al-Razi, *Mafatih al-ghayb*, 31:15–16.

65. See Robert Wild, *A Catholic Reading Guide for Conditional Immortality: The Third Alternative to Hell and Universalism* (Oregon: Resource, 2016), 9–16.

66. For annihilationism, I rely mainly on Clark H. Pinnock, "The Destruction of the Finally Impenitent" in *Rethinking Hell: Readings in Evangelical Conditionalism*, Christopher Date, Gregory G. Stump, and Joshua W. Anderson, eds. (Eugene, OR: Cascade Books, 2014), 56–73; Pinnock, "Annihilationism" in *The Oxford Handbook of Eschatology*, Jerry L. Walls, ed. (Oxford: Oxford University Press, 2008), and Pinnock, "The Conditional View" in

Four Views on Hell, Stanley N. Gundry and William Crockett, eds. (Grand Rapids, MI: Zondervan, 1996), 135–66 with responses at 167–78. I also use James Spiegel, "Making the Philosophical Case for Conditionalism" as well as Adam Murrell, "Divine Sovereignty in the Punishment of the Wicked" both in *A Consuming Passion: Essays on Hell and Immortality in Honor of Edward Fudge*, Christopher Date and Ron Highfield, eds. (Eugene, OR: Pickwick, 2015), 80–89 and 141–55, respectively. The contours of my own theological and philosophical account of annihilationism in this section broadly echo what is in the article by Claire Brown and Jerry Walls, "Annihilationism: A Philosophical Dead End?" in *The Problem of Hell: A Philosophical Anthology*, Joel Buenting, ed. (London: Routledge, 2016), 45–64 and its summary discussed by Wild in *A Catholic Reading Guide*, see 87–91. For the most sustained defense of annihilationism within Christianity, see www.rethinkinghell.com and the resources there.

67. Brown and Walls, "Annihilationism," 47.
68. See Inati, *The Problem of Evil: Ibn Sina's Theodicy*, 65–102, and Adamson, "From the Necessary Existent to God," 185–88.
69. Inati, *The Problem of Evil*, 65.
70. Inati, *The Problem of Evil*, 65–66.
71. Inati, *The Problem of Evil*, 66.
72. Brown and Walls, "Annihilationism," 47. On this kind of view, see Paul J. Griffiths, *Decreation: The Last Things of All Creatures* (Waco, TX: Baylor University Press, 2014), and Griffiths, "Self-Annihilation or Damnation? A Disputable Question in Christian Eschatology" in *Liberal Faith: Essays in Honour of Philip Quinn*, Paul J. Weithman, ed. (Notre Dame, IN: University of Notre Dame Press, 2008), 83–117. Cf. Kvanvig, *The Problem of Hell*, 146–47.
73. Steel, "Avicenna and Thomas Aquinas on Evil," 177–79.
74. Pinnock, "The Destruction of the Finally Impenitent," 67–69; Spiegel, "Making the Philosophical Case," 82–85, and Brown and Walls, "Annihilationism," 53–61.
75. Pinnock, "The Destruction of the Finally Impenitent," 67.
76. Pinnock, "The Destruction of the Finally Impenitent," 68.
77. On narrations related to the *jahannamiyun* and how monotheists will exit hell with posthumous salvation, see the extensive study by Feras Hamza, "Temporary Hellfire Punishment and the Making of Sunni Orthodoxy" in *Roads to Paradise: Eschatology and Concepts of the Hereafter in Islam*, volume 1, Sabastian Gunther and Todd Lawson, eds. (Leiden: Brill, 2017), 371–406. For brief remarks, see Lange, *Paradise and Hell*, 154–64.
78. Muslim, *Sahih* in al-Nawawi's commentary *al-Minhaj sharh sahih muslim b. al-hajjaj* (Cairo, 1929), 3:37–39.

79. al-Qurtubi, *al-Tadhkira*, 770 (Jeddah: Dar al-Minhaj edn.) and *al-Tadhkira* (abridged Eng. edn.), 180 (no. 232–33). Cf. Samuela Pagani, "Ibn 'Arabi, Ibn Qayyim al-Jawziyya, and the Political Functions of Punishment in the Islamic Hell" in *Locating Hell in Islamic Traditions*, Christian Lange, ed. (Leiden: Brill, 2015), 188, fn. 60.

80. Brown and Walls, "Annihilationism," 55. See as well Seymour, *A Theodicy of Hell*, 182–86.

81. Brown and Walls, "Annihilationism," 61–63, and Murrell, "Divine Sovereignty," 141–55. On divine sovereignty within Islamic theology, see the discussion above on the sovereignty thesis for the justification of hell.

82. Murrell, "Divine Sovereignty," 148. Emphasis in the original.

83. Murrell, "Divine Sovereignty," 148. Emphasis in the original. Take, for example, the vivid *hadith* on the consequence of suicide related by al-Tirmidhi and other compilers in his *Sunan* (Riyadh: Maktabat al-Ma'arif, 1996):

> Whoever kills himself with (an instrument of) iron, his iron will be in his hand, to continually stab himself in his stomach with it, in the fire of hell, dwelling in that state forever. And whoever kills himself with poison, then his poison will be in his hand, to continually take it in the fire of hell, dwelling in that state forever. And whoever throws himself from a mountain to kill himself, then he will be continually throwing himself in the fire of hell, dwelling in that state forever (no. 2043).

> Commentators highlight that this narration and others with near identical and similar wording contain a number of related points: (i) punishment is proportionate to the act (*al-jaaa' min jins al-'amal*), (ii) an act of suicide does not excommunicate a person from the faith of Islam, (iii) the terms "unending," "eternally," and "forever" (*khalid, mukhallad, abadan*) are not to be read as perpetual, that is, quantitatively unending, because all believers will eventually exit hell, and (iv) temporal acts affect salvation. See al-Qurtubi, *al-Mufhim*, 1:311–12 and 'Ali al-Qari, *Mirqat al-mafatih*, 8:2457 (no. 3453). On suicide, see Franz Rosenthal, "On suicide in Islam," *Journal of the American Oriental Society* 66 (1946): 239–59, and Franz Rosenthal, "al-Intihar" in *Encyclopaedia of Islam* (Second Edition), 3:1246–48.

84. Pinnock, "The Destruction of the Finally Impenitent," 68, and Spiegel, "Making the Philosophical Case," 85–87.

85. See A. J. Wensinck, *The Muslim Creed*, 121 and 165–67, and Marco Demichelis, "*Fana' al-Nar* within Early Kalam and Mysticism. An Analysis Covering the Eighth and Ninth Centuries," *Archiv Orientální* 83 (2015): 392–94.

86. al-Maturidi, *Sharh fiqh al-akbar* (Deccan: Matba'at Majlis Da'irat al-Ma'arif al-Nizamiya, 1904, repr. Qatar: Shu'un al-Diniya, n.d.), 45. On the textual history of the *Sharh* and whether it is authentically attributable to al-Maturidi, see Hans Daiber's assessment in *The Islamic Concept of Belief in the 4th/10th Century: Abul-Layth al-Samarqandi's Commentary on Abu Hanifa (died 150/767) al-Fiqh al-Absat* (Tokyo: ILCAA, 1995) and Rudolph's summary discussion in *Al-Maturidi and The Development of Sunni Theology*, 325–28. For analyses on the *Fiqh al-Akbar* text, see Wensinck, *The Muslim Creed*, 102–124; Josef Van Ess, *Theology and Society in the Second and Third Centuries of the Hijra*, trans. John O'Kane and Fierro, Maribel, M. Şükrü Hanioğlu, Renata Holod and Florian Schwarz, eds. (Leiden and Boston, Brill, 2017), 1:237–43; "Al-Fiqh al-Akbar" in *Encyclopedia of Islamic Civilisation and Religion*, Ian Richard Netton, ed. (London and New York: Routledge, 2008), 175–77 (David Thomas) and Demichelis, "Fana' al-Nar within Early Kalam," 388–94.
87. See the survey by Thomas O'Shaughnessy, *Muhammad's Thoughts on Death: A Thematic Study of the Qur'anic Data* (Leiden: Brill, 1969), 14–25.
88. O'Shaughnessy, *Muhammad's Thoughts on Death*, 15–19.
89. Badawi and Haleem, *Arabic–English Dictionary*, s.v., 141.
90. See al-Baydawi, *Anwar al-tanzil*, 2:35 and al-Tabari, *al-Jami' al-bayan*, 18:128 and 30:64 cited in O'Shaughnessy, *Muhammad's Thoughts on Death*, 17.
91. Referring to the angel who is hell's gatekeeper. See Brooke Olsen Vuckovic, *Heavenly Journeys, Earthly Concerns: The Legacy of the Mi'raj in the Formation of Islam* (New York: Routledge, 2005), 36–39 and Christian Lange, "Revisiting Hell's Angels in the Quran" in *Locating Hell in Islamic Traditions*, 89–91.
92. Badawi and Haleem, *Arabic–English Dictionary*, s.v., 763–64.
93. O'Shaughnessy, *Muhammad's Thoughts on Death*, 18–19.
94. For a historical account of universalism within the Western theological context, refer to Laurence M. Blanchard, *Will All Be Saved: An Assessment of Universalism in Western Theology* (Milton Keynes: Paternoster, 2015). On one of the most incisive treatments within Christian theology, refer to Robin A. Parry, *The Evangelical Universalist* (Eugene, OR: Cascade Books, 2012), especially 11–35.
95. I assume here that the text given in the title *al-Radd 'ala man qala bi-fana' al-janna wa-l-nar wa-bayan al-aqwal fi dhalik*, Muhammad b. 'Abd Allah al-Samhari, ed. (Riyadh: Daa al-Balansiya, 1995; abbreviated henceforth as *Fana' al-nar*) is authored by Ibn Taymiya. On discussions over its authenticity and attribution to him, see the remarks by the editor of the text al-Samhari, 12–16 and 'Abd Allah b. Salih al-Ghusn, *Da'awa al-munawi'in li-Shaykh al-Islam Ibn Taymiya: 'ard wa naqd* (al-Dammam: Dar Ibn al-Jawzi,

2003), 617–24. On Ibn Taymiya's universalism, see Nasir al-Din al-Albani's introduction to al-San'ani's *Raf' al-astar li-ibtal adillat al-qa'ilin bi-fana' al-nar* (Beirut: al-Maktab al-Islami, 1984), 5–52; Jon Hoover, "Islamic Universalism: Ibn Qayyim al-Jawziyya's Salafi Deliberations on the Duration of Hell-Fire," *Muslim World* 99 (2009): 181–91, Jon Hooever, "Against Islamic Universalism: 'Ali al-Harbi's 1990 Attempt to Prove that Ibn Taymiyya and Ibn Qayyim al-Jawziyya Affirm the Eternality of Hell-Fire" in *Islamic Philosophy, Theology and Law: Debating Ibn Taymiyya and Ibn Qayyim al-Jawziyya*, Birgit Krawietz and Georges Tamer, eds. (Berlin and Boston: Walter De Gruyter, 2013), 377–99, and Jon Hooever, "Withholding Judgment on Islamic Universalism: Ibn al-Wazir (d. 840/1436) on the Duration and Purpose of Hellfire" in *Locating Hell*, 208–211, Mohammad H. Khalil, *Islam and the Fate of Others: The Salvation Question* (New York: Oxford University Press, 2012), 92–102, Demichelis, *Salvation and Hell*, 147–54, and Mohammad H. Khalil, "The Fate of others in Fourteenth-Century Hanbalism: Ibn Taymiyya (d. 1328/728), Ibn Qayyim al-Jawziyya (d. 1350/750) and the Fana' al-Nar" *Annale de Scienze Religiose* 9 (2016): 271–94.

96. Ibn Taymiya, *Fana' al-nar*, 62–63. See al-Subki, *al-I'tibar bi-baqa' al-janna wa-l-nar* (Damascus: Matba'at al-Turki, 1347 H), 73–74, al-San'ani, *Raf' al-astar* (Beirut and Damascus: al-Maktab al-Islami, 1984), 87–90, and al-Shawkani, "Kashf al-astar fi ibtal qaql man qala bi-Fana' al-Nar" in *Kitab Fath al-Rabbani min fatawa al-Imam al-Shawkani* (San'a: Maktabat al-Jil al-Jadid, n.d.), 803–805, where he mentions five meanings of the word *ahqab*: (1) a finite length of time that can be quantified like eighty years where one year in the afterlife corresponds to a full lunar year in this world or the equivalent of a thousand days in this world or an unspecified quantity, (2) an infinite length of time, meaning unending, (3) different ages, cycles, or periods of punishment, (4) a long period of time, and (5) a state of deprivation, disorder, loss, and cessation. On the last meaning, see Lane, *Arabic–English Lexicon*, Bk. 1, 610.

97. Ibn Taymiya, *Fana' al-nar*, 68.

98. See al-Zamakhshari's remarks on this conditionality thesis in *al-Kashshaf*, trans. in Gätje, *The Qur'an and its Exegesis*, 181–83; al-Subki, *al-I'tibar*, 70–73 and the discussion by Hamza, "To Hell and Back," 96–117. Al-Shawkani in Hud, verses 106–107 mentions two responses to the meaning of this verse. The first response is that the heavens and earth mentioned in the verse are a reference to the hereafter based on: (a) the earth being transformed into a new earth mentioned in Ibrahim, verse 48, *on the day earth will be replaced by another earth* as well as (b) the fact that people in paradise will require earth to walk on and the sky to shade them. The second response is that the expression *as long as the heavens and the earth*

endure is one that the Arabs use to denote perpetuity and endlessness. God addressed the Arab audience with this expression as it would have been familiar to them in their language. Al-Shawkani then discusses fourteen interpretations with points and counter points on the exception clause *except what your Lord wills* in verse 107 bringing together all previous exegetical readings. See "Kashf al-astar," 793–802.

99. Ibn Taymiya, *Fana' al-nar*, 68–69: 'Amr ibn al-'As, "there will come a time in hell when its doors will close and no-one will remain in it."

100. Ibn Taymiya, *Fana' al-nar*, 69: Ibn Mas'ud, "there will come a time in hell where no-one will remain."

101. Ibn Taymiya, *Fana' al-nar*, 53–55. For discussions on the authenticity of these various narrations attributed to the companions and the generation immediately following them, see al-Subki, *al-I'tibar*, 73–76; al-San'ani, *Raf' al-astar*, 62–87 and al-Shawkani, "Kashf al-astar," 805–819.

102. Ibn Taymiya, *Fana' al-nar*, 53. For a thorough critique of Ibn Taymiya's use of this report, see al-San'ani, *Raf' al-astar*, 62–71.

103. Ibn Taymiya, *Fana' al-nar*, 53–55.

104. Ibn Taymiya, *Fana' al-nar*, 80–83.

105. Ibn Taymiya, *Fana' al-nar*, 83. See as well Lange, *Paradise and Hell in Islamic Traditions*, 169–71.

106. See Ibn Qayyim al-Jawziya, *Hadi al-arwah ila bilad al-afrah*, MuHammad ibn Ibrahim al-Zaghli, ed. (Dammam: Ramadi li-l-Nashr, 1997), 569–626; *Shifa' al-'alil*, M. A. al-Shalabi, ed. (Jeddah: Maktabat al-Sawadi li-l-Tawzi', 1991), 2:223–55 and *Mukhtasar al-sawa'iq al-mursala 'ala al-jahmiya wa-l-mu'attila*, abridgment by Muhammad ibn al-Mawsili and H. al-'Alawi, eds. (Riyadh: Adwa' al-Salaf, 2004). For analyses, see Jon Hoover, "Islamic Universalism: Ibn Qayyim al-Jawziyya's Salafi Deliberations on the Duration of Hellfire," *Muslim World* 99 (2009): 191–209; Jon Hoover, "A Muslim Conflict Over Universal Salvation" in *Alternative Salvations: Engaging the Sacred and the Secular*, Hannah Bacon, Wendy Dossett, and Steve Knowles, eds. (London: Bloomsbury, 2015), 160–71; Demichelis, *Salvation and Hell*, 154–61; Pagani, "Political Functions of Punishment," 184–87, and Khalil, *Islam and the Fate of Others*, 92–102.

107. Although note Khalil's remarks on *yawm* mentioned in Qaf, verse 34, *Islam and the Fate of Others*, 95, fn.145.

108. Khalil, *Islam and the Fate of Others*, 95–96.

109. Ibn Qayyim, *Hadi al-arwah*, 599–600 and his *al-Sawa'iq al-mursala*, 2:671 as cited in Hoover, "Islamic Universalism," 195.

110. Ibn Qayyim, *Hadi al-arwah*, 606–607 cited in Khalil, *Islam and The Fate of Others*, 96.

111. Ibn Qayyim, *Hadi al-arwah*, 369 cited and trans. in Pagani, "Political Functions of Punishment," 185.
112. Hoover, "A Muslim Conflict Over Universal Salvation," 167.
113. Ibn Qayyim, *al-Sawa'iq al-mursala*, 2:663 cited in Hoover, "Islamic Universalism," 196.
114. Ibn Qayyim, *Hadi al-arwah*, 606–607 cited and trans. in Hoover, "Islamic Universalism," 190.
115. Ibn Qayyim, *Hadi al-arwah*, 599–603.
116. Ibn Qayyim, *Hadi al-arwah*, 600–603. See Khalil, *Islam and the Fate of Others*, 96–98.
117. Al-Subki, however, does not make an explicit declaration of excommunication against Ibn Taymiya but only that the idea he subscribes to would merit it. On the meaning and origins of the notion of *takfir*, see Hussam S. Timani, *Takfir in Islamic Thought* (London: Lexington Books, 2018), 1–27.
118. Khalil al-Subay'i, ed. (Beirut: Dar Ibn Hazm, 1998), 61–77.
119. Because al-Shawkani's text is less known, I shall briefly summarize it. On *al-I'tibar*, see Khalil, *Islam and the Fate of Others*, 89–92 and 190–91. On another Yemeni Ibn al-Wazir who took a conciliatory approach that leaned more toward agnosticism over eternal chastisement, see Hoover, "Witholding Judgment," 218–37. Al-Shawkani composed "Kashf al-astar" in response to a request by one of the erudite scholars of Yemen and his teacher who granted him numerous religious authorization *(ijaza)* al-Husayn b. Yusuf Zabara (d. 1231) regarding the controversy of hell's annihilation (787). The text first discusses the three key verses of the Qur'an featured in the controversy—al-Naba', verse 23 and Hud, verses 107–8—focusing on how the word *ahqab* and the conditional thesis involving the exceptive clauses were interpreted to propose hell's annihilation by its proponents (787–89). This is then followed by al-Shawkani rehearsing at length the standard counter-exegetical responses from earlier scholars against this annihilationist reading citing only al-Razi by name including as well his own source and transmitter evaluation of the various reports containing opinions attributed to the Prophet's companions that suggest hell's finite chastisement and duration (789–816). He then presents his own preferred gloss on the key verses and his conclusions (816–19). A full translation of the treatise into English is forthcoming.
120. Cf. Benyamin Abrahamov, *Islamic Theology: Traditionalism and Rationalism* (Edinburgh: Edinburgh University Press, 1988), 12, 54, and Abrahamov, "The Creation and Duration of Paradise," 96.
121. al-Subki, *al-I'tibar*, 60–67.
122. al-Shawkani, "Kashf al-astar," 814–19.

123. al-Subki, *al-I'tibar*, 77.
124. al-Subki, *al-I'tibar*, 75–76.
125. Khalil labels Ibn 'Arabi as a "quasi-universalist"; see *Islam and the Fate of Others*, 72.
126. On al-Jahiz, see the entry in *The Biographical Encyclopaedia of Islamic Philosophy*, Oliver Leaman, ed. (London: Bloomsbury Academic, 2015), 245–55 (Oliver Leaman).
127. See Sadra as discussed in Muhammad Rustom, *The Triumph of Mercy: Philosophy and Scripture in Mulla Sadra* (Albany: State University of New York Press, 2012), 85–98 summarized in Rustom, "A Philosopher's Itinerary for the Afterlife: Mulla Sadra on Paths to Felicity" in *Roads to Paradise*, 534–51.
128. al-Ash'ari, *Maqalat al-Islamiyin*, 475 (Ritter's ed.).
129. Demichelis, *Salvation and Hell*, 70–71.
130. See al-Shahrastani, *al-Milal wa-l-nihal* (Beirut: Dar Ibn Hazm, 2007), 49–50/al-Jahiziya and al-Khayyat, *Kitab al-intisar*, 17, 18, and 83–84 cited in Demichelis, *Salvation and Hell*, 70.
131. See al-Baghdadi, *al-Farq bayn al-firaq*, M. 'Abd al-Hamid, ed. (Cairo: Dar al-Turath, 2007), 1:60.
132. See A.E. Affifi, *The Mystical Philosophy of MuHyid Din-Ibnul 'Arabi* (Cambridge: Cambridge University Press, 1939), 163–70; Rom Landau, *The Philosophy of Ibn 'Arabi* (London: George Allen & Unwin, 1959), 61–3; William C. Chittick, *Ibn 'Arabi: Heir to the Prophets* (Oxford: Oneworld, 2005), 123–44; Pagani, "Political Functions," 187–94; Khalil, *Islam and the Fate of Others*, 62–69 and the creed of Ibn 'Arabi from *al-Futuhat al-makkiya*, 1:162–72 cited and trans. Gibril Fouad Haddad in *Correct Islamic Doctrines Volume 2—Ibn Khafif and Shaykh Muhyi al-Din Ibn 'Arabi* (Fenton, MI and Damascus: As-Sunna Foundation of America, 1999), 27–44, art. 177–78.
133. Ibn Qayyim, *Hadi al-arwah* (Cairo: Maktabat al-Mutanabbi, n.d.), 246. Cf. as well, al-Saffarini, *al-Buhur al-zakhira fi 'ulum al-akhira* (Kuwait: Ghiras, 2007), 2:521.
134. William C. Chittick, *Sufism: A Beginners Guide* (Oxford: Oneworld, 2008), 59.
135. Khalil, *Islam and the Fate of Others*, 63, and cf. Rustom, *The Triumph of Mercy*, 113–15.
136. See William C. Chittick, *Imaginal Worlds: Ibn al-'Arabi and the Problem of Religious Diversity* (Albany: State University of New York Press, 1994), 113 and Ibn 'Arabi, *al-Futuhat al-makkiya*, 3:77 cited in *Imaginal Worlds*. Cf. as well Abrahamov, "The Creation and Duration of Paradise and Hell in Islamic Theology," 94.
137. Ibn 'Arabi, *al-Futuhat al-makkiya*, 3:25 cited and trans. in Chittick, *Heir to the Prophets*, 128–29.

138. Ibn 'Arabi, *al-Futuhat al-makkiya*, 3:466, cited and trans. in Chittick, *Heir to the Prophets*, 137.

139. Ibn 'Arabi, *al-Futuhat al-makkiya*, 3:9, cited and trans. in Chittick, *Heir to the Prophets*, 132.

140. Muslim, *al-Sahih* (no. 185).

141. Ibn 'Arabi, *al-Futuhat al-makkiya*, 2:447, cited and trans. in Chittick, *Heir to the Prophets*, 142.

142. Ibn 'Arabi, *al-Futuhat al-makkiya*, 3:25, cited in William C. Chittick, *The Self-Disclosure of God: Principles of Ibn al-'Arabi's Cosmology* (Albany: State University of New York Press, 1998), 188.

143. Ibn 'Arabi, *al-Futuhat al-makkiya*, 2:207, cited and trans. in Chittick, *Heir to the Prophets*, 140.

144. Ibn 'Arabi, *al-Futuhat al-makkiya*, 3:463, cited and trans. in Chittick, *Heir to the Prophets*, 142.

145. Al-Sha'rani, for example, accuses certain factions of interpolating heretical doctrines (*al-'aqa'id al-za'igha*) into Ibn 'Arabi's major works, one such being the account of hell just discussed above. It is inconceivable for him that Ibn 'Arabi's stature as a knower of God of the highest station subscribes to doctrines that appear flagrantly to contradict the Islamic source texts on hell's eternality and its unending torment. See *al-Yawaqit wa-l-jawahir*, 2:165. 'Abd al-Ghani al-Nabulusi (d. 1731), however, affirms that Ibn 'Arabi did hold such a view but that it is not contrary to any overt orthodox Islamic doctrine. The depth and subtlety of the view is what brings about misunderstandings as those with superficial grasp of the religion fail to fathom his exact points. See his *Sharh fusus al-hikam*, 401. One of the most vociferous attacks against Ibn 'Arabi's doctrine was penned by Ibn Taymiya.

146. Alexander Knysh, "The Realms of Responsibility in Ibn 'Arabi's *Futuhat al-Makkiya*," *Journal of the Muhyiddin Ibn 'Arabi Society* 31 (2002): 97.

147. As defined by William Lane Craig in "'No Other Name': A Middle Knowledge Perspective on the Exclusivity of Salvation through Christ," *Faith and Philosophy* 6 (1989): 172–88.

148. I maintain the tripartite typology proposed by Alan Race in *Christians and Religious Pluralism* (London: SCM Press, 1983). The Islamic soteriological pluralist (ISP) position is an outlook that moves beyond mere pragmatic recognition of religious diversity as a fact to upholding the truth claims of all religions as valid and their having salvific efficacy. It has two central motivations:

   1. There is genuine value and connectedness with an ultimate transcendent reality found in all the teachings and experiences of the

established religions.

2. Preservation of the dignity and integrity of all religions because of the historical occurrence of religious violence, oppression, and subjugation.

ISP is identified with the following core claims:

1. religious diversity is providential, meaning God is the cause of it,
2. non-Islamic religions have salvific efficacy, which is that salvation can be attained through that religion,
3. non-Islamic religious systems are not fully abrogated by Islam but only corroborated by it, which involves a denial of strict supersessionism and religious favoritism,
4. adherents of non-Islamic religious systems are virtuous and this is recognized by Islam,
5. there is parity in the truth claims about reality between Islam and all non-Islamic religions, and
6. God's mercy is encompassing to include the sincere endeavors of non-Islamic religious persons. On the ISP view, there is no worry of eternal damnation for non-Muslims because all religions are valid salvific structures—all will be saved.

See the following chapters in *Between Heaven and Hell*: William C. Chittick, "The Ambiguity of the Qur'anic Command," 65–86; Sajjad H. Rizvi, "Oneself as the Saved Other? The Ethics and Soteriology of Difference in Two Muslim Thinkers," 180–203; Farid Esack, "The Portrayal of Jews and the Possibilities for their Salvation in the Qur'an," 207–33, and Jerusha T. Lamptey, "Embracing Rationality and Theological Tensions: Muslima Theology, Religious Diversity, and Fate," 235–38 and her *Never Wholly Other: A Muslim Theology of Religious Pluralism* (New York: Oxford University Press, 2014). For a discussion on contemporary Muslim pluralists, see Khalil, *Islam and the Fate of Others*, 135–41 and Jakob W. Wirén, *Hope and Otherness: Christian Eschatology and Interreligious Hospitality* (Leiden and Boston: Brill, 2018), 141–231.

149. See as well universalism as defined and explained by Reza Shah-Kazemi for his approach argued at length in *The Other in Light of the One: The Universality of the Qur'an and Interfaith Dialogue* (Cambridge: Islamic Texts Society, 2006), 140–278 and summarized in "Beyond Polemics and Pluralism: The Universal Message of the Qur'an" in *Between Heaven and Hell*, 87–105.

150. For details, refer to Yasir Qadhi, "The Path of Allah or Paths of Allah: Revisiting Classical and Medieval Sunni Approaches to the Salvation of

Others" in *Between Heaven and Hell*, 111–21; Arif Kemil Abdullah, *The Qur'an and Normative Religious Pluralism: A Thematic Study of the Qur'an* (London: International Institute of Islamic Thought, 2014), 23–44, and Khalil, *Islam and the Fate of Others*, 132–35. See as well Robert McKim, *On Religious Diversity* (New York: Oxford University Press, 2014), 52–71 and 101–30 for a survey of exclusivism.

151. McKim, *On Religious Diversity*, 72–100.

152. Muhammad Legenhausen, "Non-Reductive Pluralism and Religious Dialogue" in *Between Heaven and Hell*, 153–79.

153. For details on this, see Timothy Winter, "The Last Trump Card: Islam and the Supersession of Other Faiths," *Studies in Interreligious Dialogue* 9 (1999): 151, and "Realism and the Real: Islamic Theology and the Problem of Alternative Expressions of God" in *Between Heaven and Hell*, 136–40.

154. Muhammad Shafi Usmani, *Iman aur Kufr: Qur'an ki Roshani Mein* (Karachi: Idarat al-Ma'arif, 2008), 17. Cf. the discussion by al-Barzanji, *Sadad al-din wa sidad al-dayn fi ithbat al-najat wa-l-darajat li-l-walidayn* (Beirut: Dar al-Kutub al-'Ilmiya, 2006), 35–51.

155. al-Baghawi, *Ma'alim al-tanzil* (Riyadh: Dar al-Tayba, 1988), 1:64.

156. See al-Ghazali, *Faysal al-tafriqa bayn al-Islam wa-l-zandaqa*, trans. Sherman Jackson as *On the Boundaries of Theological Tolerance in Islam* (Karachi: Oxford University Press, 2002), 92–93.

157. Al-Ghazali, *Faysal al-tafriqa* = Jackson, *On the Boundaries of Theological Tolerance in Islam*, 64–66, and 120–32. On surveys of al-Ghazali's soteriology, see Khalil, *Islam and the Fate of Others*, 31–39, Mohammad H. Khalil, "Islam and the Salvation of Others" in *Religious Perspectives on Religious Diversity*, Robert McKim, ed. (Leiden: Brill, 2016), 156–59, and Demichelis, *Salvation and Hell*, 136–46.

158. Al-Ghazali, *Faysal al-tafriqa* = Jackson, *On the Boundaries of Theological Tolerance in Islam*, 127–28.

159. On eleven types of disbelief, see Timani, *Takfir in Islamic Thought*, 7–8.

160. On the first four types of disbelief, see al-Khazin, *Lubab al-ta'wil fi ma'ani al-tanzil* (Beirut: Dar al-Kutub al-'Ilmiya, 2004), 1:26 and al-Barzanji's explanation of them in *Sadad al-din*, 39–42. See as well Shah 'Abd al-'Aziz al-Dihlawi, *Fatawa-i-'Azizi*, 1:42 cited in Usmani, *Iman aur Kufr*, 40–41, and al-Birgivi, *The Path of Muhammad: A Book on Islamic Morals and Ethics*, trans. Tosun Bayrak al-Jerrahi (Bloomington, IN: World Wisdom, 2005), 113–19.

161. On these first four types of disbelief, see al-Baghawi, *Ma'alim al-tanzil*, 1:64. On the theological and legal arguments surrounding whether ignorance is a ground for valid excuse, see Sultan al-'Umayri, *Ishkaliyat al-i'dhar bi-l-jahl fi-l-bahth al-'uqdi* (Beirut and Riyadh: Dar al-Wujuh, 2012).

162. Ibn 'Arabi, *al-Futuhat al-makkiya*, 3:469, trans. Chittick in *Imaginable Worlds*, 156–57, and Khalil, "Islam and the Salvation of Others," 154–55.

163. Ibn al-Qayyim, *Tariq al-hijratayn wa bab al-sa'adatayn* (Mecca: Dar 'Alam al-Fawa'id), 902. See as well Rashid Rid's interpretation in *al-Manar*, discussed in Khalil, *Islam and the Fate of Others*, 120–23.

164. On the issue of whether Islamic theology can accommodate nonculpable and rational disbelief, and whether a revisionist strategy is needed to redefine the notion of *kufr*, see Imran Aijaz, "The Islamic Problem of Religious Diversity" in *Religious Perspectives on Religious Diversity*, 162–75, and Imran Aijaz, "Belief, Providence, and Eschatology," *Philosophy Compass* 3 (2008): 235–40, and Zain Ali, *Faith, Philosophy and the Reflective Muslim* (New York: Palgrave Macmillan, 2013), 138–50. Cf. as well Robert McKim, "I'm Okay, You're Okay (More or Less)" in *Religious Perspectives on Religious Diversity*, 244–46.

165. Johnathan Brown, "The Fate of Non-Muslims: Perspectives on Salvation Outside of Islam" at https://yaqeeninstitute.org/jonathan-brown/the-fate-of-non-muslims-perspectives-on-salvation-outside-of-islam/#.XaBQ8EZKhPY (accessed July 2018). See al-Barzanji, *Sidad al-dayn*, 168–71; Ahmad Shukri, *Ahl al-fatra wa man fi hukmihim* (Damascus and Beirut: Dar Ibn Kathir, 1988), 57–63, Jamil al-Qarara'a, "Masir Ahl al-Fatra fi-l-Akhira wa Silat Aqwal al-'Ulama' fi hadhihi al-Mas'ala bi-Aqwalihim fi-l-Tahsin wa-l-Taqbih," *Umm al-Qura Journal of Islamic Sciences, Arabic Language and Literature* 18 (2006): 304–307.

166. al-Qarara'a, "Masir Ahl al-Fatra," 305–306.

167. This is the general view of the Ash'arites.

168. This is the general view of the Maturidites.

169. This is the view of Ibn Taymiya, Ibn al-Qayyim, and many Muslim scholars. Johnathan Brown, "The Fate of Non-Muslims."

170. For a discussion on agent obligation (*taklif*), refer to Arnold Y. Mol, "Divine Respite in the Ottoman *Tafsir* Tradition: Reconciling Exegetical Approaches to Q. 11:117," OSMANLI'DA İLM-I TEFSIR, edited by M.T. Boyalik and H. Abaci, eds. (Istanbul: ISAR, 2019), 539–92. I thank the author for providing me a personal copy of this article.

171. See al-Barzanji, *Sadad al-din*, 168–71.

172. See al-Isra', verse 8.

173. See al-Bayyina, verse 6.

174. See al-Isra', verse 15.

175. See al-An'am, verse 131.

176. On the theological discussion regarding gratitude, see A. Kevin Reinhart, *Before Revelation: The Boundaries of Muslim Moral Thought* (Albany: State University of New York Press, 1995), 107–160.

177. See al-Qasas, verse 47.

178. See Tas-Ha, verse 134.

179. See al-Shu'ara', verses 208–209.

180. See al-Fatir, verse 37.

181. On various interpretations of divine sanctions and the grounds for their temporal application, see Mol, "Divine Respite in the Ottoman *Tafsir* Tradition," 19–38.

182. al-Barzanji, *Sadad al-din*, 54–56. For his second argument that is a legal one framed in a syllogism and that I omit discussing here due to space, see 56–62.

183. al-Barzanji, *Sadad al-din*, 52.

184. For the narrations and a discussion, see Ibn al-Qayyim, *Tariq al-hijratayn*, 842–78; Ibn Kathir, *Tafsir al-Qur'an al-'azim* (Riyadh: Dar al-Tayba, 1999), 5:53–61; al-Suyuti, *al-Budur al-safira fi ahwal al-akhira* (Beirut: Dar al-Kutub al-'Ilmiya, 1996), 405–407 (no. 1274–90), and Shukri, *Ahl al-fatra*, 89–101.

185. al-'Ayni, *'Umdat al-qari sharh Sahih al-Bukhari* (Beirut: Dar al-Kutub al-'Ilmiya, 2001), 8:307.

186. al-'Ayni, *'Umdat al-qari sharh Sahih al-Bukhari*, 8:307. al-'Ayni judges the strength of the narration establishing this view as weak.

187. al-'Ayni, *'Umdat al-qari sharh Sahih al-Bukhari*, 8:307:307. This is the Qur'anic reference to "heights" (*al-a'raf*) in al-A'raf, verses 46–47 where there are souls that hear and address the people of Paradise but are not yet in Paradise themselves. Thus, the *a'raf* is an intermediate location that is free of suffering prior to entry into Paradise. This would entail that non-Muslim children (or non-Muslims in general) are inhabitants of Paradise. On narrations about the inhabitants of *al-a'raf*, see al-Suyuti, *al-Budur al-safira*, 396–400 (no. 1258–73). See as well "Barrier," 1:203–204 and "Barzakh" (Mona Zaki), 1:204–207 in *EQ*.

188. al-'Ayni, *'Umdat al-qari sharh Sahih al-Bukhari*, 8:307. Al-'Ayni also judges the strength of the narration for this view as weak.

189. al-'Ayni, *'Umdat al-qari sharh Sahih al-Bukhari*, 8:307–308.

190. al-'Ayni, *'Umdat al-qari sharh Sahih al-Bukhari*, 8:308. Other positions include suspending judgment on their destiny, restraining from discussing their fate, direct entry into hell, and total annihilation. See Ibn Hajar al-'Asqalani, *Fath al-bari sharh Sahih al-Bukhari* (Riyadh: Dar al-ayba, 2005), 5:178–80 (no. 1385).

191. al-'Ayni, *'Umdat al-qari sharh Sahih al-Bukhari*, 8:308.

192. Shukri, *Ahl al-fatra*, 103–104.

193. Shukri, *Ahl al-fatra*, 104.

194. Shukri, *Ahl al-fatra*, 104.

195. Shukri, *Ahl al-fatra*, 104.

196. Shukri, *Ahl al-fatra*, 78–80 and 105.

197. Ibn Hazm, *al-Fasl*, 4:135.

198. Shukri, *Ahl al-fatra*, 105.

199. Ibn Taymiya, *al-Jawab al-sahih li-man baddala din al-Masih* (Riyadh: Dar al-'Asima, 1999), 2:298, and Khalil, "Islam and the Salvation of Others," 153–54.

200. Reported by Abu Ya'la in *al-Musnad* (Beirut and Damascus: Dar al-Ma'mun, 1986), 7:225 (no. 4224). See as well al-Suyuti, *al-Budur al-safira*, 406 (no. 1291–7) for a short list of the narrations on this category.

201. Muslim, *al-Sahih* (no. 2661) and Ibn Taymiya, *al-Majmu' al-fatawa*, 4:246–47.

202. Ibn al-Qayyim, *Tahdhib al-sunan* (Riyadh: Maktabat al-Ma'arif, 2007), 4:215–16.

203. Ibn Kathir, *Tafsir al-Qur'an al-'azim*, 5:57–58.

204. Ibn al-Qayyim, *Tahdhib al-sunan*, 4:216.

205. This kind of model of foreknowledge is developed through the notion of "middle knowledge" (*scientia media*) within the Christian tradition under the theological views on providence and predestination by the sixteenth-century Spanish and Jesuit priest and scholastic Luis De Molina (d. 1600). On molinist accounts of salvation see Kirk R. MacGregor, *Luis de Molina: The Life and Theology of the Founder of Middle Knowledge* (Nashville and Grand Rapids, MI: Zondervan, 2015), ch. 3 and 4, Kenneth Keathley, *Salvation and Sovereignty: A Molinist Approach* (Nashville: B & H Publishing Group, 2010), 42–62, and John D. Laing, *Middle Knowledge: Human Freedom in Divine Sovereignty* (Grand Rapids, MI: Kregel, 2018).

206. Ahmad b. Hanbal, *al-Musnad*, Shu'ayb al-Arna'ut ed. (Beirut: Mu'assasat al-Risala, 1999), 26/228 (no. 16301) and Ibn Hibban in *al-Sahih* (Beirut: Dar al-Kutub al-'Ilmiya, 1987), 9:225–26 (no. 7313).

207. Ibn Hazm, *al-Fasl*, 4:105.

Chapter 6

1. Bethany Sollereder, "Exploring Old and New Paths in Theodicy," *Zygon* 53 (2018): 735.

2. Sollereder, "Exploring Old and New Paths in Theodicy," 735–36.

3. Sollereder, "Exploring Old and New Paths in Theodicy," 736. On this kind of pastoral approach to theodicy, see the work of John Swinton like *Raging with Compassion: Pastoral Responses to the Problem of Evil* (Grand Rapids, MI: Eerdmans, 2007). On a very similar approach that takes its cue from Peter Berger's implicit/explicit theodicy distinction, see Paul Vermeer's *Learning*

Theodicy: The Problem of Evil and the Praxis of Religious Education (Leiden: Brill, 1999).

4.   Sollereder, "Exploring Old and New Paths in Theodicy," 736.

Appendix

1.   On him, see "'Abbad B. Salman," *Encyclopædia Iranica*, I/1, 70–71, http:// www.iranicaonline.org/articles/abbad-b-salman (Madelung).

2.   al-Ash'ari, *al-Maqalat al-Islamiyin wa ikhtilaf al-musallin*, 1:319–20 (= Ritter's edn. Die dogmatischen Lehren der Anhänger des Islam, 2 vols. and index, Leipzig and Istanbul, 1929–1933; repr., Wiesbaden, 1963, 1980), 254–55.

3.   al-Ghazali, *al-Iqtisad fi al-i'tiqad* (Cairo: Mustafa al-Babi al-Halabi, 1891, repr. 1966) trans. Aladdin Yaqub, *al-Ghazali's Moderation in Belief* (Chicago, IL: University of Chicago Press, 2013), 177–78. See as well al-Ghazali's *al-Risala al-qudsiya*, Tibawi's edition in "Al-Ghazali's Sojourn in Damascus and Jerusalem," *Islamic Quarterly* 9 (1965), 89 = *Ihya'*, 1:177–93, Bk.2 trans. as *The Principles of the Creed* by K. Williams (Louisville, KY: Fons Vitae, 2016), and Nabih Faris, *Book of Knowledge* (New Delhi: India International Islamic, 1979), 83–84.

4.   See 'Abd al-Jabbar, *al-Mughni*, 13:450–60 and his *Kitab usul al-khamsa*, 28–42 in Martin, *Defenders of Reason in Islam*, 96–102, and Heemskerk, *Suffering in Mu'tazilite Theology*, 163–71.

5.   al-Razi, *Mafatih al-ghayb* (Beirut: Dar al-Fikr, 1981), 12:229–30.

6.   Ibn al-Humam, *al-Musayara*, 110–11. See as well the commentary *Kitab al-musamara*, 2:56–57.

Bibliography

Arabic Works

Abu Hayyan al-Andalusi. *al-Bahr al-muhit*. Beirut: Dar al-Kutub al-'Ilmiya, 1993.

Abu Ya'la. *al-Musnad*. Beirut: Dar al-Ma'mun, 1986.

Ahmad b. Hanbal. *al-Musnad*. Edited by Shu'ayb al-Arna'ut. Beirut: Mu'assasat al-Risala, 1999.

al-Alusi. *Ruh al-ma'ani fi tafsir al-Qur'an al-azim wa-l-sab' al-mathani*. Beirut: Dar Ihya' al-Turath al-'Arabi, 1985.

al-Ash'ari. *al-Maqalat al-islamiyin wa-ikhtilaf al-musallin*. Leipzig: Wiesbaden, 1963.

al-Ashqar. U.S. *al-Janna wa-l-nar*. Amman: Dar al-Nafa'is, 1998.

———. ed. *Sharh Ibn Qayyim asma' Allah al-husna*. Amman: Dar al-Nafa'is, 2008.

al-'Ayni. *'Umdat al-qari sharh Sahih al-Bukhari*. Beirut: Dar al-Kutub al-'Ilmiya, 2001.

al-'Azim Abadi. *'Awn al-ma'bud 'ala sunan Abi Dawud*. Amman: Bayt al-Afkar al-Dawliya, n.d.

al-Babarti. *Sharh wasiyat al-Imam Abi Hanifa*. Amman: Dar al-Fath, 2009.

al-Baghawi. *Ma'alim al-tanzil*. Riyadh: Dar al-Tayba, 1988.

al-Baghdadi. *al-Farq bayn al-firaq*. Edited by M. 'Abd al-Hamid. Cairo: Dar al-Turath, 2007.

al-Barzanji. *Sadad al-din wa sidad al-dayn fi ithbat al-najat wa-l-darajat li-l-walidayn*. Beirut: Dar al-Kutub al-'Ilmiya, 2006.

al-Baydawi. *Anwar al-tanzil wa asrar al-ta'wil*. Beirut: Dar al-Ma'rifa, 2017.

al-Bayhaqi. *Shu'ab al-Iman*. Edited by Sa'id Zaghlul. Beirut: Dar al-Kutub al-'Ilmiya, 2000.

al-Dhahabi. *Kitab al-kaba'ir*. Beirut: al-Maktaba al-Umawiya, 1970.

al-Ghazali. *Ihya' 'ulum al-din*. Beirut: Dar al-Kutub al-'Ilmiya, 2016.

———. *al-Iqtisad fi al-i'tiqad*. Cairo: Mustafa al-Babi al-Halabi, [1891] 1966.

227

————. *Maqsad al-asna sharh asma' Allah al-husna*, MS Sarajevo, Gazi Hüsrev Beg.

al-Ghusn. A. *Da'awa al-munawi'in li-Shaykh al-Islam Ibn Taymiya: 'ard wa-naqd.* Dammam: Dar Ibn al-Jawzi, 2003.

al-Hallaq, Th. *al-'Inaya al-ilahiya wa mushkilat al-sharr fi al-fikr al-falsafi.* Damascus: Dar al-Nawadir, 2014.

al-Haythami. *al-Zawajir 'an iqtiraf al-kaba'ir.* Beirut: Dar al-Kutub al-'Ilmiya, 1987.

Ibn Abi Hatim. *al-Sunan.* Mecca: Maktabat al-Nazar al-Baz, 1997.

Ibn 'Adil al-Dimashqi. *al-Lubab fi 'ulum al-kitab.* Beirut: Dar al-Kutub al-'Ilmiya, 1998.

Ibn al-'Arabi. *Ahkam al-Qur'an.* Beirut: Dar al-Kutub al-'Ilmiya, 2002.

Ibn al-Humam. *al-Musayara fi al-'aqa'id al-munjiya fi al-akhira.* Cairo: al-Maktaba al-Mahmudiya al-Tijariya, 1929.

Ibn al-Jawzi. *Zad al-masir fi 'ilm al-tafsir.* Beirut: Dar Ibn Hazm, 2002.

Ibn 'Ashur. *al-Tahrir wa-l-tanwir.* Tunis: Dar al-Tunisiya, 1984.

Ibn 'Atiya al-Andalusi. *al-Muharrar al-wajiz fi tafsir al-kitab al-'aziz.* Beirut: Dar al-Kutub al-'Ilmiya, 2001.

Ibn Hajar al-'Asqalani. *Fath al-bari.* Riyadh: Maktabat al-Malik Fahad al-Wataniya, 2001.

————. *Fath al-bari sharh sahih al-bukhari.* Riyadh: Dar al-Tayba, 2005.

Ibn Hazm. *al-Fasl fi al-milal wa-l-nihal.* Saudi Arabia: Sharikat Maktabat 'Ukkaz.

————. *Maratib al-ijma' fi al-'ibadat wa-l-mu'amalat wa-l-i'tiqadat.* Beirut: Dar Ibn Hazm, 1998.

Ibn Hibban. *al-Sahih.* Beirut: Dar al-Kutub al-'Ilmiya, 1987.

Ibn Kathir. *Tafsir al-Qur'an al-'azim.* Riyadh: Dar al-Tayba, 1999.

Ibn Nujaym. *al-Sagha'ir wa-l-kaba'ir.* Beirut: Dar al-Kutub al-'Ilmiya, 1981.

Ibn Qayyim. *Bada'i' al-fawa'id.* Edited by A. al-'Imran. Jeddah: Dar 'Alam al-Fawa'id, 2003.

————. *Bada'i' al-tafsir al-jami' li-ma fassarahu al-Imam Ibn Qayyim al-Jawziya,* 3 vols. Edited by Y. S. Muhammad and S. A. al-Shami. KSA-Cairo: Dar Ibn al-Jawzi, 1427 H.

————. *Hadi al-arwah ila bilad al-afrah.* Edited by Muhammad ibn Ibrahim al-Zaghli. Dammam: Ramadi li-al-Nashr, 1997.

————. *Miftah dar al-sa'ada wa manshur wilayat al-'ilm wa-l-irada.* 1st ed. Vol. 1. Edited by 'Abd al-Rahman b. Hasan b. Qa'id. Jeddah: Dar 'Ilm al-Fawa'id, 1432 H.

————. *Mukhtasar al-sawa'iq al-mursala 'ala al-jahmiya wa-l-mu'attila.* Abridged and edited by Muhammad ibn al-Mawsili and H. al-'Alawi. Riyadh: Adwa' al-Salaf, 2004.

————. *Shifa' al-'alil fi masa'il al-qada' wa-l-qadr wa-l-hikma wa-l-ta'lil.* Cairo: Maktabat Dar al-Turath, 1975.

————. *Tariq al-hijratayn wa bab al-sa'adatayn*. Mecca: Dar 'Alam al-Fawa'id, 2008.

————. *al-Tibb al-nabawi*. Beirut: Dar al-Fikr, n.d.

Ibn Taymiya. *al-Jawab al-sahih li-man baddala din al-masih*. Riyadh: Dar al-'Asima, 1999.

————. *Minhaj al-sunna al-nabawiya*. Edited by Muhammad Salim. Riyadh: Muhammad Ibn Saud University, 1987.

————. *al-Radd 'ala man qala bi-fana' al-janna wa-l-nar wa bayan al-aqwal fi dhalik*. Edited by Muhammad b. 'Abd Allah al-Samhari. Riyadh: Dar al-Balansiya, 1995.

Ibn Rajab. *al-Takhwif min al-nar wa-l-ta'rif bi-hal dar al-bawar*. Damascus: Maktabat al-Mu'ayyad, 1988.

al-Jurjani. *Sharh al-mawaqif* of *al-Iji*. Beirut: Dar al-Kutub al-'Ilmiya, 1998.

al-Kamal Ibn Abi Sharif, *Kitab al-musamara fi sharh al-musayara* with sub-linear notes by Qasim b. Qutlubugha. Cairo: al-Maktaba al-Azhariya, 2006.

al-Khazin. *Lubab al-ta'wil fi ma'ani al-tanzil*. Beirut: Dar al-Kutub al-'Ilmiya, 2004.

al-Lamishi. *Kitab al-tamhid li-qawa'id al-tawhid*. Edited by A al-Turki. Beirut: al-Gharb al-Islami, 1995.

al-Maturidi. *Kitab al-tawhid*. Edited by Fathalla Kholeif. Beirut: Dar al-Mashriq, 1986.

————. *Sharh fiqh al-akbar*. Deccan: Matba'at Majlis Da'irat al-Ma'arif al-Nizamiya, 1904, repr. Qatar: Shu'un al-Diniya, n.d.

————. *Ta'wilat ahl al-sunna*, 11 vols. Edited by Majdi Basallum. Beirut: Dar al-Kutub al-'Ilmiya, 2005.

al-Mawardi. *al-Nukat wa-l-'uyun*. Beirut: Dar al-Kutub al-'Ilmiya, 1992.

————. *al-Nukat wa-l-'uyun*. Beirut: Dar al-Kutub al-'Ilmiya and Mu'assasat al-Kutub al-Thaqafiya, n.d.

al-Munawi. *Fayd al-qadir sharh al-jami' al-saghir*. 2nd ed. Beirut: Dar al-Ma'rifa, 1972.

al-Nasafi, Abu al-Mu'in. *Tabsirat al-adilla fi usul al-din*. 2 vols. Edited by Hüseyin Atay and Şaban Ali Düzugün. Ankara: Nashriyat Ri'asat al-Shu'un al-Diyana li-l-jumhuriya al-Turkiya, 2003.

al-Nawawi. *al-Minhaj sharh sahih muslim b. al-hajjaj*. Cairo: al-Matba'at al-Misriya, 1929.

————. *Sharh sahih muslim*. Cairo: al-Matba'at al-Misriya, 1930.

al-Qarara'a, J. "Masir ahl al-fatra fi-l-akhira wa silat aqwal al-'ulama' fi hadhihi al-mas'ala bi-aqwalihim fi al-tahsin wa-l-taqbih." *Umm al-Qura Journal of Islamic Sciences, Arabic Language and Literature* 18 (2006).

al-Qari, Mulla. *al-Asrar al-marfu'a fi-l-akhbar al-mawdu'a*. Beirut: Dar al-Kutub al-'Ilmiya, 2018.

————. *Mirqat al-mafatih sharh mishkat al-masabih*. Beirut: Dar al-Kutub al-'Ilmiya, 2015.

―――. *Tasliyat al-aʿma ʿala baliyat al-ʿama.* Tanta: Dar Sahaba, 1993.

al-Qurtubi. *al-Asna fi Sharh asma' Allah al-husna.* Tanta: Dar al-Sahaba li-l-Turath, 1995.

―――. *al-Jamiʿ li-ahkam al-Qur'an.* Beirut: Dar al-Fikr, 1987.

―――. *al-Jamiʿ li-ahkam al-Qur'an.* Beirut: Mu'assasat al-Risala, 2006.

―――. *Kitab al-tadhkira fi ahwal al-mawta wa umur al-akhira.* Riyadh: Maktabat Dar al-Minhaj, 1425 H.

―――. *al-Mufhim li-ma ashkala min talkhis Kitab Muslim.* Damascus: Dar Ibn Kathir and Dar Kalim al-Tayyib, 1996.

al-Razi. *Mafatih al-ghayb.* 1st ed. Beirut: Dar al-Fikr, 1987.

al-Saffarini. *al-Buhur al-zakhira fi ʿulum al-akhira.* Kuwait: Ghiras, 2007.

al-Sanʿani. *Rafʿ al-astar li-ibtal adillat al-qa'ilin bi-fana' al-nar.* Beirut: al-Maktab al-Islami, 1984.

al-Shahrastani. *al-Milal wa-l-nihal.* Beirut: Dar Ibn Hazm, 2007.

al-Shawkani. "Kashf al-astar fi ibtal qawl man qala bi-fana' al-nar." In *Kitab fath al-rabbani min fatawa al-Imam al-Shawkani.* Sanaa: Maktabat al-Jil al-Jadid, n.d.

Shaykh Zadah. *Nazm al-fara'id wa-jamʿ al-fawa'id,* 1st ed. Cairo: al-Matbaʿa al-Adabiya, 1317 H.

Shukri, A. *Ahl al-fatra wa man fi hukmihim.* Damascus: Dar Ibn Kathir, 1988.

al-Subki. *al-Iʿtibar bi-baqa' al-janna wa-l-nar.* Damascus: Matbaʾat al-Turki, 1347 H.

al-Suyuti. *al-Budur al-safira fi ahwal al-akhira.* Beirut: Dar al-Kutub al-ʿIlmiya, 1996.

―――. *al-Durr al-manthur fi tafsir al-ma'thur.* Beirut: Dar al-Fikr, 2011.

―――. *al-Durr al-manthur fi-l-tafsir al-ma'thur.* Cairo: Markaz al-Hajar, 2003.

―――. *Jamiʿ al-hadith al-jamiʿ al-saghir wa zawa'iduhu wa-l-jamiʿ al-kabir.* Beirut: Dar al-Fikr, 1994.

al-Taftazani. *Sharh al-maqasid.* Beirut: ʿAlam al-Kutub, 1998.

Tattan, ʿAbd al-Karim and al-Kiylani M. eds. *ʿAwn al-murid li-sharh jawharat al-tawhid fi ʿaqidat ahl al-sunna wa-l-jamaʿa.* Beirut: Dar al-Basha'ir, 1999.

al-ʿUmayri, S. *Ishkaliyat al-iʿdhar bi-l-jahl fi-l-bahth al-ʿuqdi.* Beirut: Dar al-Wujuh, 2012.

Non-Arabic Works

Abdel-Kader, H. *The Life, Personality and Writings of Al-Junayd.* London: Luzac, 1962.

Abdul Rauf, F. "What Is Sunni Islam?" In *Voices of Islam,* 1:185–216.

Abdullah, A. K. *The Qur'an and Normative Religious Pluralism: A Thematic Study of the Qur'an.* London: International Institute of Islamic Thought, 2014.

Abrahamov, B. *Islamic Theology: Traditionalism and Rationalism.* Edinburgh: Edinburgh University Press, 1988.

Abu Rabi', I. M., ed. *Theodicy and Justice in Modern Islamic Thought: The Case of Said Nursi*. Surrey: Ashgate, 2010.

Adams, M. M. *Horrendous Evil and the Goodness of God*. Ithaca, NY: Cornell University Press, 1999.

———. "Ignorance, Instrumentality, Compensation, and the Problem of Evil." *Sophia* 52 (2013): 7–26.

Adamson, P., and G. F. Edwards, eds. *Animals: A History*. New York: Oxford University Press, 2018.

———. "From the Necessary Existent to God." In *Interpreting Avicenna: Critical Essays*, edited by P. Adamson, 185–88. New York: Cambridge University Press, 2013.

———. "Abu Bakr al-Razi on Animals." *Archiv für Geschichte der Philosophie* 94 (2012): 249–73.

Affifi, A. E. *The Mystical Philosophy of MuHyid Din-Ibnul 'Arabi*. Cambridge: Cambridge University Press, 1939.

Afnan, S. H. *Avicenna: His Life and Works*. London: George Allen & Unwin, 1958.

Aijaz, I. "Belief, Providence, and Eschatology." *Philosophy Compass* 3 (2008): 235–40.

———. *Islam: A Contemporary Philosophical Investigation*. Oxford: Routledge, 2018.

———. "The Islamic Problem of Religious Diversity." In *Religious Perspectives on Religious Diversity*, 162–75.

Akbaş, M. "Divine Retribution Again: Is the Current Economic Crisis God's Punishment?" *İstanbul Üniversitesi İlahiyat Fakültesi Dergisi* 22 (2010): 197–210.

———. *The Problem of Evil and Theodicy: In Jewish, Christian and Islamic Thought*. Saarbrücken: Scholars Press, 2013.

———. "Redemptive Suffering in Islamic Thought: A Critical Approach." *DEÜİFD* 31 (2010): 191–204.

Akhtar, S. *The Qur'an and the Secular Mind: A Philosophy of Islam*. Oxford: Routledge, 2008.

Ali, Z. *Faith, Philosophy and the Reflective Muslim*. New York: Palgrave Macmillan, 2013.

Allen, B. *Animals in Religion: Devotion, Symbol and Ritual*. London: Reaktion Books, 2016.

Andrews, K., ed. *The Animal Mind: An Introduction to the Philosophy of Animal Cognition*. London: Routledge, 2014.

Andrews, K., and J. Beck, eds. *The Routledge Handbook of Philosophy of Animal Minds*. Oxford and New York: Routledge, 2017.

Antes, P. "The First Aš'arites' Conception of Evil and the Devil." In *Mélanges offerts à Henry Corbin*, edited by S. H. Nasr, 177–89. Tehran: McGill University, Institute of Islamic Studies, Tehran Branch, 1977.

Armstrong, K. *A History of God*. London: Heinemann, 1992.

Arp, R., and B. McCraw, eds. *The Concept of Hell*. New York: Palgrave Macmillan, 2015.

Aslan, A. "The Fall, Evil and Suffering in Islam." In *The Origin and the Overcoming of Evil and Suffering in the World Religions*, edited by P. Koslowski. Dordrecht: Springer, 2001.

Attfield, R. *Creation, Evolution and Meaning*. Aldershot: Ashgate, 2009.

———. *Wonder, Value and God*. Oxford: Routledge, 2017.

Azzam, M. "Islamic Philosophy on Human Rights." In *Animal Ethics and Trade: The Challenge of Animal Ethics*, edited by J. D'Silva and J. Turner, 129–33. London: Earthscan, 2006.

Bacchus, S. *The Concept of Justice in Islam*. Victoria: Friesen Press, 2014.

Badawi, E., and M. A. Haleem, eds., *Arabic-English Dictionary of Qur'anic Usage*. Leiden: Brill, 2008.

Barnbaum, D. R. *The Ethics of Autism: Among Them but Not of Them*. Bloomington: Indiana University Press, 2008.

Bawulski, S. "The Fire That Reconciles: Theological Reflections on the Doctrine of Eternal Punishment, with Special Consideration of Annihilationism and Traditionalism." PhD. diss., University of St Andrews, 2012.

Bazna, M. S., and T. A. Hatab. "Disability in the Qur'an: The Islamic Alternative to Defining, Viewing and Relating to Disability." *Journal of Religion, Disability and Health* 9 (2005): 5–27.

Beauchamp, T. L., and R. G. Frey (ed.), *The Oxford Handbook of Animal Ethics*. New York: Oxford University Press, 2011.

Bell, W. "Horrendous Evil and the Problem of Representation." MA diss., University of Missouri, St. Louis, 2016.

Benkheira, M. H., C. Mayeur-Jaouen, and J. Sublet. *L'Animal en Islam*. Paris: Les Indes Savantes, 2005.

Bennett, G., T. Peters, M. J. Hewlett, and R. J. Russell, eds. *The Evolution of Evil*. Göttingen: Vandenhoeck and Ruprecht, 2008.

Betenson, T. "The Problem of Evil as a Moral Objection to Theism." PhD diss., University of Birmingham, 2014.

Bhatty, I., A. Moten, M. Tawakkul, and M. Amer. "Disability in Islam: Insights into Theology, Law, History and Practice." In *Disabilities: Insights from across Fields and around the World*, volume 1, edited by Catherine A. Marshall, Elizabeth Kendall, Martha E. Banks, and Reva M. S. Gover. Westport, CT: Praeger, 2009, ch.13.

al-Birgivi. *The Path of Muhammad: A Book on Islamic Morals and Ethics*. Translated by Tosun Bayrak al-Jerrahi. Bloomington, IN: World Wisdom, 2005.

Black, K. A. *Healing Homiletic: Preaching and Disability*. Nashville, TN: Abingdon Press, 1996.

Blanchard, L. M. *Will All Be Saved: An Assessment of Universalism in Western Theology*. Milton Keynes: Paternoster, 2015.

Blowers, P. "Unfinished Creative Business: Maximus the Confessor, Evolutionary Theodicy and Human Stewardship in Creation." In *On Earth as It Is in Heaven: Cultivating a Contemporary Theology of Creation*, edited by D. Meconi, 174–77. Grand Rapids, MI: Eerdmans, 2016.

Boddice, R., ed. *Anthropocentricism: Humans, Animals and Environments*. Leiden and Boston: Brill, 2011.

Bosworth, C. E. "The Rise of the Karramiyya in Khurasan." *Muslim World* 50 (1960): 6–14.

Bousquet, G. H. "Des Animaux et de leur traitement selon le Judaïsme, le Christianisme et l'Islam." *Studia Islamica* 9 (1958): 31–48.

Boyd, G. "Evolution as Cosmic Warfare: A Biblical Perspective on Satan and 'Natural Evil.'" In *Creation Made Free*, edited by T. Oord, 125–45. Eugene, OR: Wipf & Stock, 2009.

———. *Satan and the Problem of Evil: Constructing a Trinitarian Warfare Theodicy*. Downers Grove, IL: InterVarsity Press, 2001.

Brown, C., and J. Walls. "Annihilationism: A Philosophical Dead End?" In *The Problem of Hell: A Philosophical Anthology*, edited by Joel Buenting, 45–64. London: Routledge, 2016.

Bulliet, R. W. *The Patricians of Nishapur: A Study in Medieval Islamic Social History*. Cambridge, MA: Harvard University Press, 1972.

Burkhalter, S. L. "Completion in Continuity: Cosmogony and Ethics in Islam." In *Cosmogony and Ethical Order: New Studies in Comparative Ethics*, edited by Lovin, Robin and Frank E. Reynolds, 225–50. Chicago, IL: University of Chicago Press, 1985.

Capper, D. *Learning Love from a Tiger: Religious Experiences with Nature*. Oakland: University of California Press, 2016.

Chignell, A., ed. *Evil: A History*. New York: Oxford University Press, 2019.

———. "The Problem of Infant Suffering." *Religious Studies* 34 (1998): 205–17.

Chisholm, R. "The Defeat of Good and Evil." *Proceedings of the American Philosophical Association* 42 (1968): 21–38.

Chittick, W. C. *Imaginal Worlds: Ibn al-'Arabi and the Problem of Religious Diversity*. Albany: State University of New York Press, 1994.

———. *Ibn 'Arabi: Heir to the Prophets*. Oxford: Oneworld, 2005.

———. *The Self-Disclosure of God: Principles of Ibn al-'Arabi's Cosmology*. Albany: State University of New York Press, 1998.

———. *Sufism: A Beginners Guide*. Oxford: Oneworld, 2008.

———. *The Sufi Path of Love: The Spiritual Teachings of Rumi*. Albany: State University of New York Press, 1983.

————. "The Ambiguity of the Qur'anic Command." In *Between Heaven and Hell*, 65–86.

Cobb, A. "Acknowledged Dependence and the Virtues of Perinatal Hospice." *Journal of Medicine and Philosophy* 42 (2016): 25–40.

Cornell, V., ed. *Voices of Islam*, volumes 1–5. Westport, CT: Praeger, 2007.

Craig, W. L. "'No Other Name': A Middle Knowledge Perspective on the Exclusivity of Salvation through Christ." *Faith and Philosophy* 6 (1989): 172–88.

Creegan, N. H. *Animal Suffering and the Problem of Evil*. New York: Oxford University Press, 2013.

Crisp, O. "Divine Retribution: A Defense." *Sophia* 42 (2003): 35–52.

Cross, R. "Impairment, Normalcy, and a Social Theory of Disability." *Res Philosophica* 93 (2016): 693–714.

Daiber, H. *The Islamic Concept of Belief in the 4th/10th Century: Abul-Layth al-Samarqandi's Commentary on Abu Hanifa (died 150/767) al-Fiqh al-Absat.* Tokyo: ILCAA, 1995.

Darnell, R. "The Idea of Divine Covenant in the Qur'an." PhD diss., University of Michigan, 1970.

Davidson, H. A. *Proofs for Eternity, Creation and the Existence of God in Medieval Islamic and Jewish Philosophy*. New York: Oxford University Press, 1987.

Davis, S. T. *Encountering Evil: Live Options in Theodicy*. Louisville, KY: Westminster John Knox, 2001.

al-Daylami. *Kitab 'Atf al-Alif al-Ma'luf 'ala al-Lam al-Ma'tuf* ("A Treatise on Mystical Love"). Translated by Joseph Norman Bell and Hassan Al Shafie. Edinburgh: Edinburgh University Press, 2005.

Deane-Drummond, C. *Christ and Evolution: Wisdom and Wonder*. Minneapolis, MN: Fortress Press, 2009.

de Callataÿ, G. *Ikhwan al-Safa': A Brotherhood of Idealists on the Fringe of Orthodox Islam*. Oxford: Oneworld, 2005.

————. "'For Those with Eyes to See': On the Hidden Meaning of the Animal Fable in the Rasa'il Ikhwan al-Safa." *Journal of Islamic Studies* 29 (2018): 1–36.

De Cillis, M. "Avicenna on Matter, Matter's Disobedience and Evil: Reconciling Metaphysical Stances and Quranic Perspective." *Transcendent Philosophy Journal* 12 (2011): 147–68.

Dembski, W. *The End of Christianity: Finding a Good God in an Evil World*. Nashville, TN: B & H, 2009.

Demello, M. *Mourning Animals: Rituals and Practices Surrounding Animal Death*. Michigan: Michigan State University Press, 2016.

Demichelis, M. "*Fana' al-Nar* within Early Kalam and Mysticism. An Analysis Covering the Eighth and Ninth Centuries." *Archiv Orientální* 83 (2015): 385–410.

————. "The Fate of others in Fourteenth-Century Hanbalism: Ibn Taymiyya (d. 1328/728), Ibn Qayyim al-Jawziyya (d. 1350/750) and the Fana' al-Nar." *Annale de Scienze Religiose* 9 (2016): 271–94.

————. *Salvation and Hell in Classical Islamic Thought: Can Allah Save Us All?* London: Bloomsbury, 2018.

Dougherty, T. *The Problem of Animal Suffering: A Theodicy for All Creatures Great and Small*. New York: Palgrave Macmillan, 2014.

Dougherty, T., and J. P. McBrayer, eds. *Skeptical Theism: New Essays*. Oxford: Oxford University Press, 2014.

Draz, M. A. *The Moral World of the Qur'an*. London: I.B. Tauris, 2008.

Eiesland, N. *The Disabled God: Toward a Liberatory Theology of Disability*. Nashville, TN: Abingdon Press, 1994.

El-Bizri, N. *The Phenomenological Quest between Avicenna and Heidegger*. Binghamton: State University of New York Press, 2000.

El Omari, R. *The Theology of Abu'l-Qasim al-Balkhi/al-Ka'bi (d.319/931)*. Leiden: Brill, 2016.

Esack, F. "The Portrayal of Jews and the Possibilities for their Salvation in the Qur'an." In *Between Heaven and Hell*, 207–33.

Farahat, O. *The Foundations of Norms in Islamic Jurisprudence and Theology*. Cambridge: Cambridge University Press, 2019.

Farris, J., and C. Taliaferro, eds. *The Ashgate Research Companion to Theological Anthropology*. Oxford: Routledge, 2015.

Faruque, M. U. "Does God Create Evil? A Study of Fakhr al-Din al-Razi's Exegesis of Surat al-Falaq." *Islam and Christian-Muslim Relations* 28 (2017): 271–91.

Foltz, R. C. *Animals in Islamic Traditions and Muslim Cultures*. London: Oneworld, 2006.

————. "'This She-Camel Is a Sign to You'": Dimensions of Animals in Islamic Tradition and Muslim Culture." In *A Communion of Subjects: Animals in Religion, Science and Ethics*, edited by P. Waldau and K. Patton, pp. 149–59. New York: Columbia University Press, 2006.

Frances, B. *Gratuitous Suffering and the Problem of Evil: A Comprehensive Introduction*. New York: Routledge, 2013.

Francescotti, R. "The Problem of Animal Pain and Suffering." In *The Blackwell Companion to the Problem of Evil*, 113–27.

Furber, M. "Rights and Duties Pertaining to Kept Animals: A Case Study in Islamic Law and Ethics." *Tabah Paper Series* 9 (2015): 30–34.

Garrett, A. V. *Animal Rights and Souls in the Eighteenth Century*. Bristol: Thoemmes Press, 2000.

Gätje, H. *The Qur'an and its Exegesis: Selected Texts with Classical and Modern Muslim Interpretations*. Oxford: Oneworld, 2004.

Gazagnadou, D. "Note on the Question of Animal Suffering in Medieval Islam: Muslim Mu'tazilite Theology Confronted by Manichean Iranian Thought." *Anthropology of the Middle East* 11 (2016): 30–35.

Gazonneau, A. "L'Animal et L'Islam à Travers le Temps." PhD diss., National Veterinary School of Alfort, 2019.

Germann, N. "...*But Draw Not Nigh This Tree*: Evil in Early Islamic Thought." In *Evil: A History*, 198–209.

Ghaly, M. "The Convention on the Rights of Persons with Disabilities and the Islamic Tradition: The Question of Legal Capacity in Focus." *Journal of Disability and Religion* 23 (2019): 251–78.

———. *Islam and Disability: Perspectives in Theology and Jurisprudence*. London and New York: Routledge, 2010.

———. "Muslim Theologians on Evil: God's Omnipotence or Justice, God's Omnipotence and Justice." In *Theologie der Barmherzigkeit?*, 147–72.

al-Ghazali. *al-Arba'in fi Usul al-Din*. Translated by N. Abdassalam. London: Turath, 2016.

———. *Book of Fear and Hope*. Translated by William MacKane. Leiden: Brill, 1965.

———. *Book of Knowledge*. Translated by N. A. Faris. New Delhi: International Islamic, 1979.

———. *Duties of Brotherhood in Islam*. Partially translated by Muhtar Holland. Leicester: Islamic Foundation, 1980.

———. *Faith in Divine Unity and Trust in Divine Providence*. Translated by David B. Burrell. Louisville, KY: Fons Vitae, 2002.

———. *Faysal al-Tafriqa bayn al-Islam wa-l-Zandaqa*. Translated by Sherman Jackson as *On the Boundaries of Theological Tolerance in Islam*. Karachi: Oxford University Press, 2002.

———. *al-Ghazali's Moderation in Belief*. Translated by A. Yaqub. Chicago, IL: University of Chicago Press, 2013.

———. *Love, Longing, Intimacy, and Contentment*. Translated by Eric Ormsby. Cambridge: Islamic Texts Society, 2016.

———. *The Ninety-Nine Beautiful Names of God*. Translated by David Burrell and Nazih Daher. Cambridge: Islamic Texts Society, 2007.

Gillespie, N. Charles. *Darwin and the Problem of Creation*. Chicago: University of Chicago Press, 1979.

Gleeson, B. *Geographies of Disability*. London: Routledge, 1999.

Gok, H. "Said Nursi's Arguments for the Existence of God in Risale-i Nur." PhD diss., Durham University, 2014.

Goodman, L. E. *Avicenna: Arabic Thought and Culture*. Oxford: Routledge, 1992.

Goodman, L. E., and R. McGregor, eds. *The Case of the Animals versus Man before the King of the Jinn: An Arabic Critical Edition and English Translation of Epistle*

22. Oxford: Oxford University Press in association with The Institute of Ismaili Studies, 2010.

Gramlich, R. "Der Urvertrag in der Koranauslegung." *Der Islam* 60 (1983): 205–30.

Grenz, S., and R. Olson, eds. *Twentieth-Century Theology: God and the World in a Transitional Age*. Downers Grove, IL: InterVarsity Press, 1992.

Griffin, D. R. *Animal Minds: Beyond Cognition to Consciousness*. Chicago and London: University of Chicago Press, 2001.

Griffiths, P. J. *Decreation: The Last Things of All Creatures*. Waco, TX: Baylor University Press, 2014.

———. "Self-Annihilation or Damnation? A Disputable Question in Christian Eschatology." In *Liberal Faith: Essays in Honour of Philip Quinn*, edited by P. J. Weithman, 83–117. Notre Dame, IN: University of Notre Dame Press, 2008.

Gwynne, R. W. *Logic, Rhetoric and Legal Reasoning in the Qur'an*. London and New York: Routledge, 2004.

Haddad, G. F. *Correct Islamic Doctrines Volume 2—Ibn Khafif and Shaykh Muhyi al-Din Ibn 'Arabi*. Fenton, MI and Damascus: As-Sunna Foundation of America, 1999.

Hamza, F. "Temporary Hellfire Punishment and the Making of Sunni Orthodoxy." In *Roads to Paradise: Eschatology and Concepts of the Hereafter in Islam*, volume 1, edited by Gunther, Sabastian and Todd Lawson, 371–406. Leiden: Brill, 2017.

———. "To Hell and Back: A Study of the Concept of Hell and Intercession in Early Islam." PhD diss., Oxford University Press, 2002.

Haq, S. N. "Islam." In *A Companion to Environmental Philosophy*, edited by Jamieson, 111–29.

Harrison, P. "God and Animal Minds: A Response to Lynch" (1996). Available online at http://epublications.bond.edu.au/hss_pubs/71 (accessed July 2016).

Hart, D. B. *All Shall be Saved: Heaven, Hell and Universal Salvation*. New Haven and London: Yale University Press, 2019.

Harvey, R. *The Qur'an and the Just Society*. Edinburgh: Edinburgh University Press, 2018.

Heemskerk, M. T. *Suffering in Mu'tazilite Theology: 'Abd al-Jabbar's Teaching on Pain and Divine Justice*. Leiden: Brill, 2000.

Hick, J. "An Irenaean Theodicy." In *Encountering Evil: Live Options in Theodicy*, edited by Stephen T. Davis, 38–72. Louisville, KY: Westminster John Knox, 2001.

Hoover, J. "God's Wise Purposes in Creating Iblis: Ibn Qayyim al-Ǧawziyyah's Theodicy of God's Names and Attributes." In *A Scholar in the Shadow: Essays in the Legal and Theological Thought of Ibn Qayyim al-Ǧawziyyah*, edited by

Caterina Bori and Livnat Holtzman. Oriente Moderno monograph series, 90, no. 1 (2010): 113–34.

———. *Ibn Taymiyya's Theodicy of Perpetual Optimism*. Leiden: Brill, 2007.

———. "Islamic Universalism: Ibn Qayyim al-Jawziyya's Salafi Deliberations on the Duration of Hellfire." *Muslim World* 99 (2009): 181–209.

———. "Against Islamic Universalism: 'Ali al-Harbi's 1990 Attempt to Prove that Ibn Taymiyya and Ibn Qayyim al-Jawziyya Affirm the Eternality of Hell-Fire." In *Islamic Philosophy, Theology and Law: Debating Ibn Taymiyya and Ibn Qayyim al-Jawziyya*, 377–99.

———. "Islamic Universalism: Ibn Qayyim al-Jawziyya's Salafi Deliberations on the Duration of Hell-Fire." *Muslim World* 99 (2009): 181–201.

———. "A Muslim Conflict Over Universal Salvation." In *Alternative Salvations: Engaging the Sacred and the Secular*, edited by Hannah Bacon, Wendy Dossett, and Steve Knowles, 160–71. London: Bloomsbury, 2015.

———. "Withholding Judgment on Islamic Universalism Ibn al-Wazir (d. 840/1436) on the Duration and Purpose of Hell-Fire." In *Locating Hell in the Islamic Tradition*, 208–37.

———. "A Typology of Responses to the Philosophical Problem of Evil in the Islamic and Christian Traditions." *Conrad Grebel Review* 21, no. 3 (2003): 81–96.

Hunter, C. *Darwin's God: Evolution and the Problem of Evil*. Grand Rapids, MI: Brazos Press, 2001.

Hussain, M. Y. "Al-Ash'ari's Discussion of the Problem of Evil." *Islamic Culture* 64 (1990): 25–38.

Hylén, T. "The Hand of God is over their Hands (Q. 48:10): On the Notion of Covenant in al-Tabari's Account of Karbala.'" *Journal of Qur'anic Studies* 18 (2016): 58–68.

Ibn Sina. *Al-Shifa': The Metaphysics of the Healing*. Translated by M. Marmura. Utah: Brigham Young University Press, 2005.

Ibrahim, G. S. A. *Virtues in Muslim Culture: An Interpretation from Muslim Culture, Art and Architecture*. London: New Generation, 2014.

Ibrahim, L. "The Concept of Divine Justice According to al-Zamakhshari and al-BayDawi." *Hamdard Islamicus* 3 (1980): 3–17.

Inati, S. *The Problem of Evil: Ibn Sina's Theodicy*. Albany: State University of New York Press, 2000.

Izutsu, T. *The Concept of Belief in Islamic Theology: A Semantic Analysis of Iman and Islam*. New York: Other Press, 2006.

———. *Ethico-Religious Concepts in the Qur'an*. Montreal: McGill-Queens University Press, 2002.

Izzi Dien, M. *The Environmental Dimensions of Islam*. Cambridge: Lutterworth, 2000.

Jackson, S. A. *Islam and the Problem of Black Suffering*. New York: Oxford University Press, 2009.

Jaffer, T. "Is There Covenant Theology in Islam?" In *Islamic Studies Today: Essays in Honour of Andrew Rippin*, edited by M. Daneshgar and W. Saleh, 98–121. Leiden: Brill, 2016.

Jamieson, D., ed. *A Companion to Environmental Philosophy*. Oxford: Blackwell, 2001.

Jantzen, B. *An Introduction to Design Arguments*. Cambridge: Cambridge University Press, 2014.

Johns, A. H. "A Comparative Glance at Ayyub in the Qur'an." In *Deconstructing Theodicy: Why Job Has Nothing to Say to the Puzzled Suffering*, edited by David B. Burrell, 51–82. Grand Rapids, MI: Brazos Press, 2008.

Johnston, D. *Earth, Empire and Sacred Text: Muslims and Christians as Trustees of Creation*. London: Equinox, 2013.

al-Juwayni. *A Guide to Conclusive Proofs for the Principles of Belief: Kitab al-Irshad ila Qawati' al-Adilla fi Usul al-I'tiqad*. Reading: Garnet, 2001.

Kabay, P. "Is the Status Principle Beyond Salvation? Toward Redeeming an Unpopular Theory of Hell." *Sophia* 44 (2005): 91–103.

Kadi, W. "The Primordial Covenant and Human History in the Qur'an." *Proceedings of the American Philosophical Society* 174 (2003): 332–38.

———. "The Term 'Khalifa' in Early Exegetical Literature." *Die Welt des Islams* 28 (1988): 392–411.

Kaltner, J. *Introducing the Qur'an: For Today's Reader*. Minneapolis, MN: Fortress Press, 2011.

Kant, I. "On the Miscarriage of all Philosophical Trials in Theodicy." In *Religion within the Boundaries of Mere Reason and Other Writings*, translated and edited by A. Wood and G. Di Giovanni. Cambridge: Cambridge University Press, 1998.

Keathley, K. *Salvation and Sovereignty: A Molinist Approach*. Nashville, TN: B & H, 2010.

Kemmerer, L. *Animals and World Religions*. New York: Oxford University Press, 2012.

Kermani, N. *The Terror of God: Attar, Job and the Metaphysical Revolt*. Cambridge: Polity Press, 2011.

Khadduri, M. *The Islamic Conception of Justice*. Baltimore: Johns Hopkins University Press, 1984.

Khalil, M. H. *Between Heaven and Hell: Islam, Salvation and the Fate of Others*. New York: Oxford University Press, 2013.

———. *Islam and the Fate of Others: The Salvation Question*. New York: Oxford University Press, 2012.

————. "Islam and the Salvation of Others." In *Religious Perspectives on Religious Diversity*, edited by Robert McKim, 149–61. Leiden and Boston: Brill, 2016.

Khorchide, M., M. Karimi, and K. von Stasch, eds. *Theologie der Barmherzigkeit?: Zeitgemäße Fragen und Antworten des Kalam.* Münster: Waxmann Verlag Gmbh, 2014.

Kittay, F. E., and L. Carlson, eds. *Cognitive Disability and Its Challenge to Moral Philosophy.* Sussex: Wiley-Blackwell, 2010.

Knysh, A. "The Realms of Responsibility in Ibn 'Arabi's Futuhat al-Makkiya." *Journal of the Muhyiddin Ibn 'Arabi Society* 31 (2002): 87–99.

Koca, Q. "Ibn 'Arabi (1165–1240) and Rumi (1207–1273) on the Question of Evil: Discontinuities in Sufi Metaphysics." *Islam and Christian-Muslim Relations* 28 (2017): 293–311.

Krawietz, B., and G. Tamer, eds. *Islamic Philosophy, Theology and Law: Debating Ibn Taymiyya and Ibn Qayyim al-Jawziyya.* Berlin: Walter De Gruyter, 2013.

Kremer, E. J., and M. J. Laztzer, eds. *The Problem of Evil in Early Modern Philosophy.* Toronto: University of Toronto Press, 2001.

Kristen, K. et al., eds. *Eve and Adam: Jewish, Christian and Muslim Readings of Genesis and Gender.* Bloomington: Indiana University Press, 1999.

Kropf, R. *Evil and Evolution: A Theodicy.* Oregon: Wipf & Stock, 2004.

Kvanvig, J. *Destiny and Deliberation: Essays in Philosophical Theology.* Oxford: Oxford University Press, 2011.

————. *The Problem of Hell.* New York: Oxford University Press, 1993.

————. "Hell." In *The Oxford Handbook of Eschatology*, edited by J. Walls, 413–27. New York: Oxford University Press, 2016.

Laato, A., and J. de Moor, eds. *Theodicy in the World of the Bible: The Goodness of God and the Problem of Evil.* Leiden: Brill, 2003.

Laing, J. D. *Middle Knowledge: Human Freedom in Divine Sovereignty.* Grand Rapids, MI: Kregel, 2018.

Lamont, J. "The Justice and Goodness of Hell." *Faith and Philosophy* 28 (2011): 152–73.

Lamptey, J. T. *Never Wholly Other: A Muslima Theology of Religious Pluralism.* New York: Oxford University Press, 2014.

Landau, R. *The Philosophy of Ibn 'Arabi.* London: George Allen & Unwin, 1959.

Lange, C. *Justice, Punishment and Medieval Muslim Imagination.* Cambridge: Cambridge University Press, 2008.

————. ed. *Locating Hell in Islamic Traditions.* Leiden: Brill, 2015.

————. *Paradise and Hell in Islamic Traditions.* New York: Cambridge University Press, 2016.

————. "Revisiting Hell's Angels in the Quran." In *Locating Hell in Islamic Traditions*, 74–99.

Larijani, B., N. Ghasemzadeh, and M. Madani. "Animal Rights in Islam: The Use of Animals for Medical Research." In *Islamic Bioethics: Current Issues and Challenges*, edited by A. Bagheri and K. Alali, 183–96. London: World Scientific Publishing Europe, 2017.

Lasker, D. *From Judah Hadassi to Elijah Bashyatchi: Studies in Late Karaite Philosophy*. Leiden: Brill, 2008.

———. "The Theory of Compensation ('Iwad) in Rabbanite and Karaite Thought: Animal Sacrifices, Ritual Slaughter and Circumcision." *Jewish Studies Quarterly* 11 (2004): 59–72.

Leaman, O., ed. *The Biographical Encyclopaedia of Islamic Philosophy*. London: Bloomsbury, 2015.

Legenhausen, G. "Non-Reductive Pluralism and Religious Dialogue." In *Between Heaven and Hell*, 153–79.

———. "Notes Towards an Ash'arite Theodicy." *Religious Studies* 24 (1985): 257–66.

Levering, M. *Engaging the Doctrine of Creation: Cosmos, Creatures and the Wise and Good Creator*. Grand Rapids, MI: Baker, 2017.

Lewis, B. *The Political Language of Islam*. Chicago, IL: University of Chicago Press, 1988.

Lewis, C. S. *Problem of Pain*. London: HarperCollins, 2009, repr.

Linzey, A. *Why Animal Suffering Matters: Philosophy, Theology and Practical Ethics*. New York: Oxford University Press, 2013, repr.

Little, B. *A Creation-Order Theodicy: God and Gratuitous Evil*. Lanham, MD: University Press of America, 2004.

———. *God, Why This Evil?* Plymouth: Hamilton Books, 2010.

Lizzini, O. "Matter and Nature: On the Foundations of Avicenna's Theory of Providence: An Overview." *Intellectual History of the Islamicate World* 7 (2019): 7–34.

Lloyd, M. "Are Animals Fallen?" In *Animals on the Agenda: Questions about Animals for Theology and Ethics*, edited by Andrew Linzey and D. Yamamoto, 47–160. London: SCM Press, 1998.

Lobel, D. *A Sufi-Jewish Dialogue: Philosophy and Mysticism in BaHya Ibn Paquda's Duties of the Heart*. Philadelphia: University of Pennsylvania Press, 2007.

Long, M. L. "Leprosy in Early Islam." In *Disability in Judaism, Christianity and Islam: Sacred Texts, Historical Traditions and Social Analysis*, edited by D. Schumm and M. Stoltzfus, 43–62. New York: Palgrave Macmillan, 2011.

Lumbard, J. "Covenant and Covenants in the Qur'an." *Journal of Qur'anic Studies* 17 (2015): 1–23.

Lurz, R. W., ed. *The Philosophy of Animal Minds*. New York: Cambridge University Press, 2009.

MacGregor, K. *Luis de Molina: The Life and Theology of the Founder of Middle Knowledge*. Nashville, TN and Grand Rapids, MI: Zondervan, 2015.

MacIntyre, A. *Dependent Rational Animals: Why Human Beings Need the Virtues.* Chicago, IL: Carus, 1999.

Mackie, J. L. "Evil and Omnipotence." *Mind* 64 (1955): 200–12.

Madelung, W. "'Abbad B. Salman." *Encyclopædia Iranica*, I/1, 70–71. Available online at http://www.iranicaonline.org/articles/abbad-b-salman (accessed January 10, 2014).

———. *Religious Trends in Early Islamic Iran.* Albany, NY: Persian Heritage Foundation, 1988.

Maghen, Z. *Virtues of the Flesh: Passion and Purity in Early Islamic Jurisprudence.* Leiden and Boston: Brill, 2005.

al-Maghnisawi. *Imam Abu Hanifa: al-Fiqh al-Akbar Explained.* Translated by Abdur-Rahman Ibn Yusuf Mangera. Santa Barbara, CA: Whitethread Press, 2007.

Malamud, M. "The Politics of Heresy in Medieval Khurasan: The Karramiyya in Nishapur." *Iranian Studies* 27 (1994): 37–51.

Maritain, J. *On the Philosophy of History.* Edited by Joseph Evans. London: Geoffrey Bles, 1959.

Markham, I. *Engaging with Bediuzzaman Nursi: A Model of Interfaith Dialogue.* New York: Routledge, 2016.

Martin, R. C., M. Woodward, and A. Atmaja. *Defenders of Reason in Islam: Mu'tazilism from Medieval School to Modern Symbol.* London: Oneword, 1997.

Masri, B. A. *Animals in Islam.* Petersfield: Athene Trust, 1989.

———. *Animal Welfare in Islam.* Leicestershire: Islamic Foundation, 2007.

Massaro, A. "The Issue of Animal Souls within the Anglican Debate in the Eighteenth to Nineteenth Centuries." In *Mourning Animals: Rituals and Practices Surrounding Animal Death*, edited by M. De Mello, 31–38. Michigan: Michigan State University Press, 2016.

Massignon, L. "Le 'jour du covenant' (yawm al-mithaq)." *Oriens* 15 (1962): 86–92.

McBrayer, J., and D. Howard-Snyder, eds. *The Blackwell Companion to the Problem of Evil.* Oxford: Wiley Blackwell, 2013.

———. "Counterpart and Appreciation Theodicies." In *The Blackwell Companion to the Problem of Evil*, 192–204.

McClymond, M. J. *The Devil's Redemption: A New History and Interpretation of Christian Universalism.* Grand Rapids, MI: Baker Publishing, 2018.

McGinnis, J. *Avicenna.* New York: Oxford University Press, 2010.

McKim, R. *On Religious Diversity.* New York: Oxford University Press, 2014.

———. ed. *Religious Perspectives on Religious Diversity.* Leiden: Brill, 2016.

McTaggart, J. *Some Dogmas of Religion.* London: E. Arnold, 1906.

McKloskey, H. J. *God and Evil.* The Hague: Martinus Nijhoff, 1974.

———. "God and Evil." *Philosophical Quarterly* 10 (1960): 97–114.

Meisami, S. "Ibn Sina's Philosophical Interpretation of Surat al-Falaq." *Al-Bayan Journal of Qur'an and Hadith Studies* 15 (2017): 1–16.

Meister, C. *Evil: A Guide for the Perplexed*. London: Continuum, 2012.

Meister, C., and P. K. Moser, eds. *The Cambridge Companion to the Problem of Evil*. New York: Cambridge University Press, 2017.

Meister, C., P. K. Moser, and C. Taliaferro, eds. *Contemporary Philosophical Theology*. London: Routledge, 2016.

Michel Thomas, S. J. "God's Justice in Relation to Natural Disasters." In *Theodicy and Justice in Modern Islamic Thought: The Case of Said Nursi*, 219–25.

Mitchell, R. W., N. S. Thompson, and H. L. Miles, eds. *Anthropomorphism, Anecdotes and Animals*. Albany: State University of New York Press, 1997.

Mobini, M. A. "Earth's Epistemic Fruits for Harmony with God: An Islamic Theodicy." In *The Blackwell Companion to the Problem of Evil*, 296–308.

Mol, A. Y. "Divine Respite in the Ottoman tafsir Tradition: Reconciling Exegetical Approaches to Q.11:117." In *Osmanli'da ilm-i tefsir*, edited by M. T. Boyalik and H. Abaci, 539–92. Istanbul: ISAR, 2019.

Moreau, D. "Malebranche on Disorder and Physical Evil: Manichaeism or Philosophical Courage?" In *The Problem of Evil in Early Modern Philosophy*, 81–100.

Moreland, J. P., W. Grudem, C. Shaw, and S. C. Meyer. *Theistic Evolution: A Scientific, Philosophical and Theological Critique*. Wheaton, IL: Crossway Books, 2017.

Murata, K. *Beauty in Sufism: The Teachings of Ruzbihan Baqli*. Albany: State University of New York Press, 2017.

Murphy, N., R. John, and S. J. W. R. Stoeger, eds. *Physics and Cosmology: Scientific Perspectives on the Problem of Evil*, volume 1. Vatican: Vatican Observatory Publications/Center for Theology and the Natural Sciences, 2007.

Murray, M. J. *Nature Red in Tooth and Claw*. Oxford: Oxford University Press, 2008.

———. "Theodicy." In *The Oxford Handbook of Philosophical Theology*, 360–62.

Murrell, A. "Divine Sovereignty in the Punishment of the Wicked." In *A Consuming Passion: Essays on Hell and Immortality in Honor of Edward Fudge*, edited by Christopher Date and Ron Highfield, 141–55. Eugene, OR: Pickwick, 2015.

Nadler, S., ed. *The Cambridge Companion to Malebranche*. Cambridge: Cambridge University Press, 2000.

Nagasawa, Y. *Maximal God: A New Defense of Perfect Being Theism*. Oxford: Oxford University Press, 2011.

Netton, I. R., ed. *Encyclopedia of Islamic Civilisation and Religion*. London: Routledge, 2008.

———. *Muslim Neoplatonists: An Introduction to the Thought of the Brethren of Purity*. London: RoutledgeCurzon, 2013.

Niebuhr, R. *Justice and Mercy*. Edited by Ursula Niebuhr. New York: Harper & Row, 1974.

Ormsby, E. L. *Theodicy in Islamic Thought: The Dispute over Al-Ghazali's Best of All Possible Worlds*. Princeton, NJ: Princeton University Press, 1984.

———. "Two Epistles on Consolation: al-Shahid Al-Thani and Said Nursi on Theodicy." In *Theodicy and Justice in Modern Islamic Thought: The Case of Said Nursi*, 147–58.

Osborn, R. E. *Death before the Fall: Biblical Literalism and the Problem of Animal Suffering*. Downers Grove, IL: Intervarsity Press, 2014.

Osman, A. *The Zahiri Madhhab (3rd/9th-10th/16th Century): A Textualist Theory of Islamic Law*. Leiden: Brill, 2014.

O'Shaughnessy, T. *MuHammad's Thoughts on Death: A Thematic Study of the Qur'anic Data*. Leiden: Brill, 1969.

Ozkan, T. Y. *A Muslim Response to Evil: Said Nursi on the Theodicy*. Oxford: Routledge, 2016.

Pagani, S. "Ibn 'Arabi, Ibn Qayyim al-Jawziyya, and the Political Functions of Punishment in the Islamic Hell." In *Locating Hell in Islamic Traditions*, 175–207.

Parker, J. V. *Animal Minds, Animal Souls, Animal Rights*. Lanham, MD: University Press of America, 2010.

Perlo, K. W. *Kinship and Killing: The Animals in World Religion*. New York: Colombia University Press, 2009.

Pessagno, J. "The Uses of Evil in Maturidian Thought." *Studia Islamica* 60 (1984): 59–82.

Peters, T. and M. Hewlett. *Evolution from Creation to New Creation: Conflict, Conversation, and Convergence*. Nashville, TN: Abingdon Press, 2003.

Phillips, D. Z. "Theism without Theodicy." In *Encountering Evil: Live Options in Theodicy*, 145–61.

Phy-Olsen, A. *Evolution, Creationism and Intelligent Design*. Santa Barbara, CA: Greenwood, 2010.

Picken, G. *Spiritual Purification in Islam: The Life and Works of al-Muhasibi*. Oxon: Routledge, 2011.

Pigden, C., ed. *Hume on Is and Ought*. New York: Palgrave Macmillan, 2010.

Pinnock, C. "Annihilationism." In *The Oxford Handbook of Eschatology*, edited by Jerry L. Walls, 462–75. Oxford: Oxford University Press, 2008.

———. "The Conditional View." In *Four Views on Hell*, edited by Stanley N. Gundry and William Crockett, 135–66. Grand Rapids, MI: Zondervan, 1996.

———. "The Destruction of the Finally Impenitent." In *Rethinking Hell: Readings in Evangelical Conditionalism*, edited by C. Date, G. G. Stump and J. W. Anderson, 56–73. Eugene, OR: Cascade Books, 2014.

Pinnock, S. *Beyond Theodicy: Jewish and Christian Continental Thinkers Respond to the Holocaust*. Albany: State University of New York Press, 2002.

Qadhi, Y. "The Path of Allah or Paths of Allah: Revisiting Classical and Medieval

Sunni Approaches to the Salvation of Others." In *Between Heaven and Hell*, 111–21.

Al-Qoz, A. H. *Men and the Universe: Reflections of Ibn Al-Qayyem*. Riyadh: Darussalam, 2004.

al-Qurtubi, *al-Jami' li-Ahkam al-Qur'an*. Translated by Aisha Bewley. London: Dar al-Taqwa, 2003.

Rau, G. *Mapping the Origins Debate: Six Models on the Beginning of Everything*. Downers Grove, IL: InterVarsity Press, 2012.

Reinhart, A. K. *Before Revelation: The Boundaries of Muslim Moral Thought*. Albany: State University of New York Press, 1995.

Reynolds, T. E. *Vulnerable Communion: A Theology of Disability and Hospitality*. Grand Rapids, MI: Brazos Press, 2008.

Richardson, K. L. *Difference and Disability in the Medieval Islamic World: Blighted Bodies*. Edinburgh: Edinburgh University Press, 2010.

Rispler-Chaim, V. *Disability in Islamic Law*. Dordrecht: Springer, 2007.

Rizutto, Ana-Maria. *The Birth of the Living God: A Psychoanalytic Study*. Chicago: University of Chicago Press, 1979.

Rizvi, S. H. "Oneself as the Saved Other? The Ethics and Soteriology of Difference in Two Muslim Thinkers." In *Between Heaven and Hell*, 180–203.

Robinson, N. *The Sayings of Muhammad*. London: Duckworth, 1991.

Rogers, A. and N. Conroy. "The New Defense of the Strong View of Hell." In *The Concept of Hell*, 49–65.

Rose, J., R. Arlinghaus, S. J. Cooke, B. K. Diggles, W. Sawynok, E. D. Stevens, and C. D. L. Wynne. "Can Fish Feel Pain?" *Fish and Fisheries* 15 (2013): 97–133.

———. "The Neurobehavioral Nature of Fishes and the Question of Awareness and Pain." *Reviews in Fisheries Science* 10 (2002): 2–10.

Rosenthal, F. "On Suicide in Islam." *Journal of the American Oriental Society* 66 (1946): 239–59.

Rouzati, N. *Trial and Tribulation in the Qur'an*. Berlin: Gerlach Press, 2015.

Rowe, W. "The Problem of Evil and Some Varieties of Atheism." *American Philosophical Quarterly* 16 (1979): 335–41.

Rudavsky, T. "A Brief History of Skeptical Responses to Evil." In *The Blackwell Companion to the Problem of Evil*, 379–95.

Rudolph, U. *Al-Maturidi and The Development of Sunni Theology*. Leiden: Brill, 2014.

Ruse, M. *Darwinism as Religion: What Literature Tells Us about Evolution*. Oxford: Oxford University Press, 2017.

Russell, R. J. "Physics, Cosmology, and the Challenge to Consequentialist Natural Theodicy." In *Physics and Cosmology*, 109–51.

Rustom, M. "A Philosopher's Itinerary for the Afterlife: Mulla Sadra on Paths to Felicity." In *Roads to Paradise*, 534–51.

———. *The Triumph of Mercy: Philosophy and Scripture in Mulla Sadra.* Albany: State University of New York Press, 2012.

Rustomji, N. *The Garden and the Fire: Heaven and Hell in Islamic Culture.* New York: Colombia University Press, 2009.

Rutherford, D. "Malebranche's Theodicy." In *The Cambridge Companion to Malebranche,* edited by Steven Nadler, 165–89. Cambridge: Cambridge University Press, 2000.

Ryder, R. D. *Speciesism, Painism and Happiness: A Morality for the Twentieth Century.* Exeter: Imprint Academic, 2015.

Sachedina, A. *Islamic Bio-Medical Ethics: Principles and Applications.* New York: Oxford University Press, 2009.

Sachedina, A., S. J. Fitzpatrick, I. H. Kerridge, C. Jordens, L. Zoloth, C. Tollefsen, K. L. Tsomo, M. P. Jensen, and D. Sarma. "Religious Perspectives on Human Suffering: Implications for Medicine and Bioethics." *Journal of Religion and Health* 55 (2016): 159–73.

Saleh, F. "The Problem of Evil in Islamic Theology: A Study of the Concept of Al-Qabih in Al-Qadi 'Abd al-Jabbar Al-Hamadhani's Thought." MA diss., McGill University, 1992.

Sapp, J. *Genesis: The Evolution of Biology.* New York: Oxford University Press, 2003.

Scalenghe, S. *Disability in the Ottoman Arab World, 1500–1800.* New York: Cambridge University Press, 2014.

Scott, M. *Pathways to Theodicy: An Introduction to the Problem of Evil.* Minneapolis, MN: Fortress Press, 2015.

Scruton, R. *Animal Rights and Wrongs.* London: Continuum, 1999.

Seacord, B. A. "Unto the Least of These: Animal Suffering and the Problem of Evil." PhD diss., University of Colorado, 2013.

Seeskin, K. "Moses Maimonides." In *The History of Evil in the Middle Ages 450–1450,* edited by Andrew Pinsent. London: Routledge, 2018, ch.7.

Seymour, C. *A Theodicy of Hell.* Dordrecht: Springer, 2000.

Shabana, A. "The Concept of Sin in the Qur'an in Light of the Story of Adam." In *Sin, Forgiveness and Reconciliation: Christian and Muslim Perspectives,* edited by L. Mosher and D. Marshall, 40–65. Virginia: Georgetown University Press, 2016.

Shah-Kazemi, R. *The Other in Light of the One: The Universality of the Qur'an and Interfaith Dialogue.* Cambridge: Islamic Texts Society, 2006.

Shaikh, S. "Engaging Disability and Religion in the Global South," section: "A Constructive Ethical Reflection on the Quran and Disability." In *The Palgrave Handbook of Disability and Citizenship in the Global South,* 154–64. Cham, Switzerland: Palgrave Macmillan, 2018.

———. *Sufi Narratives of Intimacy: Ibn 'Arabi, Gender and Sexuality.* Chapel Hill: University of North Carolina Press, 2012.

Shehada, H. A. *Mamluks and Animals: Veterinary Medicine in Medieval Islam*. Leiden: Brill, 2013.

Shihadeh, A. "Avicenna's Theodicy and al-Razi's Anti-Theodicy." *Intellectual History of the Islamicate World* 7 (2019): 61–84.

———. *The Teleological Ethics of Fakhr al-Din al-Razi*. Leiden: Brill, 2006.

Siddiqui, M. *Hospitality and Islam: Welcoming in God's Name*. New Haven, CT: Yale University Press, 2015.

Şimsek, C. M. "The Problem of Animal Pain: An Introduction to Said Nursi's Approach." In *Theodicy and Justice in Modern Islamic Thought: The Case of Said Nursi*, 111–34.

Sollereder, B. "Animal Suffering in an Unfallen World: A Theodicy of non-Human Evolution." PhD diss., Exeter University, 2014.

———. "Exploring Old and New Paths in Theodicy." *Zygon* 53 (2018): 729–38.

———. *God, Evolution and Animal Suffering: Theodicy without a Fall*. London: Routledge, 2019.

Southgate, C. *The Groaning of Creation: God, Evolution and the Problem of Evil*. Louisville, KY: Westminster John Knox Press, 2008.

Southgate, C., and A. Robinson. "Varieties of Theodicy: An Exploration of Responses to the Problem of Evil Based on a Typology of Good-Harm Analyses." In *Physics and Cosmology: Scientific Perspectives on the Problem of Evil*, 67–90.

Southgate, C., and D. Speak. "Free Will and Soul-making Theodicies." In *The Blackwell Companion to the Problem of Evil*, 205–21.

Søvik, A. O. *The Problem of Evil and the Power of God*. Leiden: Brill, 2011.

Spiegel, J. *Hell and Divine Goodness: A Philosophical-Theological Inquiry*. Eugene, OR: Cascade Books, 2019.

———. "Making the Philosophical Case for Conditionalism." In *A Consuming Passion*, 80–89.

Steel, C. "Avicenna and Thomas Aquinas on Evil." In *Avicenna and His Heritage: Acts of the International Colloquium Leuven-Louvain-la-Neuve, September 8-September 11, 1999*, edited by Jules Janssens and Daniel De Smet, 171–96. Leuven: Leuven University Press, 2002.

Steiner, G. *Anthropocentricism and Its Discontents: The Moral Status of Animals in the History of Western Philosophy*. Pennsylvania: Pittsburgh University Press, 2005.

Steppat, F. "God's Deputy: Materials on Islam's Image of Man." *Arabica* 36 (1989): 163–72.

Stroumsa, M. "The Beginning of the Mu'tazila." *JSAI* 13 (1991): 265–93.

Surin, K. *Theology and the Problem of Evil*. Eugene, OR: Wipf & Stock, 2004.

Swinburne, R. *Mind, Brain and Free Will*. Oxford: Oxford University Press, 2013.

———. *Providence and the Problem of Evil*. Oxford: Clarendon Press, 1998.

Swinton, J. *Raging with Compassion: Pastoral Response to the Problem of Evil.* Grand Rapids, MI: Eerdmans, 2007.

al-Tabari. *The Commentary on the Qur'an.* Translated by John Cooper and edited by Wilfred Madelung and Alan Jones. Oxford: Oxford University Press, 1987.

Tibawi, A. L. "Al-Ghazali's Sojourn in Damascus and Jerusalem." *Islamic Quarterly* 9 (1965): 198–211.

Tilley, T. W. *The Evils of Theodicy.* Washington, DC: Georgetown University Press, 1991.

Timani, H. *Takfir in Islamic Thought.* London: Lexington Books, 2018.

Timothy, P., and S. J. Wykstra. "Skeptical Theism." In *The Cambridge Companion to the Problem of Evil*, 85–107.

Timpe, K., and A. D. Cobb. "Disability and Theodicy of Defeat." *Journal of Analytic Theology* 5 (2017): 100–20.

Tlili, S. *Animals in the Qur'an.* New York: Cambridge University Press, 2012.

———. "Animal Ethics in Islam: A Review Article." *Religions* 9 (2018): 1–18.

———. "All Animals Are Equal, or Are They? The Ikhwan al-Safa's Animal Epistle and its Unhappy End." *Journal of Qur'anic Studies* 16 (2014): 42–88.

Trakakis, N. "Antitheodicy." In *The Blackwell Companion to the Problem of Evil*, 363–76.

———. *The End of Philosophy of Religion.* London: Continuum, 2008.

———. "An Epistemically Distant God? A Critique of John Hick's Response to the Problem of Divine Hiddenness." *Heythrop Journal* 48 (2007): 214–26.

———. ed. *The Problem of Evil: Eight Views in Dialogue.* Oxford: Oxford University Press, 2018.

———. ed. *William L. Rowe on Philosophy of Religion: Selected Writings.* Aldershot: Ashgate, 2007.

Turner, B. S. *Regulating Bodies: Essays in Medical Sociology.* London: Routledge, 2002.

Usmani, M. S. *Iman aur Kufr: Qur'an ki Roshani Mein.* Karachi: Idarat al-Ma'arif, 2008.

Van Bekkum, K., J. Dekker, H. R. van den Kamp, and E. Peels, eds. *Playing with Leviathan: Interpretation and Reception of Monsters from the Biblical World.* Leiden: Brill, 2017.

Van den Brink, G. "God and the Suffering of Animals." In *Playing with Leviathan*, 179–99.

Van Ess, J. "Mu'tazila." In *Encyclopaedia of Religion*, edited by L. Jones. Detroit: Macmillan, 2005, 10:220–29.

———. *Theology and Society in the Second and Third Centuries of the Hijra.* Translated by John O'Kane and Fierro, Maribel, M. Şükrü Hanioğlu, edited by Renata Holod and Florian Schwarz. Leiden: Brill, 2017.

Van Inwagen, P. *The Problem of Evil.* New York: Oxford University Press, 2006.

Vasalou, S. *Ibn Taymiyya's Theological Ethics*. New York: Oxford University Press, 2016.

———. *Moral Agents and Their Deserts: The Character of Mu'tazilite Ethics*. Princeton, NJ: Princeton University Press, 2008.

Vermeer, P. *Learning Theodicy: The Problem of Evil and the Praxis of Religious Education*. Leiden: Brill, 1999.

Vuckovic, B. O. *Heavenly Journeys, Earthly Concerns: The Legacy of the Mi'raj in the Formation of Islam*. New York: Routledge, 2005.

Waldau, P. *Animal Studies: An Introduction*. New York: Oxford University Press, 2013.

Waldau, P., and K. Patton, eds. *A Communion of Subjects: Animals in Religion, Science and Ethics*. New York: Columbia University Press, 2006.

Watt, W. M. "God's Caliph, Qur'anic Interpretations and Umayyad Claims." In *Iran and Islam in Memory of the Late Vladimir Minorsky*, edited by C. Bosworth, 565–74. Edinburgh: Edinburgh University Press, 1971.

———. *Islamic Creeds: A Selection*. Edinburgh: Edinburgh University Press, 1994.

———. *Islamic Philosophy and Theology*. Edinburgh: Edinburgh University Press, 1985.

———. "Suffering in Sunnite Islam." *Studia Islamica* 50 (1979): 5–19.

Webb, S. H. *On God and Dogs: A Christian Theology of Compassion for Animals*. New York: Oxford University Press, 1998.

Wensinck, A. J. *The Muslim Creed: Its Genesis and Historical Development*. New Delhi: Oriental Books Reprint Corporation, 1979, repr.

White, D. J. "Do, Evolution and the Problem of Evil: Towards a Solution." PhD diss., University of Exeter, 2014.

Whitted, Q. J. *"A God of Justice?" The Problem of Evil in Twentieth Century Black Literature*. Charlottesville: University of Virginia Press, 2009.

Wild, R. *A Catholic Reading Guide for Conditional Immortality: The Third Alternative to Hell and Universalism*. Eugene, OR: Resource Publications, 2016.

Williams, S. M. "Horrendous-Difference Disabilities, Resurrected Saints, and the Beatific Vision: A Theodicy." *Religions* 9 (2018): 1–13.

Winter, T. "Islam and the Problem of Evil." In *The Cambridge Companion to the Problem of Evil*, 230–48.

———. "The Last Trump Card: Islam and the Supersession of Other Faiths." *Studies in Interreligious Dialogue* 9 (1999): 133–54.

———. "Realism and the Real: Islamic Theology and the Problem of Alternative Expressions of God." In *Between Heaven and Hell*, 136–40.

Wirén, J. W. *Hope and Otherness: Christian Eschatology and Interreligious Hospitality*. Leiden and Boston: Brill, 2018.

Wynne, C., and M. Udell, eds. *Animal Cognition: Evolution, Behaviour and Cognition*. Basingstoke: Palgrave Macmillan, 2013.

Yaran, S. *Islamic Thought on the Existence of God: With Contributions from Contemporary Western Philosophy of Religion.* Washington: Council for Research in Value and Philosophy, 2003.

Yong, A. "Disability and the Love of Wisdom." *Ars Disputandi* 9 (2009): 54–71.

Younos, F. *Principles of Islamic Sociology.* Bloomington, IN: Author House, 2011.

Zeni, T. M. *Revival of Piety through an Islamic Theodicy.* Turin: Independent Publication, 2020.

Zysow, A. "Karramiyya." In *The Oxford Handbook of Islamic Theology*, 252–62.

———. "Two Unrecognized Karrami Texts." *Journal of the American Oriental Society* 108 (1988): 577–87.

Index

'Abd al-Jabbar 4, 73, 78–80, 97
Adam 58, 59, 109, 115, 116
Adams, Marilyn 51, 52, 53; *see also* horrendous
  evil
ahl al-fatra 157, 160, 161, 163, 164, 165
animals: nature and status of 67–76; pain and suffering 76–78; Qur'anic view on 71–73
annihilationism 117, 136, 142; Islamic views on
  136–41
arguments: absolute seriousness 132–34; APS
  argument (Animal Pain and Suffering) 76;
  divine foreknowledge 133
al-Asha'ri 175–76
Ash'arism 19–20; Ash'arite skeptical theism
  82–83

bala' 46, 47
al-Barzanji, Muhammad b. 'Abd al-Rasul 161,
  163
al-Baydawi, 'Abd Allah b. 'Umar 35
best possible world thesis 127–28
al-Burullusi, 'Ali al-Khawwas 70

CD (causa dei) 105–106, 108
CTO (chaos to order) 106–108
counterfactuals 133, 165, 166, 167
covenant 15, 48, 49; thesis 126–27; *see also mithaq*
Creegan, Nicola Hoggard 109–11

Darwin, Charles 100–101
al-Daylami, Abu al-Hasan 70
defence 22–23; *see also* theodicy
disability 29–66, horrendous-difference disability
  51, 53–55, 63; Islamic view of 31–33; *see also*
  disability theodicy; *diyafa*
disvalues 114, 115, 205
diyafa (hospitality) 46, 55, 56

epistemic distance 114
eschatological recompense 44, 78–83; *see also*
  'iwad

evil 11–27; according to Ibn Sina 16–18; according to the Qur'an 15, 23–4; evidential problem
  12, 13, 23; the problem of 11–14; types of 14;
  soteriological problem of 155–68

free will thesis 128–29

al-Ghazali, Abu Hamid 4, 37, 58, 81, 119, 122,
  123, 127, 158, 159, 175–76
God's holiness thesis 125–26
Grenfell Tower 1–2

Harrison, Peter: typology of animal theodicies
  78, 83, 88; *see also* animal; animal theodicies
Hell 117–55; justification of 120–21; mainstream view 117–19; objections to the
  doctrine of 120–55; strong view 118–19; *see*
  also theodicy
horrendous evils 51–53
hospitality *see diyafa*

Ibn al-'Arabi, Abu Bakr 26
Ibn 'Arabi 145, 149; his naturalisation view of
  hell 153–55; his universalism 149–55
Ibn al-Humam 83, 90, 91, 179
Ibn Kathir 35, 166
Ibn Qayyim 40; his animal theodicy 92–98; his
  universalism 145–48
Ibn Sina (Avicenna) 11, 14, 16, 17, 18, 21, 119,
  137
Ibn Taymiya 33; his universalism 142–44
Ibn Umm Maktum, 'Abd Allah 30, 31
Iblis 14, 15, 84, 85, 91, 132, 149, 168
ibtila' see bala'
IET (Islamic Evolutionary Theodicy) 111–16
ISE (Islamic Soteriological Exclusivism) 156–57
ISI (Islamic Soteriological Inclusivism) 156–57
ITE (Islamic Theistic Evolution) 112
'iwad 73, 78

justice thesis 123

251

www.ingramcontent.com/pod-product-compliance
Lightning Source LLC
Chambersburg PA
CBHW071933090426
42811CB00042B/2426/J